P9-CCX-031

The Marx Brothers At The Movies

The Marx Brothers At The Movies

by **Paul D. Zimmerman**
and **Burt Goldblatt**

G. P. Putnam's Sons
New York

COPYRIGHT © 1968 BY PAUL D. ZIMMERMAN AND BURT GOLDBLATT

All rights reserved. This book, or parts thereoi, must
not be reproduced in any form without permission.
Published simultaneously in the Dominion of Canada
by Longmans Canada Limited, Toronto.

FIRST PRINTING

Library of Congress Catalog
Card Number: 68-25434
Text by Paul D. Zimmerman
Designed by Burt Goldblatt
Printed in the United States of America

For Leslie and Heather
who fight a little and laugh a lot.

We would like to acknowledge the generous cooperation of the following people and institutions without whose help this book would not have been possible: the British Film Institute; William K. Everson; Allyn Freeman; Marilyn Goldin of the Museum of Modern Art; Charles Hirsch of MCA; Sol Jacobson; Sol Jaffe of Vitaprint Corporation; King Displays; Paul D. Meyers of the Lincoln Center Library; Tess Michaels of United Artists; Arthur Perles of M-G-M; and Daniel Talbot of the New Yorker Theater. Special thanks to Barbara Zimmerman for her long hours of cruel toil and unflagging support.

Contents

The brothers and Minnie at the time of I'll Say She Is, *1924*

Groucho, Zeppo, Harpo, Chico and Gummo

Chico

Harpo

Home sweet home, 93d Street

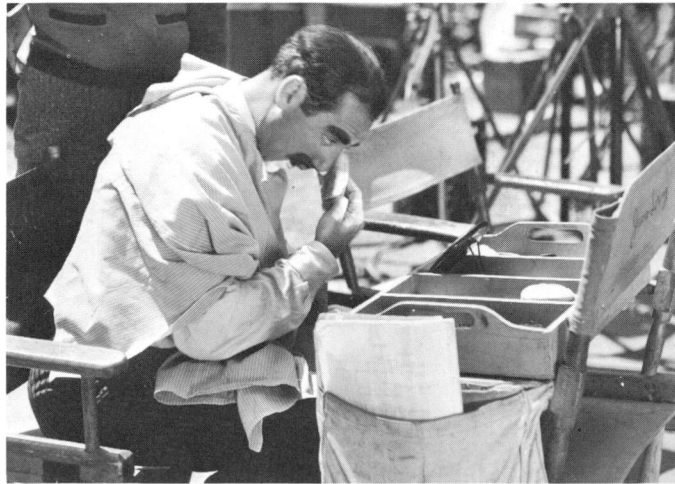

Between takes of Duck Soup, *Groucho puts on his face*

1 Introduction

High in the pantheon of American screen comedy stand three disreputable figures. The man in the swallow-tailed coat is slightly stooped, as if passing under a low doorway. He holds a plump cigar behind him, ready to flick its ash onto the nearest rug. Leering eyes, like windows to a dirty mind, look out from behind steel-rimmed glasses. A generous nose leads to an even more generous smudge that passes for a moustache. He gives the impression of a man looking for something, perhaps a ten-dollar bill on the floor or a pair of pretty legs.

The next one is all outfit and face. His shoes, fungus with buttons, open at the toe to swallow cigarette butts. His trousers, a duffel bag with legs, are tailored to conceal a hardware store, a block of ice, a burning candle. His taste in ties and shirts runs to the garish—polka dot on plaid, or plaid on plaid, or plaid on bare skin. He is swaddled in a trench coat generous enough to accommodate every known utensil, the contents of a neighborhood delicatessen and twenty settings of silver cutlery. Balanced neatly on this pyre of garbage sits the rounded head of a fallen angel—dancing eyes, puckish nose, rubber cheeks, cherubic mouth, all presided over by a free-form halo of golden hair. In one hand, he grips a taxi horn. He is about to chase something, more likely a blonde than a taxi.

The third radiates good-natured ignorance, tempered by suspicion and animated by ambition. He is clothed in corduroy from the shapeless cuffs of his skimpy suit to the pinhead hat that rides his ears. His face is soft and slack, but his shrewd eyes are busy calculating some losing wager. There is a fourth pedestal marked "Zeppo," but it has long since been vacated, with only a pair of ordinary footprints marking its owner's brief appearance by association in this comic Hall of Fame.

An improbable combination, this trio, yet there they are, alongside Chaplin, Keaton and W. C. Fields, larger and more lunatic than life, as they always were. In fact, the Marx Brothers have become a metaphor for the improbable. They were America's madmen during its age of normalcy. They were excessive and profligate through the pinched years of the Depression. Amid rising Fascism in Europe and at home they raised the banner of free spirited anarchy. (They had to raise it, otherwise Harpo would have eaten it.) They belittled intellectualism, and the intellectuals loved them most of all. They assaulted the myths and virtues of middle-class America, which dutifully flocked to their pictures to laugh at itself. They were the incarnation of lowbrow vaudeville comedy, but, though that world is dead, they are more revered and popular now than when they made their first picture forty years ago. In January, 1968, in New York, the Bleecker Street Cinema revived that film—*The Cocoanuts*—along with their *Duck Soup* and drew standing-room-only crowds for three days. Both films did only middling business when they were first released.

Why have they survived so handsomely? There are any number of reasons, all of them pretty much beside the point. It is true enough that their wildness stirs something deep within even the meekest citizen. They act on our forbidden desires, from telling off our hostess or an after-dinner speaker to kicking over a customs desk or racing after a pretty girl. It is also true that their targets—authority, the System, education, politics, sex, culture, the police, war, the upper class—are as attractive today as ever. But when the theorizing is done, the answer to their survival is simple—they are very, very funny, so funny that they transcend their time.

Like Chaplin, Keaton and Fields, their comedy was shaped by two large forces, poverty and vaudeville. Chico, Harpo and Groucho were born Leonard, Aldoph and Julius—in that order —amid the slums of Manhattan's Yorkville section in the not-so-gay nineties. The slum was a perfect breeding ground for comic anarchists. The middle sons of Sam Marx, a dapper, highly unsuccessful tailor, and Minnie Schoenberg, the stagestruck daughter of an itinerant German magician, learned at an early age that law and order were society's instruments for keeping down the poor and that money was the way out. In their movies, they ripped this order to pieces as they scurried after cash in one form or another.

Already in boyhood one can see the outlines of Chico, Harpo and Groucho. There is young Leonard learning to mimic accents as he runs the gauntlet of ethnic strongholds that lie beyond his own block on 93rd Street. Harpo remembers his older brother "learning how to bet on horse races and prize fights and how to play pinochle, learning the laws of probability by observing the neighborhood crap game." The character of the Italian hustler was taking shape. Adolph, too, was slowly changing into the silent, rubber-faced clown. Already by his own confession "not much of a talker," he learned his trade by watching. "The man who first inspired me to become an actor was a guy called Gookie," he writes in his autobiography, *Harpo Speaks.* "Gookie had nothing to do with the theater. He rolled cigars in the window of a cigar store on Lexington Avenue . . . when he got going good he was completely lost in work, so absorbed that he had no idea what a comic face he was making. His tongue lolled out in a fat roll, his cheeks puffed out, and his eyes popped out and crossed themselves. Over the years in every comedy act or movie I ever worked in I've thrown a Gookie at least once."

In a less dramatic way, Julius was becoming Groucho. With the Marx home in constant chaos, young Julius would stash himself away in some corner room, light up a cigar and read, stockpiling his incomparable verbal arsenal. For some time, he wanted to be a doctor, an ambition he finally realized on the screen as Dr. Hackenbush, the veteran veterinarian of *A Day at the Races.* From the beginning, Harpo and Chico were pals and Groucho something of a loner, and so they appear in the screen from first film to last.

It was Minnie who forged these three latent talents into the Marx Brothers. Out of the meager family till, she set aside twenty-five cents each week for Chico's piano lessons, lessons he was to pass to Harpo. Unfortunately, the teacher was competent only with her right hand and faked the left. Chico inherited her failing. In his piano solos in the brothers' films, he performs all his tricks—shooting the keys, wagging at them with an index finger, running them—with his right hand, while his left limps lamely along. It was Minnie who acquired a secondhand harp for her whimiscal son, who learned to play it himself, placing it on the wrong shoulder, and became one of the world's most celebrated soloists. It was Minnie who encouraged Groucho to launch his career as a boy tenor, delivering him into the hands of a two-bit impresario who stranded him, penniless, in Colorado. And it was Minnie who whipped her boys—including the oldest, Gummo, and her sister, Hannah, into a vaudeville act that passed through many transformations—the Four Nightingales, the Six Musical Mascots, a routine called Fun in Hi-Skule—but never fell apart.

Minnie's feat couldn't have been more demanding and hazardous had she been asked to carry her family across the high wire. The act began as a musical travesty with Gummo and Groucho singing or playing the mandolin and guitar, then grew bigger and worse when Aunt Hannah and Minnie herself sang "Two Little Girls in Blue." Harpo joined the act around 1909, but Chico went his separate way, building a modest reputation as

a trick pianist who could perform blindfolded with a sheet over the keys. The group transmogrified like an amoeba, swelling with raw recruits from outside the family, then splitting when these outsiders dropped out or wanted more money.

And while the team was finding its proper shape and style, it was touring the relentless hell of the vaudeville circuit: one-night stands in bug-infested rooms, precarious pay, beatings by suspicious and hostile local thugs, managers who delighted in fines for the least breach of the rules. The "Midwestern Vaudeville Circuit" offered an endless procession of sink-hole theaters, sheds and tents where the Marxes would perform for ten cents a show. "What I remember," wrote Harpo, "are railroad-station waiting rooms, boardinghouse dining rooms, dressing rooms, poolrooms and men's rooms . . . . It was a miracle that we stuck it out."

Knocking about such towns as Thibodaux, Donaldsville, Plaquemine and Lafayette, the Marxes began to find themselves. In Denison, Texas, Groucho promised the stage manager a comedy act to get a better price, forcing the family to invent its first comic routine. "We didn't promise the guy a good comedy act," apologized Groucho. "We just said we'd give him an act." In that act, Harpo played the stock vaudeville figure, Patsy Bolisar, a carrot-topped country moron. For the occasion, Aunt Hannah concocted a wig out of cotton and unraveled pieces of rope. Harpo and his hairpiece were never to be parted, or, as Chico might have noted, "it made him hair to a fortune."

On the same trip, the brothers stumbled onto their improvisatory

Sam Marx and sons (note expert tailoring on Harpo)

style. They were performing one night in Nacogdoches, Texas, when a mule broke loose outside the theater. The audience walked out on the Marxes to investigate the ruckus. When they returned, the angry comedians were ad-libbing their act. In the middle of one song, Groucho interrupted to let the audience know what he thought of their town. "Nacogdoches," he yelled, "is full of roaches." The ad lib became a permanent fixture of Marx comedy.

As a comic rather than musical act, the team started getting a little better work: the Keith Circuit, the Pantages theaters. Minnie called in her brother, Al Shean, of Gallagher and Shean, to work up a new routine. It was called "On the Mezzanine." Shean was astute enough to spot Harpo's genius as a mime and assigned him only three lines. The review in the Champaign-Urbana paper the next day praised Harpo's pantomine but added, "The effect is spoiled when he speaks." Shean cut out the three lines and Harpo, his vanity bruised, assented. "I knew Uncle Al had been right," he wrote later. "I simply couldn't outtalk Groucho or Chico, and it was ridiculous of me to try. I would never speak another word on stage."

About the same time, the brothers acquired their rightful names. Art Fisher, a monologist who was traveling on a train with them, often joined their poker games. At that time, a comic strip called "Knocko the Monk" was extremely popular. When it was Fisher's turn to deal, he began "a hole card for . . . Harpo. A card for, um, Chico" (because he liked the girls) . And so it went. Groucho was so dubbed for his saturnine disposition, Gummo for his rubber-soled shoes, or gumshoes.

When Gummo enlisted in the Army in 1918, Herbert, the baby of the family took his place. Each brother has a different explanation for Herbert's sobriquet. According to Harpo, Herbert was always chinning himself, like Zippo, the star of a famous chimpanzee act; so he became Zippo, then changed it to the more flattering Zeppo. Groucho claims Zeppo was named after the Zeppelins then coming into use. Gummo and Chico explain Zeppo as a variant of Zebbo, the hick name given to their brother for his brief stint on a farm the family acquired outside Chicago.

The origin of Groucho's greasepaint moustache is less obscure. One night, when the team was playing the Fifth Avenue Theater in New York, Groucho arrived back from dinner late, had no time to affix his paste-on moustache, and drew a black smear under his nose. After the show, when the manager demanded "the same moustache you gave 'em at the Palace," Groucho took it off the dressing-room table and handed it to him. He didn't wear a hirsute moustache again until *Love Happy*, some thirty years later, when it was homegrown.

As the Palace and the Fifth Avenue Theater suggest, the brothers were doing better. Their comedy, too, was doing better, after such early exchanges as: Harpo: "Yonder in the distance an island lays." Groucho: "Lays what? Eggs?" By the time S. J. Perelman heard them on tour in Rhode Island in 1916, they were developing miniature Marx Brothers movies. Groucho would descend from an ocean liner, stifle a belch and observe: "I'm certainly glad to put my feet on terra firma again. Now I know when I eat something, I wouldn't see it again."

Harpo, as Perelman recalls, then "disgorged the entire ship's cutlery from his sleeves and inspected the lingerie of several *zoftick* fellow passengers. Chico approached Groucho with his hand extended. 'I'd like to say gombye to your wife.' 'Who wouldn't?' riposted his brother." The act ended with the Marxes rowing their way offstage in a papier-maché boat, knocking over most of the cast.

But it was eight years before the brothers would make it to Broadway, and then only after their fortunes touched bottom. By breaking a contract, they had fallen out of favor with the theater barons, who blacklisted them from the vaudeville circuits. In desperation, they signed up with a tab show, a hybrid vaudeville review-musical comedy. Called *I'll Say She Is,* it played seventeen weeks in Philadelphia. The Marxes stayed with it eighteen months on the road. Finally, on May 19, 1924, the show opened in New York. It was an immediate hit, partly on the strength of an ecstatic review by *New Yorker* critic Alexander Woollcott, who spent a good deal of his mature life lionizing the team. A year later, the brothers were playing *The Cocoanuts,* which, in turn, led them to *Animal Crackers,* both of which they committed to film.

While these shows were more extended and ambitious than anything they attempted on the Keith Circuit, the brothers never strayed far from the style Perelman observed in Rhode Island. The movies of the Marx Brothers, for all their romantic subplots and dressy production numbers, remain essentially vaudeville shows on film, a string of comic bits catching each other by the tail. The team's style is wild, kinetic, cinematic, but its theatrical upbringing—the sense of footlights bordering the bottom of the screen, the musty smell of grease paint—permeates even the most elaborate of their pictures. They drew their subject matter from their own experience, as have all great comedians. In this sense, their films are autobiographical, the Marx Brothers dressed up and dramatizing themselves, acting out the irreverent role of usurpers that they learned in poverty and punched into shape in vaudeville. *The Cocoanuts* is the first installment in the thirteen-chapter history of their lives.

Chico, Groucho, Harpo, Zeppo

Zeppo Marx "Jamison"
Groucho Marx "Hammer"
Harpo Marx "Harpo"
Chico Marx "Chico"
Oscar Shaw "Bob"
Mary Eaton "Polly"
Cyril Ring "Yates"
Kay Francis "Penelope"
Margaret Dumont "Mrs. Potter"
Basil Ruysdael "Hennessy"

Mr. Hammer: GROUCHO
Harpo: HIMSELF
Chico: HIMSELF
Jamison: ZEPPO
Mrs. Potter: MARGARET DUMONT
Polly Potter: MARY EATON
Bob Adams: OSCAR SHAW
Penelope: KAY FRANCIS
Harvey Yates: CYRIL RING
Hennessy: BASIL RUYSDAEL
Also SYLVAN LEE, GAMBY-HALE BALLET GIRLS and ALLAN K. FOSTER GIRLS

* * *

Producer: Walter Wanger
Associate Producer: James R. Cown
Directors: Robert Florey and Joseph Stanley
Adaptor: Morrie Ryskind
Music and Lyrics: Irving Berlin
Original Book of Musical Play: George S. Kaufman and Morrie Ryskind
Photography: George Folsey
Editing: Barney Rogan
Music Director: Frank Teurs
Released by Paramount, August 3, 1929. 96 minutes

2 The Cocoanuts (1929)

The Cocoanuts was filmed in the spring of 1929 among the artificial palm of an Astoria, Long Island, studio. It was a hectic time for the brothers who would shoot *The Cocoanuts* in the morning and afternoon and then troupe back to New York in the evening to perform in their third Broadway hit, *Animal Crackers*. "Sometimes I'd get so punchy," recalls Groucho, "that I'd find myself spouting the dialogue from *Animal Crackers* in a scene I was doing in *Cocoanuts* and vice versa." While it's unlikely that anyone in the audience knew the difference, this double life dragged on for five months as the directors, Robert Florey and Joseph Stanley, and their crew struggled with the latest innovation in motion pictures — sound. Their pioneer equipment constantly broke down in the middle of simple scenes which often had to be reshot as many as twenty or thirty times. And, as though the shooting were following Groucho's first law of physics, what didn't break down had to break up — notably the director.

"The shooting would be interrupted every time we started improvising," Harpo recalls in his autobiography. "It wasn't that our ad libs weren't funny. The trouble was Florey couldn't help breaking up. When he laughed, he laughed so hard he drowned out everything else on the sound track." At this point, the broth-ers, never easily coralled onto one stage for very long, would break up as well. Chico would go off to call his bookie or scrounge up a pinochle game. Harpo and Groucho would search for him and get sidetracked with the girls, and precious time would be lost before the pack could be reassembled and the process of breakup and breakdown resumed. Only a drastic remedy would do—like imprisonment. The brothers were each assigned a cell from the jail set constructed for one of the last scenes. Florey was incarcerated in a glass soundproof booth where he directed with hand signals. Chico's cell was equipped with telephone and phone book so he could keep in touch with the latest three-year-old filly. It must have been quite a sight. Each time a scene was to be shot, the director would be herded into his cell and the Marx Brothers released from theirs. "We still played to Florey," Harpo re-members. "When he flew into a fit of silent convulsions we knew we had done something good. It was the weirdest audience we ever played to."

The Marx Brothers always played to an audience, whether it was Florey in his directorial goldfish booth, or the tryout audiences in Minneapolis, Cleveland and Pittsburgh whose reactions were measured before the broth-ers committed their material to film, or the movie audiences themselves, whose tastes were always analyzed in the Marx Brothers dead serious story conferences. Right from the beginning, Groucho took to addressing the audience directly. In *Horse Feathers*, for example, during Chico's piano solo, he tells the people in the theater: "I've got to stay here, but there's no reason why you folks shouldn't go out into the lobby until this thing blows over." Nowhere, however, did the audience play a more important role than in *The Cocoanuts,* which changed in its two years on Broadway from something George S. Kaufman wrote to something the Marx Brothers did to what George S. Kaufman wrote, with the approval of a nightly audience. One night, Heywood Broun tried to talk to Kaufman while the author was in the wings watching the show. Broun became irritated when he saw Kaufman wasn't listening to him and snapped: "What's the matter with you?" "I may be wrong," Kaufman replied, raising an apologetic hand. "But I thought I just heard one of the original lines."

Actually, *The Cocoanuts* had become a largely Marxian vehicle even before it roared into New York. After a disastrous performance in Boston which had run forty minutes overtime and closed to an almost empty theater, Kaufman, co-author Morrie Ryskind and songwriter Irving Berlin met in gloomy conference. Kaufman suggested that a production number, two choruses and two more songs be excised. "My God!" cried Berlin. "Any more cuts and this will be a musical without any music!" "Tell you what," said the mournful Kaufman. "You waive the songs, and I'll waive the story." One of the songs Berlin waived was "Always." *The Cocoanuts* was, as it turned out, the only show he wrote that did not contain at least one hit song. And even then, the songs he did write played second fiddle to the Marx trio. A sketch in the December 13 edition of the *New York World* depicts a disgruntled Berlin "straining to hear the words of one of his own lyrics."

This now common overhead shot drew applause from 1929 audiences

Oscar Shaw and Mary Eaton: love and hisses

"Just forget about money . . . 'cause you won't get it, anyway."

Margaret Dumont, who was to play Groucho's foil in nine of the brothers' thirteen films, affords a closer look at exactly how the Marks worked on any given night. She recalled that once, during a performance of *Animal Crackers,* the brothers had completely abandoned the script and were improvising scene after scene. After some time she decided to take her chances and enter in the middle of it all. At that moment, Chico and Harpo simply walked off the stage, leaving the great dowager face-to-face with Groucho. There were no lines prepared for this random meeting, so Groucho, with his characteristic speed of mind, gestured to a nearby divan. "Ah, Mrs. Rittenhouse," he proclaimed. "Won't you . . . er . . . lie down?" This line shows up again in the screen version of *The Cocoanuts.* It had gotten a laugh on Broadway, so the brothers simply took it with them when they traveled to the Astoria studio. "Ah, Mrs. Rittenhouse," from *Animal Crackers,* was merely changed to "Ah, Mrs. Potter," for use in *The Cocoanuts.*

The brothers' first film remains the best record we have of their vaudeville style. In fact, *The Cocoanuts* and *Animal Crackers* are really examples of the Marx Brothers at the height of their stage art rather than records of their film beginnings. Here are the characters the brothers developed night by night through some twenty years of trouping, not yet fully fleshed out, instead hungry, youthful, sometimes venomous and totally anarchistic, the pure products of hard times unmellowed by the easier life of Hollywood. Like demons from another planet, they invade the conventional, romantic precincts of the plot and demolish everything in view. *The Cocoanuts* is not built around them; it is a structure built beforehand which they enter and flatten. No one knew the incompatability of the brothers and the world of musical comedy better than George S. Kaufman, who tried to set a path for them through each plot. "How can you write for Harpo?" he asked in dismay. "All you can say is, 'Harpo enters.' From that point on, he's on his own."

The Cocoanuts is interesting also as one of the few filmed records of a 1920's musical comedy, with its highly mannered acting, drill-team dance numbers and sentimental stories. Today, many chorus girls are almost six feet tall. Forty years ago, the film shows us, most of them were just over five feet. But beyond its historical value the most remarkable thing about *The Cocoanuts* is that it is terifically funny. Generally a stage show literally transcribed onto the screen is as captivating as a filibuster. It doesn't work, foiled by the aesthetic law that tells us to expect one set of conventions from the stage and another from the screen. But the Marx Brothers, who violated all laws, logical and social, found this last one no barrier at all, mainly because they were perfect screen comedians before talkies even began. Their wild sight gags profit little from the confines of the stage. But film captures, energizes and magnifies their rapid-fire, kinetic humor. Film editing, with its quick and crazy cutting, complements perfectly the helter-skelter movements of the Marxes themselves. Someone located in the back of a theater might miss the subtle, second-to-second emotional changes that play across Harpo's face. But film close-ups turn the Marxes' mugs into visual playgrounds filled with comic events. *The Cocoanuts* is one of those happy accidents of art and technology in which cinema found sound just in time to give full voice to Groucho's wit, Chico's verbal tenacity and Harpo's silence.

Although *The Cocoanuts* was the brothers' first picture, they were al-

The world's shortest friendship

ready entering middle age. Chico had just turned forty. Harpo was thirty-eight and Groucho thirty-three. But in this film, as in nearly all those to follow, the Marxes never looked their age, or acted it. Groucho, as the owner of the Cocoanuts Hotel during the height of the Florida land boom, conveys the youthful zest of the callow embezzler eager to cheat his way to the top. His great comic lope is here only a slight, suspicious lean, and his love scenes with Margaret Dumont are those of a young adventurer fleecing the widow, with hardly a trace of the moth-eaten middle-aged lover to come. Chico is smooth-faced and resilient. And Harpo is a pixilated Pan of eternal youth, a perfect blend of playful innocence and impishness.

Like a heavily weighted freight train, *The Cocoanuts* takes awhile starting but, once launched, hits a fast comic clip. The opening sequences set forth what passes for a plot. Bob Adams, a young architect working as a clerk at the hotel, has great plans for developing the Cocoanut Grove area. Those plans include marrying Polly Potter, daughter of the wealthy, snooty Mrs. Potter. Harvey Yates, of the Boston Yates, is also interested in Polly and her mother's money. For the moment, he can't snare the one, so he plots to steal the other. His plan: to swipe Mrs. Potter's $100,000 necklace with the aid of his sleazy friend, Penelope, who shares an adjoining suite with Mrs. Potter. All this is set out in sappy song and sinister story, with an interlude for mechanized dance routines by bathing beauties supposedly doing their

Groucho lectures Dumont on septic tank technology

morning calisthenics. Apt as this might be for a dance opener, it turns out that all the other dance numbers share this same gymnastic muscularity —fine for Olympic training but likely to bedazzle a Balanchine.

Before things get altogether too sweaty, we meet Groucho for the first time, doing what he likes best, conning cash from the unsuspecting. The bellboys and bellgirls are clamoring for their wages. At first, Groucho tries to pay them off with paper promises of a great future in Florida. "Three years ago," he tells them, "I came to Florida without a nickel in my pocket. Now I have a nickel in my pocket." When the Horatio Alger approach is greeted with grumbles, he suddenly joins the world of organized labor in order to defeat it. "You want to be wage slaves?" he asks them. "Answer

Harpo's menu: buttons, sponge à la paste, ink and plastic

me that. No, of course not. Well, what makes wage slaves? Wages! I want you to be free...." But free in what sense? Groucho makes it abundantly clear: "Just forget about money...don't think about it... 'cause you won't get it anyway." They cheer him wildly and return to their work willingly, models of obedience to their union leader.

Groucho is the true democrat, willing to swindle anyone regardless of race, color, creed or checkbook. The Cocoanut Grove area, he tells Margaret Dumont (Mrs. Potter) as he tries to sell her worthless property, "is only 2,200 miles by train from midtown New York, only 1,600 as the crow flies and only 1,400 as the horse flies." Having hit his stride as the crooked real estate man par excellence, he asks her: "Do you know that property values have increased 1929 since 1,000 percent?" "Mr. Hammer," Miss Dumont finally beseeches him, "will you let me say something?" "I hardly think so," ripostes Groucho, following the first law of salesmanship,

as he goes on to demonstrate the wonders of a new sewage pipe to be installed in the area, an item he knows will surely offend Miss Dumont's snobbish sensibilities. He leaves her holding the pipe, so to speak, and she trails rather pitifully after him.

Enter Harpo and Chico, prototypes of the con men who work the resort hotels. Groucho immediately recognizes them as one of his own breed when they ask for a room but no bath. "I see," he says. "You're just here for the girls." The bellhop tries to take their bag, but Harpo won't let go of it. Finally, it pops open. "You know," says Groucho, "that suitcase is empty." "I know," returns Chico. "We fill it up before we leave." After systematically emptying the cubbyholes of their mail and ripping the letters in half, Harpo takes a lunch break. First he plucks the buttons from a bellboy's uniform and pops them into his mouth, savoring them like fresh berries. He munches on a desk sponge, seasons it with glue and swills it down

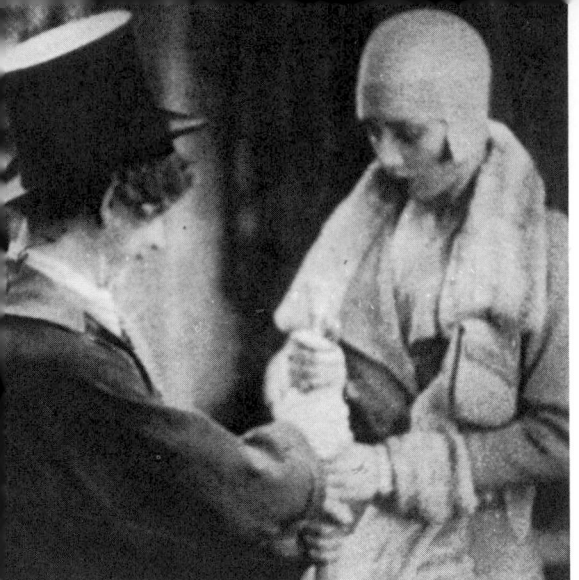

First "dibbs up" on a cane

then a waltz with Cyril King

with some vintage ink. A nice midday snack, but not quite filling enough, so Harpo nibbles on the telephone awhile. Groucho is called away from the desk, leaving Chico and Harpo in charge. "Don't forget, the register," he reminds them. They hop the counter and empty the register. Harpo rings the desk bell. A lovely bellgirl arrives and salutes. He rings it again. Another girl arrives. He has discovered Aladdin's lamp. He rings and rings and rings. Beautiful girls keep popping out of nowhere. Then he stops ringing, his eyes saucers of delight, and starts moving slowly toward his prey, like a slightly demented child approaching Christmas toys. Finally, he springs over the counter and runs madly in various directions as the girls scatter.

Penelope, played with the slither of the serpent of Eden by Kay Francis, must have a fall guy or guys at the scene of the necklace theft, so she arranges a rendezvous with Chico in her room at eleven o'clock, first softening him up by telling him that he looks like the Prince of Wales. Tempting Harpo is another matter. She appeals

to his chivalry, dropping her handkerchief. He simply pockets it. When she asks him if he's seen it, his face becomes an aureole of innocence as he shakes his head. Penelope switches to flirting. "Did anyone ever tell you you look like the Prince of Wales?" she asks. Yes, Harpo nods, smiling. People have told me that thousands of times, his face explains. "Oh," says the foiled Penelope. "I thought I was the first one." Harpo purses his lips and shakes his head briskly. Realizing subtlety will not do, Penelope is forced to lay it on the line. "Do you know my name?" she asks. Harpo, still grinning a lurid little grin that lets her know he's seen her type before, shakes his head. "Do you know my room number?" she asks. This he knows, and the rendezvous is set, but only on Harpo's terms, which reduce Penelope to a nameless body in a numbered room. To complete her humiliation, Harpo picks off her breast handkerchief with his teeth, keeps it, and mocks her swagger as she heads for the elevator.

Groucho is busy courting Margaret Dumont. He assaults her with his claims of love in the first of their many seduction scenes, all calculated to destroy the language of romance forever. "Did anyone ever tell you look like the Prince of Wales?" he asks her. "I don't mean the present Prince of Wales. One of the old Wales. And believe me when I say whales, I mean, whales. I know a whale when I see one." He imagines a cottage where they could "bill and cow, I mean, bull and cow." When Mrs. Potter contends that Groucho wouldn't love her if she were poor, he replies: "I might, but I'd probably keep my mouth shut." He goes on to conjure up domestic bliss for two: "I can see you, bending over the stove. Only I can't see the stove." Finally, he takes to the oldest dodge of all, comparing her to the moon, but with a novel twist. "Just think," he says, "tonight, tonight, when the moon is sneaking around the clouds, I'll be sneaking around you. I'll meet you tonight under the moon. Oh, I can see you tonight, under the moon ... you

wear a necktie so I'll know you."

As things turn out, Penelope winds up hosting all three brothers who rotate into her room and disappear into the one next door, like figures on an invisible carrousel. She manages to steal the necklace but accidentally drops the map of where she is going to stash the booty into Harpo's hat. Groucho is busy with a theft of his own, but one that works within the forms established by so-called decent, ordinary people. He will auction his lots. Just to make sure they bring a good price, he recruits Chico to keep raising the bids, promising him he'll get a nice commission. "How about some money?" asks Chico, who knows the value of Groucho's commissions. "You can have your choice," replies Groucho. Then he spreads out a blueprint of the area. "Do you know what a blueprint is?" he asks. "Sure," says Chico, always confident in his ignorance, "oysters."

Groucho, undaunted, proceeds.

Mary Eaton sentenced to marry Cyril King

Harpo consoles her in her hour of happiness

"Here's Cocoanut Grove," he says, "and here's Cocoanut Heights—it's a swamp—and here, where the road forks, is Cocoanut Junction." "Where," asks Chico, "is Cocoanut Custard?" "Over by the forks." Groucho makes the grievous error of pointing out a viaduct. Chico seizes on it immediately: "Why-a duck, why-a no chicken?" The more Groucho tries to explain it, the more tenacious Chico becomes. After fifteen explanations, Chico is still fixated. "All right," he says, "I catch on why-a horse, why-a chicken, why this, why that: I no catch on why-a duck."

Groucho surrenders. "I was only fooling," he says. "I was only fooling. They're going to build a tunnel there in the morning. Now is that clear to you?" "Yes," Chico returns, "everything except why-a duck." If this scene is trying once, imagine what it must have been for the Marx Brothers, who not only performed it nightly for two years, but who had to repeat it twenty-seven times in the filming because the crackling of the blueprints drowned out the dialogue. Finally the director hit on the idea of soaking the blueprints in water. The twenty-eighth take was quiet and kept.

Groucho hasn't seen the last of Chico. At the auction, his pupil catches on well at first, bidding $200 on the lot. But like the student in Ionesco's *The Lesson*, who can add anything but subtract not at all, Chico can't stop raising his bid. He purchases the first lot, the second and the third. When someone bids $700, he bids $800. As he explains it, "Six hundred, seven hundred, eight hundred, what the heck do I care . . . I've got plenty of numbers." Groucho gets so furious at his pariah that he yells, "Get away from that tree before it dies." Discouraged by Groucho's ingratitude at a job overdone, Chico slinks off. Groucho takes over, in the best tradition of American salesmanship. "What am I offered for lot twenty-five?" he asks, and nobody answers. "What am I offered for lot twenty-five and a year's subscription to *Youth Companion*?" No response. "Will somebody take a year's subscription? I'm trying to work my way through college." No takers. "Will somebody take a six months' subscription? I'll go to high school." Stony si-

Harpo staggers to the safety of the punch bowl

lence. "Does anybody want to buy a lead pencil?" Nothing. Finally Groucho challenges them all: "I'll wrestle anybody in the crowd for five dollars."

Mrs. Potter rushes onto the scene to announce that her necklace has been stolen. She offers a $1,000 reward. "Two thousand," bids Chico. Harpo finds the necklace, located on the very site of the bidding. Mrs. Potter kisses him, then, overcome with joy, announces she must kiss him again. This time, however, Harpo is ready, his face twisted into a sneer, his right arm ready to wallop her. The dowager reconsiders.

Good Bob Adams, who has won the lot, is jailed when Penelope implies that he stole the necklace for love of her. Mrs. Potter, who has always considered Adams social riffraff, announces that Polly will wed Boston-bred Harvey Yates, and an engagement masquerade celebration is announced. Adams remains in jail about six-

Watching Harpo booze it (l to r): Groucho, Chico, M. Dumont, C. King, K. Francis, M. Eaton

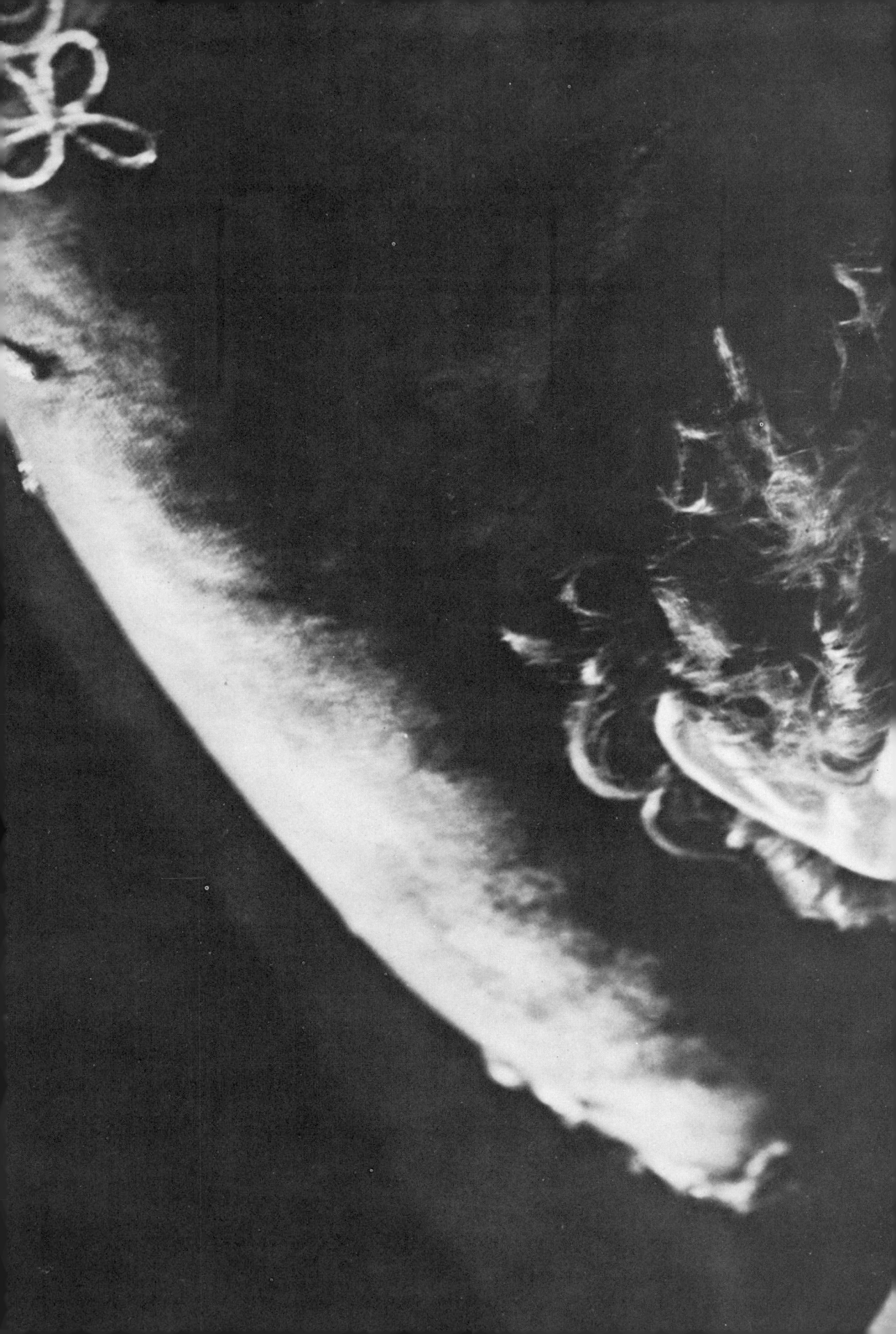

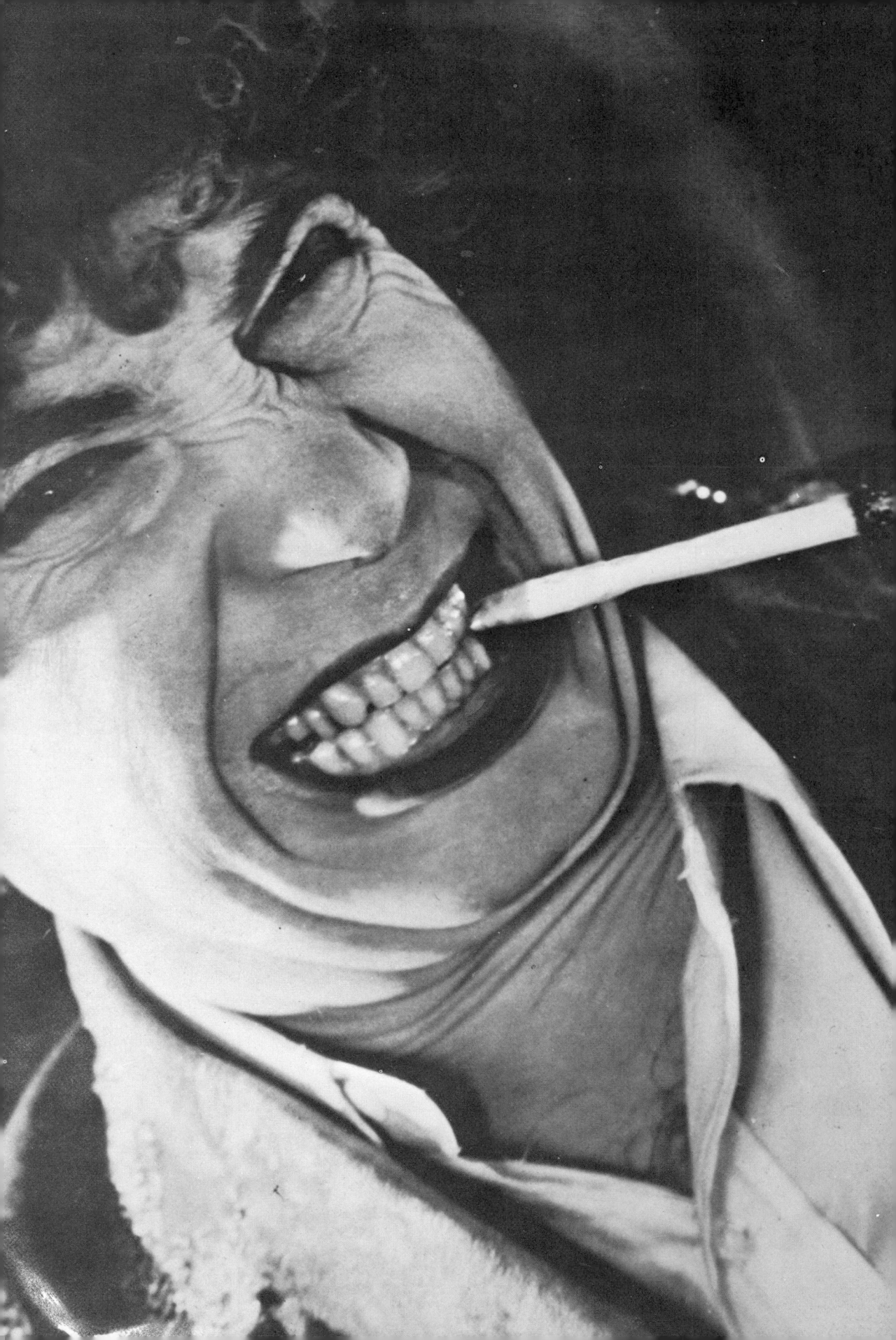

teen seconds, or just long enough for Harpo to pick the detective's keys to the cell and free him. The banquet itself is a model satire on all boring sit-down ceremonials. Groucho begins with a capsule takeoff on that repellent social menace, the after-dinner emcee. "Ladies and gentlemen," he begins. "Two hundred dollars," replies Chico.

Groucho goes on. "I want to welcome you to the Rotary Club of Waukegan . . . in recognition of my twenty years of service to the railroad . . . which reminds me of the story of the Irishman." Groucho doesn't even have to tell the story itself. He laughs, and the audience laughs heartily as well. As Groucho continues, Harpo, in gaucho getup for the lavish affair, staggers away from the table, his face, swollen with boredom and disgust, resembling that of a puff adder with

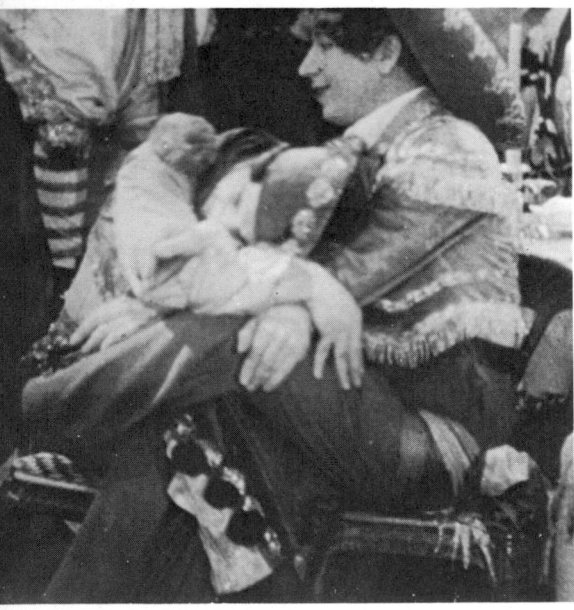

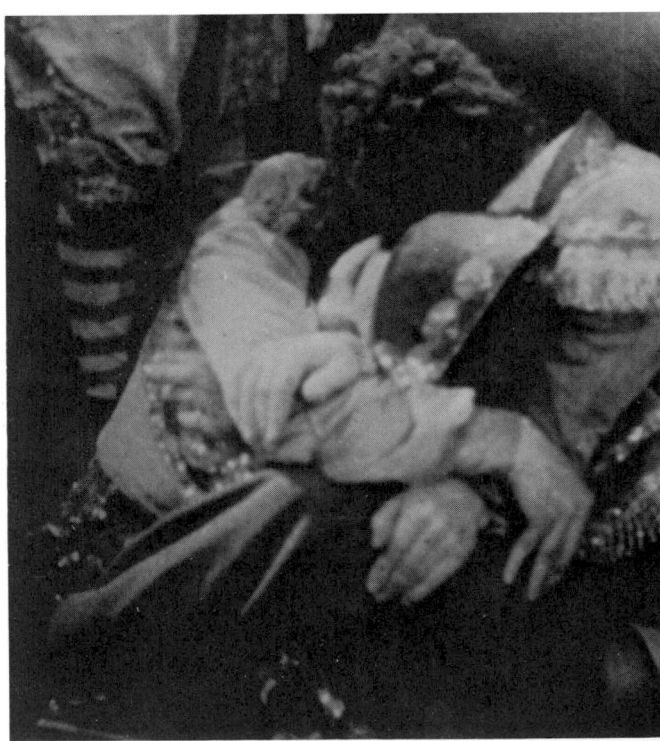

Harpo and Chico double up with boredom at banquet

heartburn. Each time a new speaker begins his remarks, Harpo puffs up and strides off to the punch bowl, returning a bit merrier and more anesthetized than before. Harvey Yates gets up to speak, and Harpo is off once more. "Thank you for calling on me," he says to Groucho, who is wearing a hat that turns him into a walking tree house. "Not at all," returns Groucho. "You must call on me sometime." Yates goes on. "I really don't know what to say." "Then shut up," barks Chico, expressing the hidden sentiments of all victims of dull dinners.

Everything, of course, is knotted up at the end, with sweet Bob winning sweet Polly to live sappily ever after; Penelope and Yates are whisked off to the clink with no avenging Marx Brothers to set them free. The final shot belongs to the lovers, smiling blandly at the audience. It was the first and last time the Marx Brothers did not steal the final frame as well as the picture.

The film was a success. Nobody missed Zeppo, who had a minuscule role as Groucho's assistant. The camera work, which showed all the mobility of a concrete fire hydrant caught in a winter freeze, was noted by the New York *Times* reviewer but dismissed, quite rightly, as harmless. Even the amputation of Berlin's score was looked on with good cheer. "Fun puts melody in the shade in the audible pictorial transcription of the musical comedy 'The Cocoanuts,'" wrote the man from the *Times,* grappling to find words for this strange hybrid. For the first time, the Marxes, who had played all over America, city by city, town by town, suddenly played everywhere at once.

Justice triumphs

Chico, Groucho, Harpo, and Zeppo

Margaret Dumont

Robert Grieg

Hal Thompson and Lillian Roth

Louis Sorin

Margaret Irving

Captain Jeffrey T. Spaulding:	GROUCHO
The Professor:	HARPO
Signor Emanuel Ravelli:	CHICO
Horatio Jamison:	ZEPPO
Mrs. Rittenhouse:	MARGARET DUMONT
Arabella Rittenhouse:	LILLIAN ROTH
Roscoe W. Chandler:	LOUIS SORIN
John Parker:	HAL THOMPSON
Mrs. Whitehead:	MARGARET IRVING
Grace Carpenter:	KATHRYN REECE
Hives, the Butler:	ROBERT GRIEG
Inspector Hennessy:	EDWARD METCALF
Six Footmen:	THE MUSIC MASTERS

* * *

Director: Victor Heerman
Screenplay: Morrie Ryskind
Original book of Musical Play: George S. Kaufman and Morrie Ryskind
Continuity: Pierre Collings
Music and Lyrics: Bert Kalmar and Harry Ruby
Photography: George Folsey
Released by Paramount, September 6, 1930. 98 minutes

3 *Animal Crackers* (1930)

The Cocoanuts was the first of five pictures the brothers contracted to make for Paramount. *Animal Crackers* was the natural second. The boys had lived with it for a year while it was the melba toast of Broadway, then had taken it on tour. As with *The Cocoanuts*, all they needed to do was haul the entire production before the Astoria studio cameras, and *voila*—instant movie. Certainly the price was right. For nine Broadway performances a week, the brothers were paid $2,000 each. For a couple of months, work at Astoria, they would each clear $50,000. So they deserted Broadway, never to darken its towels again. It is hard to believe that Groucho was sorry to go. His description of life during the Broadway run of *Animal Crackers,* as related to his friend and future collaborator Arthur Sheekman, reads like the diary of a man caught in a revolving door. "I arise in the morning, and before I have had my clothes on ten minutes," he writes, "I am over at the theater doing the ordering scene. Then follows thirty minutes of Harpo climbing up Dumont's leg, and the shirt scene, and then to the dressing room for what I imagine is going to be a good long rest. I am no more than seated with the *Morning World* when the buzzer rings, and I am downstairs again doing the ordering scene, and Harpo is back again at Dumont's leg. After four shots of this, I stagger to my hotel, go to bed, and the alarm rings and I rush over to the theater and do the ordering scene again."

The ordering scene never made the film, and the half hour Harpo spent climbing up Margaret Dumont's leg was snipped to a few seconds. But even so, the movie ran ninety-eight minutes and seems even longer. It contains Groucho's greatest monologue, his most celebrated character, his familiar theme song, marvelous encounters with Chico, and Harpo's famous silverware-dropping routine. Nevertheless, it holds together poorly and, toward the end, drags badly. The principal problem seems to be the plot. In *Animal Crackers* the brothers do not play against the plot, as they did in *The Cocoanuts.* Nor do they jettison it completely, as they were to do in their next three Paramount films. Instead they either wriggle through cracks in its makeup or ignore it when they can. The result is a film with a heavy, silly, complicated plot featuring three comics who pretend it isn't there. There are many definitions of good comic structure. This is none of them. So *Animal Crackers* survives as an old-fashioned "laff riot" with all the sense of discipline and organization that that rubric implies.

In contrast to the rest of the film, the opening sequence is a model of form, precise and economical as it sets

Hoorah for Captain Spaulding, the African explorer

up the action. We learn that Mrs. Rittenhouse, once again Margaret Dumont at her most theatrical, is holding a party at her mansion to honor the return of Captain Spaulding, the African explorer. On the same evening, she is to unveil the famous Beauregard oil painting, "The Hunt," donated by the philanthropist Roscoe W. Chandler. We also learn that her daughter, Arabella, is in love with a penniless artist named John Parker. (Arabella is played by Lillian Roth, whose celebrated descent into alcoholism lends her fresh, energetic but hopelessly hammy performance a tragic cast.)

Our appetite for Captain Spaulding whetted, the opening scene goes on to establish the characters of the brothers in classic fashion. Zeppo enters first, as Groucho's secretary Jamison, announcing that his boss is about to arrive. In comes Groucho, attired in a questionably spotless explorer's outfit and borne on a stretcher by four African natives, another pair in the rear carrying his guns. "What? From Africa to here, a dollar eighty-five?" he cries in the outraged tone of the piker haggling with his cabbie. "I told you not to take me through Australia. It's all chopped up. You should have come right up the Lincoln Boulevard." Then he swivels to face Mrs. Rittenhouse; "You're the most beautiful woman I've ever seen, which doesn't say much for you." "It is indeed an honor to welcome you to my poor home," says Mrs. Rittenhouse. "Oh, it isn't so bad," Groucho replies, sizing up the joint. "Wait a minute. I think you're right. It is pretty bad. As a matter of fact, it's one of the frowziest joints I've ever seen. You let this place run down, and what's the result? You're not getting the class of people you used to. Why, you've got

What? From Africa to here a dollar eighty-five?"

people here that look like *you*. Now I'll tell you what we'll do. We'll put up a sign outside—Placed Under New Management. We'll set up a seventy-five-cent meal that will knock their eyes out. After we knock their eyes out, we can charge anything we want." Most people are rude in one of two ways, but Groucho can be rude with endless variation. He doesn't eat and run. He runs almost before he arrives, as he explains in the song "I Must Be Going," in which he states: "Hello, I must be going/I cannot stay, I only came to say/I must be going." The crowd, as always, replies to Groucho's rudeness by extolling him in song and cheer. "Hurrah for Captain Spaulding" afterward became Groucho's theme song, used to introduce each episode of his TV quiz show, "You Bet Your Life."

Enter Chico as Signor Emanuel Ravelli, one of the musicians, who, in contrast to Groucho, eats almost before he arrives. His opening line: "Where's the dining room?" Before he utters another word, he and Groucho have hooked up in one of their nonsense duels. "What do you get an

hour?" Groucho asks. "For playing, we get-a ten dollars an hour." "I see. What do you get for not playing?" "Twelve dollars an hour," says Chico. "Now for rehearsing, we make special rates. That's-a fifteen dollars an hour." "And what do you get," asks Groucho, "for not rehearsing?" "You couldn't afford it. You see, if we don't rehearse, we don't a-play. And if we don't a-play, that runs into money." "How much would you want to run into an open manhole?" "Just-a the cover charge." "Well, drop in some time." "Sewer," says Chico. "Well, I guess we cleaned that up," concludes Groucho.

Finally, Harpo is introduced as the Professor, though professor of what is never made clear. He descends the main stairway in high hat, cape and taxi horn. "The gates swung open," announces Groucho," and a Fig Newton entered." Harpo, like the other brothers, wastes no time telling us who he is. He blows solid puffs of smoke, turning them brown when Groucho requests chocolate. "He's a-got everything," comments Chico. Well, not quite. Hives, the butler, removes Harpo's cape, revealing him in T-shirt and shorts. Once, during the Broadway run, Harpo arrived at the theater late, forgot to put on the shorts, and appeared onstage at this point sheltered only by a minuscule G-string. Groucho saved the day. "Tomorrow night," he announced, "he's not going to wear anything, so get your tickets early."

As the crowd scatters in dismay, Harpo turns the lobby into his private shooting gallery. First he takes aim at the pendulum of the wall clock, spinning it with each shot. Then he sights on the pet canary, which chirps for a

"If we dont a-play, that runs into money"

A fig newton enters

bit, then lets out an ominous groan. Finally he knocks the hats off a pair of passing ladies. When a blonde rushes through, he drops his rifle and takes chase.

With the brothers all on hand, operating true to form in their natural habitats, the story continues on schedule with THE COMPLICATIONS. A neighbor, Mrs. Whitehead, jealous of Mrs. Rittenhouse's gala party, enlists Hives to substitute a phony Beauregard for the real one. At the same time, Arabella convinces Harpo and Chico to substitute John Parker's copy of the Beauregard for the real one, hoping that philanthropist Chandler will recognize Parker's skill and offer him a scholarship. At this point, the movie breaks into pieces, hilarious pieces, but pieces nonetheless.

Groucho always keeps his motor running in case money speeds by. At the first opportunity, he cruises after Mrs. Rittenhouse. "You've got beauty, charm, money," he tells her. "You have got money, haven't you? 'Cause

Harpo, in full academic dress, shows the better part of his nature

if you haven't, we can quit right now. Ever since I've met you," he declares, "I've swept you off my feet. Something has been throbbing within me, like an incessant tom-tom in the primitive jungle. There's something I must ask you. Would you wash out a pair of socks for me?" Just as Groucho has Mrs. Rittenhouse on the "five-yard line" as he poetically puts it, Mrs. Whitehead enters. He immediately shifts his strategy. "You know, you girls have everything," he begins. "You're tall and short and slim and stout and blond and brunet." He concludes with a proposal of marriage to both of them. "Why, that's bigamy," exclaims Mrs. Rittenhouse." "Yes," says Groucho, "and it's big-a-me, too." Mrs. Rittenhouse will have none of it. Marriage, she says, is a noble institution. "Yeah," Groucho replies, "but the trouble is, you can't enforce it. It was put over on the American people while our boys were over there and our girls were over here."

Later Groucho tries to put the bite on Roscoe W. Chandler. "You have heard of me?" says the flattered philanthropist. "Yes," answers Groucho, "I've heard of you for a great many years, Mr. Chandler, and I'm getting good and sick of it. How would you like to finance a scientific expedition?" "Well, *that's* a question," remarks Chandler. "Yes, that *is* a question. You certainly know a question when you see one. I congratulate you." It turns out that Groucho wants Chandler to finance "the one thing I always wanted to do before I quit—retire. Now, would you be interested in proposition of that kind? You know, I've always felt that my retirement would be the greatest contribution to science the world has ever known." "The nickel today is not what it used to be ten years ago," says Chandler, indicating what he think's Groucho's retirement is worth. Groucho counters with an economic theory keener than Keynes: "Do you know what this country needs today? A seven-cent nickel. Yessiree, we've been using the five-cent nickel in this country since 1492, and that's pretty near a hundred years' daylight saving. Now why not give the seven-cent nickel a chance? If it works out, next year we could have an eight-cent nickel. Think what that would mean. You could go to the newsstand, buy a three-cent newspaper and get the same nickel back again. One nickel carefully used would last a family a lifetime!" No sale. Chandler announces that he will be sailing for Uruguay shortly."Well," says Groucho. "You go Uruguay and I'll go mine."

The Marx Brothers movies bristle with Groucho's attacks on one kind of formal language or another. In addition to this salvo on economic words-

One morning I shot an elephant in my pajamas."

Hal Thompson and Lillian Roth

The great garter theft

"Just send the stamp airmail."

Getting a leg up before the bridge game

manship, Captain Spaulding also decimates the jargon of the business letter. "Gentlemen, question mark," he tells Zeppo, dictating a letter to his lawyers, Hungadunga, Hungadunga, Hungadunga and McCormack. "Harrumph." He clears his throat. "Do you want that harrumph in the letter?" "No," replies Groucho, "put it in an envelope. Now then, in re yours of the fifteenth, yours to hand, brackets, that we have gone over the ground carefully and we seem to believe, i.e., to wit, e.g., in lieu, that despite all our precautionary measures that have been involved, we seem to believe that it is hardly necessary for us to proceed unless we receive an *ipso facto* that is not negligible at this moment, quotes, unquotes, quotes, hoping to find you, I beg to remain, as of June 9, cordially yours." Groucho asks Zeppo to read back the letter, but Zeppo has omitted everything he

Something fishy going on

didn't understand. "You just omitted the body of the letter," cries Groucho, taking a wild swing at his head. "Well, send it that way and tell them the body will follow." Should Zeppo put that in brackets? "No, the body will never get there in brackets. Better put it in a box. Now I want you to make two carbon copies of that letter and throw the original away. And when you're through with that, throw the copies away. Just send the stamp airmail. You may go, Jamison. I may go."

Groucho's greatest achievement is his thoroughgoing lampoon of the African adventure saga, recited to the guests at Mrs. Rittenhouse's soiree. "Africa is God's country, and He can have it," he begins. "Well, sir, we left New York drunk and early on the morning of February 2. After fifteen days on the water and six on the boat, we finally arrived on the shores of Af-

rica. The first morning saw us up at six, breakfasted and back in bed at seven. This was our routine for the first three months. We finally got so we were in bed at six thirty. The principal animals inhabiting the African jungle," he goes on, "are moose, elks and Knights of Pythias. Of course, you know what a moose is. That's big game. The first day, I shot two bucks. That was the biggest game we had. [The brilliant hand of playwright George S. Kaufman is evident here.] The elks, on the other hand, live up in the hills, and in the spring they come down for their annual convention. It is very interesting to see them come to the water hole. And you should see them run when they see it's only a water hole. What they're looking for is an elkahole. One morning I shot an elephant in my pajamas. How he got in my pajamas, I don't know. Then we tried to remove the tusks, but they were embedded in so firmly that we couldn't budge them. Of course, in Alabama, the Tuskaloosa. But that's entirely irrelephant to what I was talking about. We took some pictures of native girls, but they weren't developed, but we're going back again in a couple of weeks." This onslaught is halted by Chandler, who calls, "Three cheers for Captain Spaulding, three cheers for Captain Spaulding!"

"Abie, the fishman!"

Would you take a check?

Art critics at work

Harpo obliges with three chairs for Captain Spaulding.

Like Groucho, Chico and Harpo have come to the Rittenhouse mansion for profit rather than fun. A first, they try blackmail. Chico has discovered by the birthmark on Chandler's forearm that he was once Abie Cabibble, the Czechoslovakian fish peddler. "How did you get to be Roscoe W. Chandler?" Chico asks. "How did you get to be an Italian?" replies Chandler, spotting Chico's ethnic disguise for the first and last time in a Marx movie. Groucho had the same kind of fun with Chico's Italian ancestry during the stage run of *Animal Crackers*. When Chico would protest that he was Groucho's brother, Groucho would reply in a drawl: "How come you're an Italian and I'm from the Deep South?" At any rate, here Chico brushes off Chandler's question with a terse "Never mind. Whose confession is this?" He starts chanting, "Abie, the fish man, Abie the fish man" until Chandler offers him $500 to keep him quiet. Chico refuses. Chandler returns the money to what he thinks is his pocket but turns out to be Harpo's. Finally, he offers a $5,000 check. Harpo drops it on the floor. It bounces back to his hand. The brothers settle for smaller stakes. They steal Chandler's handkerchief, garters and birthmark, which Harpo transfers somehow to his own forearm.

Extortion, apparently, is only a sideline. Harpo and Chico depend on cardsharking for their livelihood. Business up to this point has been slow. "We keep this up, we wind up in the old ladies' home. How you like that?" says Chico. Harpo grins luridly. The con team at last engages Mrs. Rittenhouse and Mrs. Whitehead

A low regard for a Beauregard

in a game of bridge, but not before Harpo has handed the dowager his leg several times, taken a swipe at her, and recovered, with the help of Chico, who serves as his second. Finally, after having fumed, puffed and snorted, he punches her in the stomach. At last, the quartet sits down to bridge. "How do you want to play," asks Chico, "honest?" They draw for partners. Chico picks an ace of spades. Harpo also picks an ace of spades. "Two aces of spades?" asks Mrs. Rittenhouse. "Yeah," says Chico, "he's got thousands of 'em." Harpo, having drawn the highest card (apparently his ace of spades is higher than Chico's), has his choice of seats. He plops himself on Mrs. Whitehead's lap. "He thought it was contact bridge," explains Chico. Harpo must shuffle the cards. The silent partner grabs half the deck in each hand, riffles them separately, and returns them unmixed Then, wetting his left thumb, he deals with his right hand, offering Chico a look at each card. When Chico likes one, he keeps it. When he doesn't, Harpo deals it to Mrs. Rittenhouse, who is busy arranging her hand. To make matters more improbable, Mrs. Rittenhouse emerges with the good hand. So Harpo swipes it. He bids one. "One what?" asks Mrs. Rittenhouse. "Never mind," says Chico, who bids two of the same. Harpo leads his ace of spades. "No spades, partner," warns Chico. Harpo tries again. "No spades, partner!!!" Harpo finally shrugs and rips his ace of spades to bits. But, as Chico says, he has thousands of them. He plays thirteen aces and wins the hand. "He plays a good game," Chico tells Mrs. Rittenhouse. The two ladies leave the table in a huff. Harpo, it turns out, has not only won the game, but Mrs. Whitehead's shoes, which he totters off in.

The gala evening arrives. The Beauregard is unveiled, only it is the fake that Hives has placed there. Within minutes, not only is the original missing, but the two copies as well. Mrs. Rittenhouse calls in the police under the direction of Hennessey, the same name used by the detective in *The Cocoanuts*. Groucho introduces himself as Captain Scotland of Spaulding Yard and sets out to solve the case. Chico offers his help. He

Reprise (l to r): R. Grieg, L. Sorin, H. Thompson, M. Dumont, L. Roth, E. Metcalf

knows the motive behind the theft: robbery.

"Something was stolen," he says, following his own involuted logic. "Stolen where? In-a this house. Stolen by who? Somebody in this house. Now to find the painting, all you got to do is go to everybody in the house and ask 'em if-a they took it." "Suppose nobody in the house took the painting?" posits Groucho. "Go to the house next door," says Chico. "That's great. Suppose there isn't any house next door?" "Well, then of course we gotta build one." Groucho wants a modest dwelling, "someplace you can call home and tell the wife you won't be home for dinner." Chico has just the place, a cottage with the roof in the basement, "so when-a it rains, the chimney won't get wet." Before they finish designing this castle in the air, Chico has solved the mystery. "The painting," he proclaims, "was eaten by left-handed moths. That's a-my solution." "Yeah," says Groucho, "and I wish you were in it. You ought to lie down for a couple of years."

Harpo is the left-handed moth who has taken the paintings. In the final sequence, he returns all three. Chandler recognizes the skill in John Parker's copy and offers him a scholarship. Hennessey steps in to arrest Harpo but decides to give him some friendly advice instead. "You're running around with the wrong kind of people," says the officer. "Do you want to be a crook?" Harpo nods and smiles. Undaunted, the detective goes on, counseling Harpo to return to his dear mother. In his autobiography, Harpo describes this classic sequence which he first developed in the vaudeville act "On the Mezzanine": "Impressed by sparing me from a life of crime, the detective shakes my hand. A knife falls out and bounces on the floor. The detective shakes harder. Three more knives fall out. He shakes both hands, and still more silver comes spilling out. When I first did the bit, I had twenty pieces up my sleeves. I eventually worked up to dropping three hundred knives, with a silver coffee pot tumbling out of my coat for a finish." By *Animal Crackers*, Groucho knew the act well enough to remark on screen: "I can't understand what's delaying the coffee pot." Out it comes. The detective goes to arrest Harpo, but Harpo flits knockout juice over the entire company, including his brothers. Then, following his wild logic to its inevitable conclusion, he knocks himself out to end the film.

Predictably, *Animal Crackers* was a hit. After all, the show had been a roaring success on Broadway and on the road. The film was little more than a canned version of the play. And the brothers had already proven in *The Cocoanuts* that they could make a play work on the screen. "Their popular brand of comedy pervades the picture," wrote the critic for *Film Daily*, the business journal of the movie industry, "So much, in fact, that there is little footage left for a love plot of any importance. While most of the repartee is nonsense, it gets laughs, and that's what counts." If the *Film Daily* critic was dismayed by the nonsense and minimal romance of this early picture, he was to be blown out of his seat by what was to come. Up to this point, the brothers had been bound by the limits of the stage. With their success in *Animal Crackers*, Paramount unleashed them.

A knockout of an ending: Harpo in heaven

Chico, Zeppo, Groucho, and Harpo

Otto Fries

Harry Woods

Rockcliffe Fellowes

Thelma Todd

Ben Taggart

The Stowaways:	GROUCHO
	HARPO
	CHICO
	ZEPPO
Lucille:	THELMA TODD
Joe Helton:	ROCKCLIFFE FELLOWES
Gibson:	TOM KENNEDY
Mary Helton:	RUTH HALL
Alky Briggs:	HARRY WOODS
The Captain:	BEN TAGGART
Second Mate:	OTTO FRIES
Manicurist:	EVELYN PIERCE
Opera Singer:	MAXINE CASTLE

* * *

Director: Norman McLeod
Story: S. J. Perelman and Will B. Johnstone
Additional Dialogue: Arthur Sheekman
Photography: Arthur L. Todd
Released by Paramount, September 19, 1931. 77 minutes

4 Monkey Business (1931)

With *Monkey Business,* the Marx Brothers set up shop in Hollywood. The Astoria studio had been adequate for "audible pictorial transcriptions" and had allowed the brothers to carry on their stage career. But the two Astoria films suffered from an acute case of cinematic claustrophobia, that disease of the screen caused by lack of real sunshine, real grass, real trees and real doors that open onto something more expansive than backstage. Not that the Marxes ever took great advantage of "location shooting." No comedians ever used so little of the out-of-doors. But Astoria was clearly not the film capital of the world. The brothers needed a bigger sound stage and an occasional outdoor setting. And they needed to operate close to the home studio, where the best producers, directors and actors were located. If they needed a good comic writer who lived in New York, they could import him. His name was S. J. Perelman.

Perelman, a regular contributor at that time to *Judge,* a humor magazine, and author of *Dawn Ginsberg's Revenge,* and Will B. Johnstone, who wrote *I'll Say She Is,* collaborated on both *Monkey Business* and *Horse Feathers.* Perelman etched his imprimatur indelibly on both films and on the brothers' style in the movies that followed. His influence in *Monkey Business* is felt everywhere—in the highly literate script, in the

beautifully honed edge on Groucho's puns, in the methodical madness and mordant tone of the film. It is no accident that two films Perelman worked on are the most verbal the brothers made and among the best.

Not that the brothers took to Perelman as a duck takes to soup. Comedy was their business. It was nothing to laugh about, as Perelman found out when the Marxes returned to Hollywood after playing the Palladium in London and listened to their new writer read them his script. Perelman recorded this encounter in a piece in *Show* magazine several years ago. His chilling account should disabuse the most fanatical Marx buff of any notion that the brothers' story conferences were a carnival of chuckles. The Marxes, accompanied by their girl friends, gag writers and dogs, filed in to hear Perelman read the 126-page script. "When I counted noses and paws before ringing up the curtain," Perelman recalls, "there were twenty-seven people and five dogs confronting me . . . I had not proceeded very far before I began to sense a distinct change in the mood of my listeners. At first it was pliant—indulgent, so to speak—and there was an occasional polite ripple. This soon ceased and they became watchful—not hostile as yet, but wary. It was as if they were girding themselves, flexing for trouble they knew was inevitable. Then, by slow degrees, an attitude of sullen re-

Four kippered herring

sentment stole into their faces . . . and they grew vengeful. *Some* of them got vengeful, that is; the majority got sleepy, for by then, I had stopped inflecting my voice to distinguish one character from another and had settled into a monotonous lilt lika a Hindu chanting the Bhagavad-Gita."

"When I finally croaked 'fade-out,' " Perelman concludes, "at the end of my ninety-minute unspectacular there was no sound except the stertorous breathing of the dogs. After an aeon, Chico stretched, revolved in his chair, and addressed Groucho. 'What do you think?' he growled. With the deliberation of a diamond cutter, Groucho bit the end off his cigar and, applying a match, exhaled a jet of smoke. 'It stinks' he said, and arose. 'Come on.' " The next day, however, "our critics capriciously reversed themselves,"

Perelman reports, "and decided that traces of our handiwork could be salvaged."

Perelman was but the first of many writers to sweat out a stone-cold story conference with the Marx Brothers. "They never laughed during a story conference," Margaret Dumont once remarked. "Like most expert comedians, they involved themselves so seriously in the study of how jokes could be converted to their own style that they didn't even titter while appraising their material." It is impossible, of course, to tell how much of Perelman's material passed through the Marxes' converter. Groucho insists that Perelman was not as smoothly geared to the brothers' style as Kaufman and Ryskind or, as Groucho puts it, "He wasn't a constructionist for the stage." But if Perelman was more literary than theatrical, his jaundiced attitude toward language flowed easily through Groucho's character. In *Monkey Business* and *Horse Feathers* each one of Perelman's lines is perfectly tailored to Groucho, and Groucho, in turn, accords each line its proper balance and bite. "I was doing this kind of comedy long before I met S. J. Perelman," Groucho once said, describing the ideal situation for a perfect marriage of writer and comic.

In *Monkey Business* the Marx Brothers work for the first time with a script written especially for the screen. But their break with the stage is by no means complete. In fact, even in their movies of the 1940's, the influence of vaudeville and Broadway is apparent. The typical Marx Brothers scene invariably takes place in a stateroom or hotel room or backstage dressing room not far in spirit from the

Cocoanuts Hotel. The whole of *Monkey Business* could be played, with slight alterations, on the stage. But these alterations are important. The film contains scenes in which close-up and chase are part of the comedy. Settings switch quickly from stateroom to stateroom, from ship to shore, from baronial estate to barn. The characters no longer declaim to some phantom audience beyond an invisible proscenium arch. Their gestures are less baroque, knowing that the camera is sensitive to smaller responses. On balance, *Monkey Business* is conceived of and executed as a moving picture in the literal sense of the word.

The camera can no longer sit on its hindquarters and absorb the action; it must chase madly after the Marxes.

The chase begins almost immediately. The brothers are stowaways on an ocean liner, each living in his own kippered herring barrel. They pass the time singing "Sweet Adeline," with Harpo mouthing merrily. They are discovered by the crew when their barrels are hoisted away—Zeppo, Chico and Groucho preparing a breakfast of eggs and toast and Harpo industriously giving the coffee pot a shoeshine. The brothers flee to the deck with the crew straggling after, rush into the first-class lounge and

Each brother in his favorite key

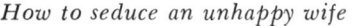

How to seduce an unhappy wife

render an instant impersonation of the band. Chico plays the piano while the other brothers break into a cacophony of swing numbers, each in his own key, on three different saxophones. The audience, always ignorant and obliging in Marx movies, lustily cheers the musical mess.

The chase continues throughout the film. The Marx Brothers are either chasing blondes and brunettes or being chased by criminals and crew. The smell of Prohibition days hangs heavily over the picture with the whole plot strung on the efforts of the bad guy, a bootlegger named Alky Briggs, to move in on the territory of the good guy, another bootlegger (retired) named Joe Helton. Groucho is

interested in moving in on Briggs' territory, namely Mrs. Briggs. She is played by Thelma Todd, a coltish blonde who received Groucho's blandishments in both Perelman films. While not as imposing a receptacle of indignities as Margaret Dumont, she shared the Marx Brothers' sense of fun and boundless energies and, in her own playful way, served equally well as a foil for Groucho. She died in 1935, three years after *Horse Feathers* was finished.

The closet scene between Miss Todd, as Lucille Briggs, and Groucho remains one of the masterpieces of Marxian repartee. Groucho, escaping from the pursuing crew, barges into the Briggs' stateroom with the line

and wind up with an unhappy husband

"Pardon me while I step in the closet." Undeterred, Briggs and Lucille carry on their marital war, a series of battles in the spirit of Jean Harlow and Wallace Beery that pop up throughout the film. When Briggs walks out in a huff (a small blue huff, Groucho might add), Lucille knocks on the closet. "What are you doing in there?" she asks. Out pops Groucho's head, eyes rolling lasciviously, cigar aflame. "Nothing, come on in." She suggests that he can't stay in there forever. "I can't, can I?" Groucho challenges, then adds in a burst of logic: "Just remember, my little cabbage, if there weren't any closets, there wouldn't be any hooks, and if there weren't any hooks, there wouldn't be any fish,

which would suit me fine." Not only will Groucho not leave the closet, he is not even in it, he insists, proving his point with the skill of an attorney framing an innocent man. "Did you see me go in that closet?" he asks, hopping out. "No," she says. "Am I in that closet?" he demands. "Well, no," she answers. "Well, how do you know I was *in* the closet?" he concludes in triumph, throwing himself on her bed. "Your Honor, I rest my case." "You're awfully shy for a lawyer," Lucille observes. "You bet I'm shy," says Groucho. "I'm a shyster lawyer." He has a strictly dishonest plan that will free her of her tyrannical husband. "Madame," he states, "before I get through with you, you will have a

Harpo, Punch and Judy

clear case for divorce, and so will my wife. Now the first thing to do is arrange for a settlement. You take the children. Your husband takes the house. Junior burns down the house, you take the children and," he adds amorously, "I take you. I know you're a woman who's gotten nothing but dirty breaks," he tells her. "We can clean and tighten those brakes, but you'll have to stay in the garage overnight."

Groucho and Lucille celebrate her liberation with a tango that leaves him spinning into the arms of Alky Briggs, returned unexpectedly. Groucho is best at moments like these. "How dare you, sir. This is an outrage," he cries, "breaking into a man's home. I'm not in the habit of making threats, but there'll be a letter about this in the *Times* tomorrow morning." Briggs doesn't read the *Times*, but he does lay people out. "Oh, you're gonna lay me out pretty, eh?" says Groucho, "That's the thanks I get for freeing an innocent girl who, though she is hiding in the closet at the moment, has promised to become the mother of her children." Briggs insists that he is wise to what's been going on. "You're wise, eh?" challenges Groucho. "Well what's the capital of Ne-

braska? What's the capital of the Chase National Bank? . . . Now I'll try you on an easy one. How many Frenchmen can't be wrong?" "I know," says Briggs, trapped into the little quiz game. "You were wrong," says Groucho, not waiting for the answer. Then he adds in a tone prophetic of the quiz master he was to become, "But don't be discouraged. With a little study you'll go a long way, and I wish you'd start now." Briggs is a sore loser. He's going to kill Groucho but has the decency to allow him a few last words. "I'd like to ask you a question," says Groucho. Then, slipping into the whine of a teen-age girl, he goes on. "Do you think girls think less of a boy if he lets himself be kissed. I mean, don't you think that, although girls go out with boys like me, they always marry the other kind?" Briggs finally surrenders and, impressed with Groucho's nerve, decides to take him on as his bodyguard. Clearly Groucho is a man you want on your side, even if it's only to make sure he isn't against you. "I think we could get along well together," Briggs says. "Well," counters Groucho, now grown into a newlywed, "the first year we might have our little squabbles, but that's inevitable, don't you think?"

Harpo also enjoys one of his most brilliant and imaginative sequences aboard the good ship *Monkey Business*. With the crew hot on his worn heels, he seeks refuge in a Punch 'n' Judy show being held for the kids. Clipping a pair of puppet's legs to his collar like a necktie, he pokes his head

The great Gookie

Harpo's version of I am a Camera

onstage and becomes the third puppet, a perfectly inanimate "Gookie" frozen on his face. The transformation is so dazzling, in fact, that someone entering the theater at this point would be hard pressed to know whether he was watching Harpo playing a puppet or a puppet playing Harpo. The captain is puzzled as well. He goes to touch Harpo's face but winds up tapping the papier-maché mask Harpo has put on the back of his head for just such a verification. The first mate has stuck Harpo's bottom with a pin, so he knows puppet from pretender, but he can't convince the captain, which gives the kids a good laugh. Finally, the captain catches on—to Harpo's leg and starts pulling. The going gets tough, so Harpo runs out to join them, and the three of them pull the artificial limb loose. While the captain and mate wrestle with the leg on the floor, Harpo exists in style on a roller cart,

waving to the cheering throng.

Later in the film, Harpo manages another spectacular transformation. A supercilious grande dame—one of a handful of instant substitutes for Margaret Dumont used by the brothers when the great dowager wasn't with them—is about to have her picture taken by the press. The photographer peers under his black cloth and pushes the bulb. HONK! The cloth falls away, and there is Harpo, a pair of crutches and one leg forming the tripod, a midget box Brownie simulating the lens. The "camera" rushes off and Groucho rushes in to interview the diva, at once satirizing the stupid questions posed by the press and assaulting the star with insults. "Is it true you're getting a divorce as soon as your husband recovers his eyesight?" he asks. "Is it true you wash your hair in clam broth? Is is true you used to dance in a flea circus?"

A fro

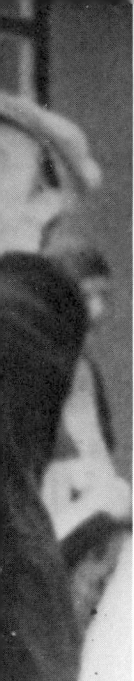

In this sense, the three balance like a logical equation. In the beginning of the film, Chico and Groucho take over the captain's quarters. Chico hasn't eaten for three days. "Three days?" questions Groucho, who plays the straight man for Chico and nobody else in the Marx Brothers films. "I'd didn't eat yesterday," explains Chico. "I didn't eat today. And I'm not gonna eat tomorrow. That makes-a three days." Actually, Chico has come up to see the captain's bridge. "I'm sorry," says Groucho. "He always keeps it in a glass of water while he's eating. Would you like to see where he sleeps?" "I saw that," Chico replied. "That's the bunk."

Chico manages to get along in any situation. He kills time in the ship's barbershop getting his nails manicured. "Would you like your nails trimmed long?" asks the manicurist. "Oh, about an hour and a half. I got nothing to do," Chico replies. Then, when a member of the crew enters, sporting a handlebar moustache, Chico adapts immediately, impersonating the barber. He and Harpo pro-

Chico's moments are always tied to one of the other brothers. Groucho and Harpo thrive on their encounters with strangers, but Chico rarely blossoms without help from the family. On the other hand, while Groucho and Harpo rarely play together, Chico works beautifully with both of them.

One snoop-a too much

roat

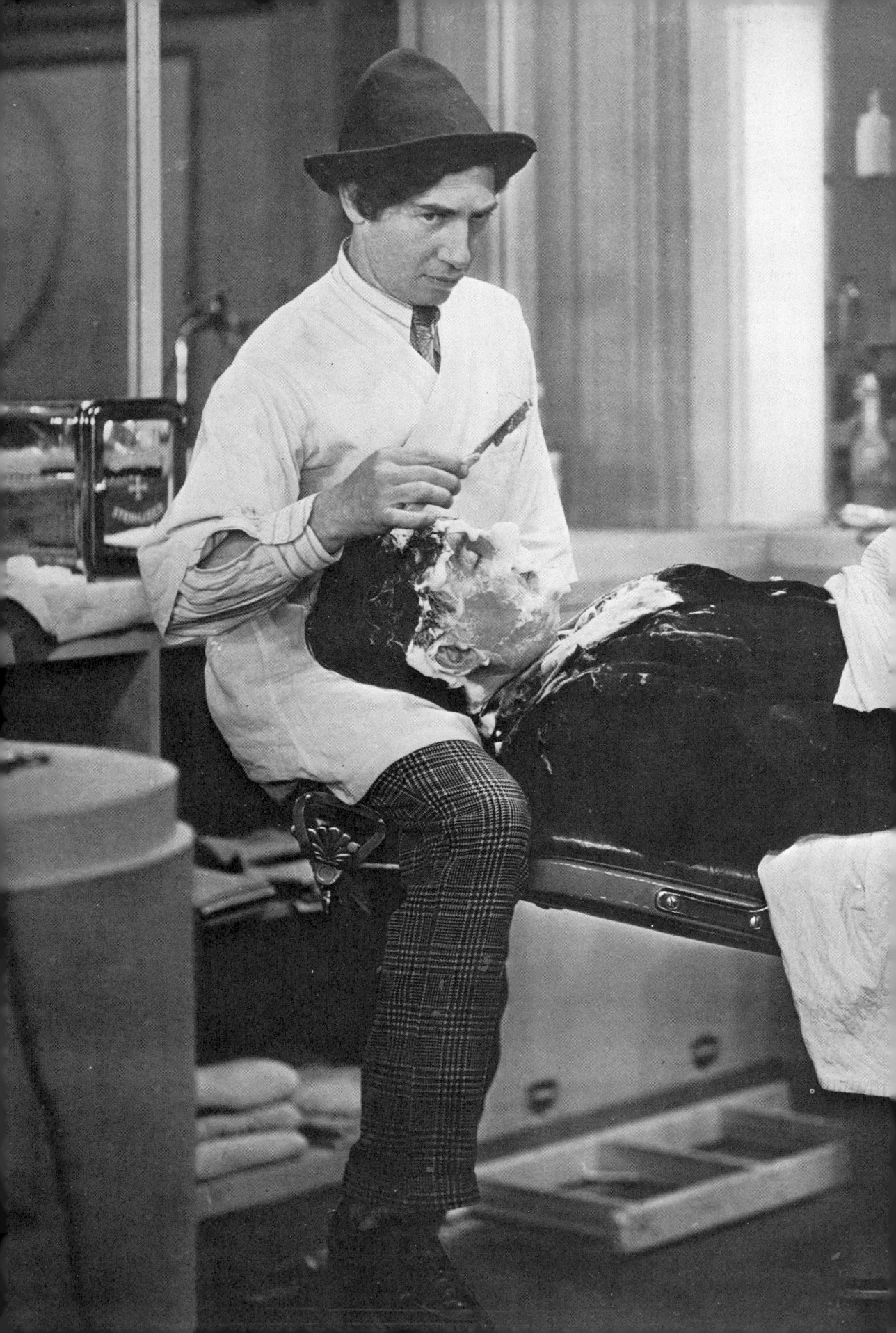

ceed to give him a shave and a trim. Harpo snips off one side, then the other. They pull out tape measures to check each side. "It's a foot too long," proclaims Chico from his side of the moustache. Harpo instantly tries to yank off the man's foot. Finally, after a snip here and a snip there, the moustache has shrunk to an adolescent version of Hitler's. A final snip takes care of that. "Hey, you know," observes Chico, always helpful, "I think you gave him one snip-a too much."

Harpo and Chico remain a team throughout the movie. Briggs has taken as bodyguards Groucho and Zeppo (why not Zeppo? He never seems to have anything to do). Helton needs two of his own. "All right, how much you pay?" asks Chico, offering his services and those of Harpo, who heaves and snorts and makes ugly faces to show how rough he is. "Well, just how tough are you?" asks Helton skeptically. "Well," says Chico, who never undersells anything, "you pay a little bit, we're a little tough, pay very much, very much tough. You pay too much, too much tough." Hired! Helton, surrounded by his new henchmen, then walks on deck, displaying his "protection." His protec-

The four Chevalier Brothers:
Harpo turns in a record performance

tion, however, starts following anyone who vaguely resembles Helton. Harpo and Chico wind up on the wrong deck with the wrong man, a bearded elderly gentleman. "Hey," cries Chico. "It's-a the boss. He's gotta disguise. Take off-a the whiskers, we know you." Harpo mimes a laugh and playfully yanks the beard, triggering pipsqueak cries of "Officer! Officer!" and the brothers are on the run again.

Groucho, who describes himself as a man who has "licked his weight in wild caterpillars, decides that four bodyguards are too many. Approaching Helton, he puts forth a plan to cut costs in the thug business. "Now there are two fellows trying to attack you, aren't there? And there are two fellows trying to defend you. Now that's fifty percent waste. Now why can't you be attacked by your own bodyguards? Your life will be saved, and that's . . . that's one hundred percent waste. *Now* whaddya got? You

still got me, and I'll attack you for nothing." Groucho admits that the savings wouldn't be spectacular, but it's a penny here and a penny there. "Look at me," he says. "I worked myself up from nothing to a state of extreme poverty."

As it must to all stowaways, the moment of disembarkation arrives, and the brothers are stuck without passports. They hit on what only four insane men would call a good idea. Zeppo has gotten hold of Maurice Chevalier's passport, and the brothers, their Manhattan mugs twisted into Gallic grimaces, push to the front of the customs line. First Zeppo, then Chico, then Groucho put their best Chevalier touch to singing "If a Nightingale Could Sing Like You." Each one is tossed to the back of the line. Then Harpo marches up to the customs table, kicking papers as he goes. He presents the Frenchman's passport and bursts into full song,

arpo puts his stamp on the scene

"The sweetest little thing . . . in the whole wide world"

sounding every bit as Chevalieresque as the master himself. The customs man, no brighter than any other official in a Marx movie, shifts his eyes from the passport to Harpo and back to the passport, trying to square what he sees with what he hears. Just as it looks as though Harpo has triumphed, his "voice" starts winding down into a molasses baritone. He desperately reaches behind him to wind up the phonograph he has strapped to himself like a papoose but the jig is up, and his beaming face crumples into a smashed pillow of exasperation. Undaunted, he tosses the piles of papers neatly arranged on the table before him into a snowstorm of bureaucratic garbage. Three guards cannot stop him from stamping everything—hands, tables, papers and finally the bald dome of the head *douanier*.

The brothers escape at last when a man faints on deck. Dr. Groucho, after taking the pulse of an onlooker, finally declares: "I can't do anything for that man. He's fainted. What he needs is an ocean voyage. In the meantime, get him off and have his baggage examined." The stretcher bearing the ailing man off the ship winds up carrying the brothers. The scene shifts to Joe Helton's estate, where the softened criminal is holding a swank coming-out party for his daughter, Mary. The setting gives Harpo a chance to play the harp, albeit as accompanist for a shattering messy soprano named Mrs. Smallhausen, whose piercing tones drive Harpo to finish the number with his head buried for protection in his overcoat. Harpo also gets his right hand stuck in the strings, so he simply unscrews it and throws it away, producing a new hand from his sleeve. Chico has his chance to tickle the ivories. And Groucho gets a last chance to tickle Lucille Briggs. "Oh, no, don't," she cries, as they bull and cow on the veranda. "My husband might be outside. If he finds me here, he'll wallop me." "Always thinking of your husband," sighs Groucho. "Couldn't I wallop you just as well? Oh, why can't we

"We can lodge with my fleas in the hills."

Groucho delivers the play-by-play from a safe distance as Chico and Harpo handle the henchmen

break away from all this?" he cries. "We can lodge with my fleas in the hills. I mean flee to my lodge in the hills." But she will have none of it, although she admits she is miserable. "I've been married four years," she complains. "Four years of neglect. Four years of battling, four years of heartbreak." "That makes twelve years," comments Groucho, the literalist. "You must have been married in Rompers. Mighty pretty country there." Before the party is over, Helton has presented his daughter as "the sweetest little thing in the whole wide world," only to have Harpo mince through a huge floral wreath, a rose caught between his teeth.

Briggs kidnaps Mary Helton and spirits her off to a barn, where the film ends, Harpo and Chico knocking out Briggs' henchmen and spinning a wagon wheel turned wheel of fortune to determine who Harpo will bop next. Zeppo takes on Alky Briggs, and Groucho, courageous as ever, broadcasts the fight from a distant loft. The last frames show the brothers pitching through the straw searching "for a needle in a haystack."

The wheel of fortune:

Monkey Business was well received by the critics, despite the fact that it opened at the unMarxly hour of 10:30 in the morning. Mordaunt Hall of the *Times* wrote: "Whether it is really as funny as 'Animal Crackers' is a matter of opinion. [He does not give us his.] Suffice it to say that few persons will be able to go to the Rivoli and keep a straight face." Another critic warned: "This picture should not be missed if you like sophisticated insanity, which is it's own excuse for being. They have added a plot to this picture, but you would hardly know it." Students of S. J. Perelman will recognize his hand in lines like "lodge with my fleas in the hills" and "you must have been married in Rompers." While Marx fans debate whether *Monkey Business* and the two films that followed, or more structured movies like *A Night at the Opera,* are the brothers' best, there is no doubt that this film is one of their good ones. Many critics of the brothers claim that their comedy is too wild, too unbelievable. They are referred to the following customs form Groucho filled out on a transatlantic crossing a few years before *Monkey Business* was made.

Name: Julius H. Marx
Address: 21 Lincoln Road, Great Neck, L.I.
Born: Yes
Hair: Not much
Occupation: Smuggler
List of Items Purchased out of the United States, Where Bought and the Purchase Price: Wouldn't you like to know.

...ico, Harpo and boppo!

Zeppo, Groucho, Harpo, and Chico

Nat Pendleton

David Landau

Robert Craig

Thelma Todd

James Pierce

Professor Quincey Adams Wagstaff:	GROUCHO
Pinky:	HARPO
Barovelli:	CHICO
Frank Wagstaff:	ZEPPO
Connie Bailey:	THELMA TODD
Jennings:	DAVID LANDAU
The Biology Professor:	ROBERT CRAIG
Mullen:	JAMES PIERCE
MacHardie:	NAT PENDLETON
Retiring President of Huxley College:	REGINALD BARLOW
Peggy Carrington:	FLORINE McKINNEY
Professors in Wagstaff's Study:	E. J. LeSAINT
	E. H. CALVERT

* * *

Director: Norman McLeod
Screenplay: Bert Kalmar, Harry Ruby, S. J. Perelman and Will B. Johnstone
Photography: Ray June
Music and Lyrics: Bert Kalmar and Harry Ruby
Released by Paramount, August 19, 1932. 68 minutes

5 Horse Feathers (1932)

In their vaudeville days, the Marx Brothers had Fun in Hi-Skule, their first comedy act, which cast Groucho as the professor and Harpo as the teacher's pet peeve. The humor was rough, a variation on an old routine by vaudevillian Gus Edwards, but in 1915 it brought down the house in places like Denison, Texas, and Waukegan, Illinois. Groucho would ask Harpo to describe the shape of the world. "What is the shape of my cuff buttons?" he would ask, trying to give his slower than slow learner a hint. "Square," Harpo would proclaim. "I mean the cuff buttons I wear on Sunday," Groucho would explain. "Now what is the shape of the world?" "Round on Sunday, square on weekdays," was Harpo's reply. It is little wonder he fled to silence. The act was also livened with horseplay. Harpo customarily brought the teacher an orange, which he kept in a clean place, under his hat. But one night in Waukegan, he tossed it at the piano player, and the rest of the family, moved by the same demonic spirit, dumped everything from books to stilettos into the pit. Later, when Chico launched into an extended Italian-American ad lib, the violin player split into howling convulsions, nearly stopping the show. His name was Benny Kubelsky, later to become Jack Benny.

Finally, some fifteen years later, the Marx Brothers managed to graduate from hi-skule to kollege. But while *Horse Feathers*, as a satire of American education, is incomparably more sophisticated, elaborate and finely edged than their hi-skule hi-jinx, it is fired by the same wild irreverence and contempt for the classroom as that first comedy act. Even the parts are the same: Groucho plays the professor in one scene and Harpo and Chico his incredibly dense pupils. They bring the teacher a present—a watermelon this time instead of an orange—and they still have a limitless fund of wrong answers. "Now then, baboons," Groucho asks at one point, "what is a corpuscle?" "That's easy," cries Chico, his face shining with the confidence of the wholly ignorant. "First there's a captain. Then there's a lieutenant. Then there's a corpuscle." "That's fine," returns Groucho. "Why don't you bore a hole in yourself and let the sap run out?"

It is a measure of just how lowly the Marxes looked on college that Harpo is allowed to sign his enrollment papers with an "x." In a number of Marx Brothers films, Harpo is cast as not only dumb but totally unlettered. This suits his character as the instinctive, natural and lovable child-man, but beyond this, it suited Harpo as Harpo. He never got past the second grade, the victim of a bully who would drop him out the second-floor window. Harpo, as he explains it in his autobiography, simply got tired of trying to explain to the teacher on his return from the pavement how he had left the room without permission. His illiteracy was not only a comic device but a fact. Harpo, the silent one, was indeed a stranger to the world of words. Once he was the "murderer" in a little game of crime the critic Alexander Woollcott used to play with his weekend guests. As Woollcott set it up, the murderer would approach his victim and declare, "You are dead." It was the job of the rest of the guests to find the body and discover the killer. Harpo wrote his declaration in lipstick on a square of toilet paper. Alice Duer Miller, the poetess, was the unwitting victim and remained trapped in silence in the bathroom until eleven in the evening. When she was finally discovered, the identity of the killer was solved instantly. Harpo had written "You are ded."

Horse Feathers marks a cinematic advance for the brothers. The settings are more spacious and occasionally move outdoors, the football-game finale belongs to the mainstream of American film comedy and a number of other set pieces are written with the more fluid possibilities of the screen in mind, most notably the moment when Harpo and Chico fall through the ceiling into a bridge party. Perelman and Johnstone are joined by Bert Kalmar and Harry Ruby, who contribute two sparkling musical numbers. "Everyone Says 'I Love You' " is echoed at one point or another by all four of the brothers—Harpo whistles it to a horse—and serves as a lyrical leitmotiv that helps to unify the film, much in the same fashion as the melodies of the early René Clair movies. *Horse Feathers* isn't quite as fierce and relentless as *Monkey Business* but it casts a wider

Whatever it is, he's against it

net, encompassing virtually every aspect of college life, with room left over for Prohibition satire and the usual burlesque of romance.

Groucho plays Professor Quincy Adams Wagstaff, whose moniker places him in the great New England tradition of college presidents hired to produce winning football teams. Groucho, like every college president, is torn between academic necessities and athletic imperatives. He can't decide which is less important. But the fact that Huxley College has fired a different president each year since 1888, the last year the college had a winning football team, brings out the survivalist in him and sends him seeking gridiron recruits.

The film opens in the college auditorium, where Groucho takes a break from shaving to address the students and faculty. The dean introduces him, and Groucho launches his regime:

"Members of the faculty, faculty members, students of Huxley and Huxley students—I guess that covers everything. I thought my razor was dull until I heard this speech. And that reminds me of a story so dirty that I'm ashamed to think of it myself. As I look over your eager faces, I can readily understand why this college is flat on its back." Noble motives have drawn him to Huxley. "I came into this college to get my son out of it," he explains. His son is Zeppo, who is sitting in the audience with a girl on his lap. "Young lady," calls Groucho, beginning one of the most grievous puns in any Marx movie, "would you mind getting up so I could see the son rise?"

The dean urges Groucho to outline his program for the school. "Why don't you go home to your wife?" Groucho tells him, then has second thoughts. "I'll tell you what, I'll go home to your wife and, outside of the improvement, she'll never know the difference." "Now that you've stepped into my shoes," the dean tries once again. "Oh, so that's what I stepped into," says Groucho, checking his soles. "I wondered what it was. If these are your shoes, the least you could do was have them cleaned." Finally Groucho strikes the tone of his new administration—nihilism. In "I'm Against It," Groucho states succinctly his feelings about suggestions from the faculty. "I don't know what they have to say. It makes no difference anyway. Whatever it is, I'm against it." As with the bellboys in *The Cocoanuts*, the guests in *Animal Crackers* and the lounge audience in *Monkey Business*, the professors support Groucho's nonsense without question. Their feet shuffling in rhythm, their beards bouncing, their hands polish-

...he son about to rise

Chico and Groucho woo the student body

ing invisible windows in an antiquarian version of a soft-shoe routine, they follow him about slavishly as he sings a song of ridicule and contempt for them.

Groucho and son Zeppo then have a heartless-to-heart talk in which Dad berates Sonny for courting Connie Bailey, the college widow, and getting a bad name for himself. If anyone is going to get a bad name, Groucho implies, it will be the president. As it turns out, Groucho does try his hand at wooing Connie, but under the most trying circumstances: with the other three brothers trying to make love to her at the same time. Thelma Todd is back as Connie, but she and Groucho do not cross swords as they did in *Monkey Business*. Perhaps the writers were afraid of repeating themselves or, worse, of failing to repeat the brilliant romantic repartee of their last film. Or maybe they were interested in aiming Groucho at a different satiric target. Whatever the case, Groucho spends most of his time wrestling with the college instead of Connie. As a result, Chico and Harpo play a more prominent role in this film than in any before.

Like some aging alumnus, Groucho has not only turned away from sex, but toward football. Zeppo tells him that he can buy two gridiron stars at the local speakeasy. "Isn't that against the law," Groucho remarks, mocking the outraged citizen, "selling football players in a speakeasy?" If the players are Harpo and Chico, it is. At least that's who Groucho winds up recruiting. Two lugs named Mullen and MacHardie are the real ringers, but *Horse Feathers* wouldn't have been much of a picture starring Groucho, Mullen and MacHardie.

Chico works in the back room of the joint, filling orders and filling bottles. If somebody orders Scotch, Chico pulls out the finest bottle he can find and fills it with rotgut from the speakeasy keg. Chico also watches the door on occasion, with strict orders not to let anyone in who doesn't know the password. The secret word, as Groucho would later say on his quiz show, is "swordfish." But this film predates "You Bet Your Life" by several decades, so Groucho is lost when he arrives at the door. "I give you three guesses," Chico says through the slot. "It's the name of a fish." Groucho asks

Harpo ordering a small Scotch

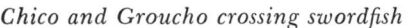

Chico and Groucho crossing swordfish

if it's "Mary." "That's-a no fish," says Chico. "She isn't," Groucho concedes, "but she drinks like one." "Sturgeon" is Groucho's next guess, but sturgeon, as Chico explains, "is a doctor cuts you open when you sick." How about "haddock"? "That's-a funny," says Chico, "I gotta headache, too." Finally Chico gives his victim a tiny hint. "You can't come in here unless you say 'swordfish.'" "I think I've got it," cries Groucho. "Is it 'swordfish'?" Chico comes out to congratulate his guest, and Groucho slips inside, slamming the door. Now Chico must guess the password. "Swordfish," he proclaims confidently. "No," says Groucho. "I got tired of that. I changed it." But since he can't remember what he changed it to, he comes outside and locks himself out, too. Harpo finally rescues them. He produces a live fish with an excalibur in its mouth at the door and waltzes in, Chico and Groucho following behind.

Harpo is right at home in the speakeasy. He plucks a button off his coat and feeds it to the one-armed bandit, pushing aside a poor sap who has invested his life's savings nourishing the machine. Harpo hits the jack-

pot immediately. As the coins pour out in a gush, he drinks deeply of his success and spits the coins in his hat. Later he goes to the phone, plays a nickel, and hits the jackpot again. The bartender asks him what he'll have to drink, and Harpo breaks into a Highland fling—Scotch. He pours the drink into a shot glass with a tube for a bottom that leads to a bottle Harpo keeps in his trousers. Soon the bar's bottle is empty and Harpo's is full. For Harpo, the speakeasy is a wonderland of soft touches and games and magic. He moves through its confines like a great glowing sun through darkness. When he passes by a pair of tough poker players, one growls, "Cut the cards." Harpo immediately drives a hatchet through the pack and the table.

Harpo has a number of jobs in this film. He delivers ice for the speakeasy, depositing it in wall safes so it won't be stolen. Occasionally he spends his time dropping ice out the window, retrieving it and delivering it again. But his official title is Town Dogcatcher, a job he has developed into a science. He carries with him in his horse-drawn cart a number of portable fire

70

Hitting the jackpot

hydrants to attract stray dogs. At one point, he is feeding his beloved gray horse a bouquet of salted roses and, in the spirit of true horsehood, sharing the same oat supply, when a policeman rushes toward him and points out that his truck is holding up an endless line of angry motorists. Harpo zips up an unfinished banana while the cop writes him a ticket. Always prepared, like the most conscientious Boy Scout, Harpo writes the cop a ticket. The cop tears up Harpo's ticket. Harpo tears up the cop's ticket, his face mirroring the emotions of the policeman's. The cop shows Harpo his badge. Harpo shows the cop an armada of badges pinned to the inside of his coat. Such foolishness can't go on forever while there are still dogs loose in the world. Harpo takes off after one stray, runs him into the large cage that forms the back of his truck and slams the back door, leaving the pursuing policeman trapped with the dogs. He then hops out and pulls down a sign: "POLICE DOG FOR SALE."

The film is at its best when punching holes in academia. In one scene, Groucho manipulates a pair of profes-

sors like a champion working two yo-yos. Beneath their dignified robes the scene tells us, the college professor, no less than the businessman, wears the gray flannel suit of conformity. "The trouble is, we're neglecting football for education," Groucho tells his two bearded Babbitts after cracking open a bag of walnuts with the telephone. "Exactly, the professor is right," the toadies declare, in unison. "Oh, I'm right, am I?" Groucho returns. "Well, I'm not right. I'm wrong. What I meant to say is that there's too *much* football and not *enough* education." The professors agree. "Oh, you do, do you?" cries Groucho. "You're wrong again. Where would this college be without football? Have we got a stadium?" Yes. "Have we got a college?" Yes. "Well, we can't support both," Groucho decides. "Tomorrow we start tearing down the college." But, Professor," the flunkies dare to ask, "where will the students sleep?" "Where they always slept," replies President Wagstaff. "In the classroom." Groucho's secretary rushes in to announce that a dean who has been waiting to see Groucho is furious with impatience. "The dean is furious. He's waxing wroth," she cries. "Is Roth out there, too?" says Groucho. "Tell Roth to wax the dean for a while." (This line, a classic among Marx buffs, is a perfect example of Perelman's style working flawlessly through Groucho's character.)

The classroom scene provides Groucho with his second direct assault on education. Having enrolled Harpo and Chico, he leads them to their first class, presided over by Robert Grieg, the butler in *Animal Crackers* and later used by director Preston Sturges as the incarnation of

stuffy dignity (not to be confused with Stuffy McInnes, who played first base for Philadelphia). "Well, let us go on with our lecture," Grieg declares. "I wish you'd go on without your lecture," taunts Groucho, voicing the feeling of every student stuck with a dud professor. Grieg asks Groucho to peer into his microscope. "What do you think of that slide?" he asks. "Well," says Prexy Groucho, "I think he was safe at second, but it was very close." Grieg then embarks on a complicated lecture on the heart. "Any questions?" he asks. "Yeah," says Chico, suddenly interested. "When you gonna cut the watermelon open?" Finally, when Groucho

Harpo and his beloved

Harpo and police dog

challenges Grieg's facts, the professor assures him, "My students will bear me out." This is the moment Chico and Harpo have been waiting for, and they bear Grieg out—into the hall.

Groucho takes over and unburdens himself of a lecture on the blood and heart. He characterizes the blood carriers as "a hill-dwelling tribe that live in the Alps" and reminds his class that "the Lord Alps those who Alp themselves," a line directly stolen from *I'll Say She Is.* "Now in studying your basic metabolism," he goes on, "we first listen to your heartbeat. And if your heart beats anything but your diamonds and clubs, it's because your partner is cheating, or your wife." Harpo is compelled throughout the film to cover every available surface with a poster of a circus ballerina he has fallen in love with. In this instance, he tacks it over Groucho's anatomy chart. Groucho demands to know who played this trick. As Harpo rises, his hand raised, his eyes manufacturing the tears of a trained delinquent, Groucho tells him, "Young man, you'll find as you grow older you can't burn the candle at both ends." Harpo stops crying instantly, smiles slyly, and produces from his trenchcoat a candle blazing at both ends. But Groucho won't relent; punishment must be dealt out. Groucho orders the prettiest girl in the class to stay after school. The scene ends with a return to the primitive days of Fun in Hi-Skule: Chico and Harpo zapping at the professor with peashooters and the professor descending to their level—actually descending behind the desk—to pelt them back with a peashooter of his own.

In a more general way, *Horse*

"We're neglecting football for education."

Fun in kollege

The comedy of anatomy

Harpo using force and persuasion

Feathers satirizes the whole rah-rah mania of colleges for winning teams. The film will lose its punch the day colleges stop cutting corners, compromising standards and cheating to lure athletic talent—or, as it appears now, roughly when the sun burns out. The only difference between 1931 and today is method. Today, inducements to athletes go under antiseptic titles like "athletic scholarship." In the 1930's, the same practices went under the heading of bribery and, in the case of the brothers, kidnapping.

The brothers resort to kidnapping only after bribery has failed, failed for Huxley, that is, but paid off for arch-rival Darwin which has signed Mullen and MacHardie to play in the big game. Groucho dispatches Harpo and Chico to abduct the two ringers. Chico explains that he usually kidnaps people by phoning them first and sending his car and chauffeur around for them. But unfortunately, Chico goes on, a chauffeur and car were too expensive, so he sold the car. "Well, that shows you how little I know," says Groucho. "I would have kept the car and sold the chauffeur." "That's-a no good," Chico unex-

plains. "I gotta have a chauffeur to take me to work in the morning." "Well, if you've got no car," asks straight man Groucho, "how can he take you to work?" "He don't have to take me to work. I gotta no job." (The exchange is just crazy enough to survive the Depression audience it was obviously aimed at.)

This time Chico doesn't do anything so foolish as telephoning the victims. He tips off the man who hired them instead. So, when Harpo and Chico arrive by taxi on the afternoon of the big game, Mullen and MacHardie are ready. "You sister, she's a very sick man," Chico begins. "You better come with us. Come, we take you in our car." "You will, eh?" says Mullen. "Well, I have no sister." "That's all right," Chico points out. "We gotta no car." Harpo goes through one of his menacing acts, heaving and snorting, his eyes crossed with rage until, confronting both bullies, he delivers a crashing pit-pat on the cheek of each and winds up being pitched across the room. "You better think of something else," Chico advises. The kidnappers' next approach shows more sense. They run away as fast as possible, but the thugs simply lock them in an upstairs room. Harpo produces a rope. "Tie on-a the bed and throw it out the window," Chico commands. Harpo puts his tie on the bed and throws the rope out the window. The two then saw a circle in the floor, with themselves in the middle, and fall through into the bruisers' room again. Mullen and MacHardie proceed to strip the pair down to their skivvies, where we will leave them for the moment, cringing with modesty. (Harpo is so modest he has

even turned his poster of the ballerina toward the wall.)

While Harpo and Chico are getting their brains knocked around, Groucho is enjoying the modest pleasure of a rowboat ride on a duck pond with Connie Bailey, who as a Darwin spy is out to discover Huxley's football signals. Every assignment has its price. In this case, Connie is doing the paddling while Groucho serenades her on the guitar. As soon as that romantic ploy is exhausted, Groucho simply heaves the instrument overboard. Con-

Harpo and Chico stripped to their bare essentials

nie, however, is intent on intrigue, not amour. Drifting into cutesy baby talk, she asks, "Is gweat big stwong man gonna show liddle icky baby all about those bad footbawl signals?" Startled, Groucho asks, "Was that you or the duck? 'Cause if it was you, I'm gonna finish this ride with the duck." Undaunted, Connie goes on. "If icky baby don't learn about the footbawl signals, icky baby gonna cwy." Groucho pipes back, twice as infantile and twice as sappy, "If icky girl keep on tawking that way, big stwong man kick all her teef wight down her thwoat." The age of chivalry gives its final death rattle in the next few frames. Connie goes to hug Groucho as a pretext for snatching the signals. Groucho pushes her overboard. When she cries for a lifesaver, he pulls a peppermint out of his pocket and throws it slightly out of her reach, so even the candy will sink before she gets to it. He ends the trip, as promised, with the duck in the boat.

The big game is in progress, but Chico and Harpo are still prisoners in underwear. They finally escape by sawing their way through the floor into a ladies' card party. Harpo snatches a white sash from one of the shocked matrons, wraps it around his head like a gladiator's headdress and, along with Chico, leaps into a waiting chariot—a garbage truck drawn by two white steeds. The two arrive in the arena in the grand manner of Ben Hur just as the first half of the game is coming to a close, with Darwin leading 12–0. "Hurry up," cries Chico to Harpo, "we still have time to play." And the two rush to the bench and launch into a spirited game of pinochle. Finally they charge into the huddle. The huddle breaks. And they

Groucho serenades Thelma Todd while Chico and Harpo cut themselves in on a bridge game

are still playing pinochle.

The football game is an unfair contest—eleven talented football players against four Marx Brothers, who happen to have control of the script. Groucho takes time out from flirting with a beauty in the stands to tackle a Darwin player headed for a touchdown. "That'll teach him to pass a lady without tipping his hat," he comments. Later Groucho joins the backfield, where Chico, notorious for his dazzling ability to keep a secret, is calling the signals. "Hey diddle diddle, the cat and the fiddle, this time I think we go up the middle." Another call is what might be termed in modern sports parlance an automatic: *"Uno, due, tre, vendi,* this-a time we go left endi." The Marxes manage to get one touchdown back when Harpo attaches a rubber band to the ball.

He fades to pass and throws to Chico. When the Darwin team heads for the pass receiver, Harpo simply summons the ball back and runs for the score. Zeppo, who always seems to manage to return just as the film is ending, pats Harpo on the back and asks him if he's tired. No, Harpo says, by shaking his head with bravado, and promptly faints. Since the Marx Brothers own the picture, Darwin must play by their rules. More precisely, after Darwin scores, Huxley gets the ball, but after Huxley scores, Huxley also gets the ball. This time, Zeppo runs toward the goal line, Harpo scattering banana peels behind him to trip up the Darwin pursuers. But lack of proportion is part of Harpo's charm. Delighted with his success, he throws a banana peel under Zeppo before he reaches the goal

Gladiators grabbing the garbage express

Harpo scoring four quick touchdowns

line. Time is running out. Suddenly a dog bursts out from the sidelines, stirring the deepest primitive urges in Harpo the dogcatcher. He leaps into his cart and charges down the field with the football, his brothers riding sidecar. When he crosses the goal line, he touches down the football: 12–12, and another, 18–12, and another, 26–12, and keeps on making touchdowns as fast as Groucho can feed him the footballs. Huxley wins by some astronomical figure.

Apparently as a reward for their victory, Chico, Harpo and Groucho all marry Connie Bailey at once. (Zeppo, one imagines, had to finish his education.) She says "I do," and the three tuxedoed Marx Brothers begin what promises to be the oddest

marriage of the century by kissing, mauling and piling onto their new bride.

The film delighted the growing number of Marx fans among the critics, although their response in print was something close to surrender before a kind of formless phenomenon that paralyzed their critical equipment. "The business of reviewing a Marx Brothers film," wrote Richard Watts of the New York *Herald·Tribune* after the opening, August 10, 1932, "need consist of saying little more than whether or not the boys are keeping to their stride. Any effort to tell too much about their latest inventions will result only in confusion for the reviewer and the picture." Other critics merely chucked the whole business of analysis and deferred to their own basic instincts, like William Bocknel of the New York *Telegram*, who simply stated, "I laughed last night as I have seldom laughed before." But perhaps more interesting than the raves was the virulent reaction of the critic for the Sunday London *Times*, who wrote: "I have in my experience been condemned to sit out many absurdities in the cinema but never have I encountered a more banal and unintelligent waste of time and money than in 'Horse Feathers.'" Which is only to say that the Marx Brothers, even among those who hadn't the vaguest notion of what they were doing, never drew an indifferent response. Perhaps the most intelligent comment came from the Los Angeles *Times* reviewer, Philip K. Scheuer, who wrote: "The current Marx comedy is the funniest talkie since the last Marx comedy, and the record it establishes is not likely to be disturbed until the next Marx comedy comes along. As for comparisons, I was having too good a time to make any." Scheuer's instinct about the early films was right. While buffs compare Keaton and Chaplin films and various other great American comedies, no one has ever found anyone to compare the Marxes to, for better or for worse. Scheuer's prediction about the next film's breaking *Horse Feathers'* record for lunacy was also on target. The next film was *Duck Soup*.

"I do!" "I do!" "———!"

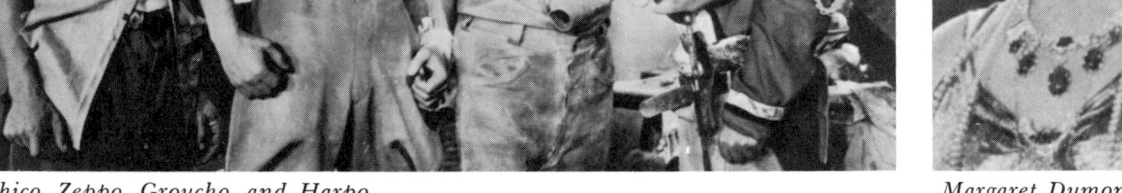

Chico, Zeppo, Groucho, and Harpo

Margaret Dumont

Louis Calhern

Raquel Torres

Edgar Kennedy

Rufus T. Firefly:	GROUCHO
Pinkie:	HARPO
Chicolini:	CHICO
Bob Rolland:	ZEPPO
Mrs. Teasdale:	MARGARET DUMONT
Ambassador Trentino:	LOUIS CALHERN
Vera Marcal:	RAQUEL TORRES
The Lemonade Seller:	EDGAR KENNEDY
Zander:	EDMUND BREESE
First Minister of Finance:	WILLIAM WORTHINGTON
Secretary of War:	EDWIN MAXWELL
Agitator:	LEONID KINSKY
Secretary:	VERNA HILLIE
First Judge:	GEORGE MacQUARRIE
Second Judge:	FRED SULLIVAN
Second Minister of Finance:	DAVISON CLARK
Prosecutor:	CHARLES B. MIDDLETON
Third Judge:	ERIC MAYNE

* * *

Director: Leo McCarey
Screenplay: Bert Kalmar and Harry Ruby
Additional Dialogue: Arthur Sheekman and Nat Perrin
Photography: Henry Sharp
Art Direction: Hans Dreier and Wiard B. Ihnen
Editing: LeRoy Stone
Music and Lyrics: Bert Kalmar and Harry Ruby
Music Direction: Arthur Johnston
Released by Paramount, November 17, 1933. 68 or 70 minutes

6 Duck Soup (1933)

"Acting in 'Duck Soup,' our last picture for Paramount, was the hardest job I ever did," Harpo has written. "It was the only time I can remember that I worried about turning in a bad performance. The trouble was not with the script, the director, or the falls I had to take (I never used a stunt man or a double). The trouble was Adolf Hitler. His speeches were being rebroadcast in America. Somebody had a radio on the set, and twice we suspended shooting to listen to him scream." Harpo responded in his private life by changing his name from Adolph to Arthur. The brothers responded with *Duck Soup*.

Hitler was not the only specter that lurked in the wings while the shooting went on. Present also was the real collapse of the American economy, the crisis of confidence in the European democracies and our own, and a climate of doubt and despair over the breadlines that seemed to stretch from New York all the way to Hollywood. *Duck Soup* is not a programmatic political vision or a utopia stood on its head. It is not even a direct attack on Fascism alone. The brothers' minds did not run on political tracts. Instead, they operated from a nucleus of strongly felt instincts—disregard, dislike and distrust of authority, impatience with form and ceremony, and a hardened suspicion of wealth and power, personal or political. Like strips of litmus paper, these instincts took on the coloration of the times. *Duck Soup's* buckshot satire touches every discontent of the day, from suspicion of all forms of government and a growing skepticism of war as an instrument of policy to a more humdrum dissatisfaction with politicians in general and a pervasive fatigue and despair over the miseries of the Depression.

To these pressures the brothers responded with a fantasy of freedom in which sheer creative human energy, corrupt and imperfect as it is, triumphs. The scoundrels who rule are exposed and expelled, and diplomacy is bared as a battle of vain men and chiselers for personal glory. Many critics have called the Marx Brothers revolutionaries. Their vision may be anarchic, but their banner carries slogans of personal freedom beyond any political label. As such, they represented in spirit a threat to all authoritarian movements. In the fall of 1939, Benito Mussolini condemned the Marx Brothers and ordered his subjects not to laugh at them. The same year, at a meeting in New York of the pro-Nazi German-American Bund, a speaker cited the brothers as exemplars of the full flower of Communist culture which must be destroyed. The brothers, who never considered their films as political salvos, must have been both dismayed and flattered by all the attention.

Shooting the trial sequence

Duck Soup was the last film the brothers directed toward minority taste. The script banishes sentiment ·and romance entirely, provides no soft corners for those who seek reassurance as part of their entertainment, and presents the Marx Brothers comedy in its most unrelieved and undiluted form. For these reasons and because of the totally uncompromising opposition viewpoint it presents, it is the favorite of the purists among Marx Brothers fans. While it is one of the two Marx films the Museum of Modern Art includes in its library of classics (*A Night at the Opera* is the other), *Duck Soup* did only middling business at the box office, a fact that had an enormous impact on the brothers' career. Nonetheless, *Duck Soup* remains the high-water mark in the quartet's early work and a source of endless delight for those who like their Marx Brothers comedy straight.

Originally titled *Cracked Ice* and then changed to conform in name to the menagerie of Marx films that pre-

ceded it, *Duck Soup* is the most expensive of the Paramount productions. In an era of national deprivation, films with lavish decors, like the Busby Berkeley musicals, satisfied America's appetite for opulence. Paramount was quick to apply this truth to *Duck Soup,* which opens in a setting teeming with pretty girls, gallant court guards, casts of hundreds if not thousands, dancing, singing and splendor everywhere. The occasion is the conferring of the Presidency of Fredonia on a man destined to lead it down the drain—Rufus T. Firefly, alias Groucho Marx. Groucho has been forced on the bankrupt kingdom by Margaret Dumont, who as Mrs. Teasdale, the multimillionairess, wields the power of the purse. Flattered by Groucho's attentions, she puts the state in his hands, and he shakes it up.

There is only one man missing at Groucho's coronation — Groucho. Zeppo, as his secretary, assures Mrs. Teasdale that the great statesman will arrive "when the clock on the wall strikes ten." He and the assembly launch into a song to that effect. On either side of the path that His Excellency is to tread, royal guards line the way, their swords crossed, forming a canopy. Dancing girls spread a red carpet of rose petals. The entire court bursts into an inspirational rendition of the national anthem, "Hail Freedonia," and—no Groucho. There is a momentary pause. The anthem is resumed with even more vigor. All eyes turn toward the royal entrance. Still no Groucho. Suddenly, upstairs, an alarm clock sounds. Groucho sits up in bed, doffs his nightshirt, and fully tuxedoed, slides down a fireman's pole into the rear of the hall. He approaches one of the guards quietly and asks, "Expecting somebody?" Then he joins the row of guards and waits for himself, his swordless arm lifted with the rest. (In the original script, Groucho was supposed to direct the line "Expecting somebody?" to one of the dancing girls, who would answer "Yes." But when the moment came, the young lady was so rattled by the presence of the microphone and the lecherous advances Groucho was making that she automatically shouted "No!" Groucho cracked up, the scene had to be reshot and the line was assigned to a guard.)

Finally Mrs. Teasdale spots him at the end of the line and implores him to lead Fredonia to the pinnacle it occupied when Mr. Teasdale was President. "Promise me you will follow in the footsteps of my husband," she beseeches him. "How do you like that?" says Groucho to the camera. "I haven't been on the job five minutes, and already she's making advances to me." Then he turns to Mrs. Teasdale. "What about your husband?" "He's

Relaxing on the set

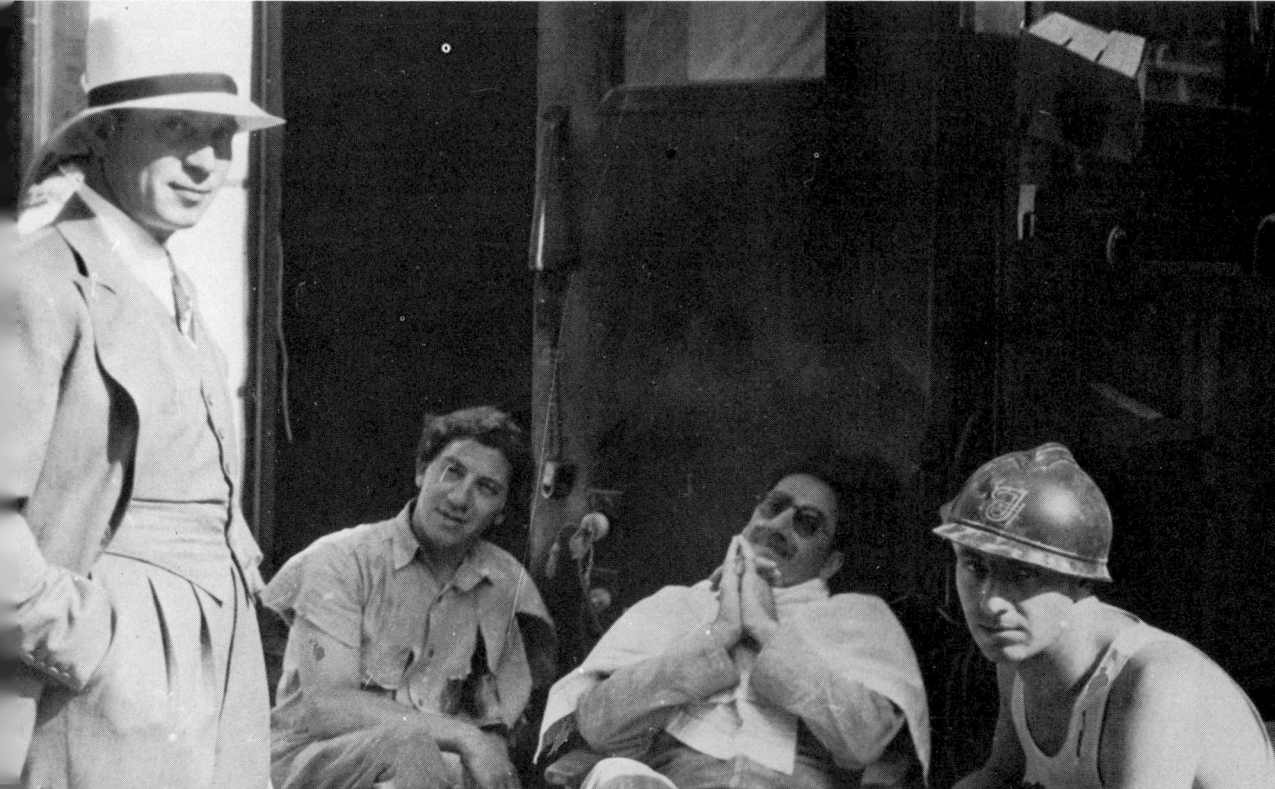

Groucho: following the footsteps of her husband

"Just Wait 'Til I Get Through with It"

dead," she replies. Groucho is skeptical. "He's just using that as an excuse." "I was with him to the end," Mrs. Teasdale assures. "No wonder he passed away." "I held him in my arms and kissed him," she reminisces. "So it was murder, eh?" cries Groucho, but he changes his tune when Mrs. Teasdale adds, "He left me his entire fortune." "Can't you see what I'm trying to tell you?" intones Groucho, who can shift his line more nimbly than a fly fisherman. "I love you." "Oh, Your Excellency," mutters the matron. Replies Groucho. "You're not so bad yourself." *Duck Soup* finds Groucho maturing from the seedy young Lothario he was in the earlier films to the mangy, flea-bitten older lover he is generally remembered as being. His famous stoop, only a modest tilt in *The Cocoanuts*, has by this film assumed its classic inclination.

One of the great virtues of the three Paramount films in Hollywood is the integration of the plot and the music. The songs belong to the comedy and the story. Here Groucho outlines his administration in a number by Kalmar and Ruby called "Just Wait 'til I Get Through With It." Gliding across the set like Hans Brinker, occasionally transforming his legs into kicking corkscrews, Groucho announces: "If anyone's caught taking graft and I don't get my share/ We'll line 'em up against the wall and pop goes the weasel." In summation, he declares: "If you think this country's bad off now, just wait 'til I get through with it." "This is a gala day for you," says Mrs. Teasdale, congratulating him. "That's plenty," Groucho replies. "I don't think I could handle more than a gal a day."

Many of the villains in the later films are second-rate Hollywood heav-

Enter two common house spies

Harpo lighting up, Calhern sitting down

ies who drape themselves about the plot like lead weights. But *Duck Soup* is graced with two excellent bad guys, Louis Calhern and Edgar Kennedy. Calhern, suave, debonair and beautifully poised, plays Trentino, the leader of rival Sylvania. He seeks to control Fredonia by marrying Mrs. Teasdale. First, however, he must discredit Firefly. He dispatches two secret weapons, Chicolini and Pinky, to spy on the prexy, only to find he has unleashed a brace of boomerangs. The spies, of course, are Chico and Harpo. They appear on the threshold of Trentino's office in disguise. Harpo wears a beard and rotating pinwheels for eyes, all on the back of his head. They charge into the office, leap in Trentino's chair just as he is about to sit down, cut his coattails, and fake lighting a cigar with his telephone receiver. When Trentino asks for Groucho's record, Harpo flings a phonograph record at the ceiling, pulls out a pistol and shoots it like a skeet. Trentino needs a light for his cigar. Harpo pulls a flaming acetylene torch from his omnibus trench coat. Once the cigar is lit, Harpo surreptitiously snips it in half.

Chico and Harpo have done as brilliant a job of tailing Firefly as they did of trailing Helton in *Monkey Business*. "Well, you remember you gave us a picture of this man and said, 'Follow him'?" explains Chico. "Well, we get on-a the job right away and in one hour, even less than one hour—" "Yes?" says Trentino, alive with expectation. "We lose-a the picture," concludes Chico. "That's pretty good work, eh?" Trentino wants details. "All right, I tell you," Chico begins. "Monday we watch-a Firefly's house, but he no come out. He wasn't home. Tuesday we went to a ball game, but he fool us. He no show up.

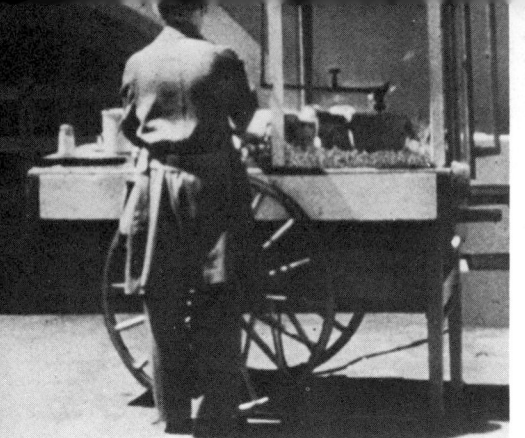

Harpo versus Kennedy

Wednesday *we* go to the ball game, and *we* fool *him*. We no show up. Thursday was a doubleheader. Nobody show up. Friday it rained all day. There was no ball game, so we stay home and listen to it on-a the radio." "Then you didn't shadow Firefly?" cries Trentino indignantly. "Sure we shadow Firefly, we shadow him all-a day," assures Chico. "What day was that?" "Shadowday," laughs Chico. "Some joke, eh, boss?"

They have other jokes for Trentino. A telegram arrives. Harpo opens it, looks it over and then, in a rage, rips it to pieces. "He gets mad because he can't read," Chico explains. But he guarantees that Harpo is an excellent sleuth. "My friend, he's got the nose of a bloodhound," says Chico, "and the rest of his face isn't so good either." They leave the office in triumph with Trentino absolutely baffled, the daily newspaper pasted to his bottom so he'll always be on top of world events. The biggest joke on Trentino, however, is that both his spies are in the employ of Firefly.

Harpo is Groucho's chauffeur. He roars into the film on a motorcycle and sidecar. Groucho hops into the sidecar. Harpo roars off. The sidecar stays. After Groucho is suckered twice this way, he pulls a switch on Harpo, taking the motorcycle himself and relegating Harpo to the sidecar. Groucho fires the engine and the sidecar roars off, leaving him frozen on the motorcycle. Chico is an important member of Groucho's Cabinet, a post he wins in a little quiz game. "What is it that has four pair of pants, lives in Philadelphia and it never rains but it pours?" asks Groucho, laughing behind his hand with confidence. "That's a good question," replies Chico, turning the tables. "I give you three guesses." Groucho is stumped. "Okay, I give you one," says Chico. "Who has a big black moustache, smokes a cigar and is a big pain in the neck?" Groucho puzzles the question for a while, then gets furious. "Just for that," he says, "you can't have the job I was going to give you." "What job was that?" Chico asks. "Secretary of War." "Good," shouts Chico, "I'll take it." And Groucho, slamming an imaginary gavel, yells, "Sold!"

Two jobs are not enough for Harpo and Chico. In addition to spying and government work, they run a peanut and hot dog stand outside the Fredonian palace, next to a lemonade stand run by the master of the slow burn, Edgar Kennedy. In their first encounter with Kennedy, who likes to help himself to the brothers' goods without paying, Harpo starts up a crazy shell game with hats. He knocks Kennedy's off and, as the victim is about to replace it on his head, sub-

stitutes his own hat. Soon Harpo has the hats dancing on different heads faster than Kennedy can follow, until the lemonade seller is wearing Chico's pointed dunce cap. The game is settled when Harpo roasts Kennedy's skimmer on his hot dog spit. In a later sequence, this little war between Harpo and Kennedy that mirrors the larger war to come suddenly escalates. Kennedy starts helping himself to Harpo's peanuts. When Harpo holds out his hand to be paid, Kennedy paints it with mustard. Harpo wipes his hand clean on Kennedy's apron and snips off the used portion. The lemonade vendor grabs another bag of peanuts; Harpo knocks it on the ground and, as Kennedy goes to pick it up, roasts his new hat. Kennedy contemplates his fate, his eyes blazing, his hand wiping fate itself from his face. Finally he retaliates by capsizing the peanut stand and, satisfied, returns to sell lemonade. A long line is waiting. Business is good. But suddenly the line disperses in horror. Kennedy can't understand it. He implores them to stay. Then he looks up. There is Harpo, with his pants rolled up, perched on the edge of the lemonade tank gleefully kicking his filthy legs through the brew like a kid at the edge of a swimming pool.

Groucho makes a mockery of all forms of government, democratic as

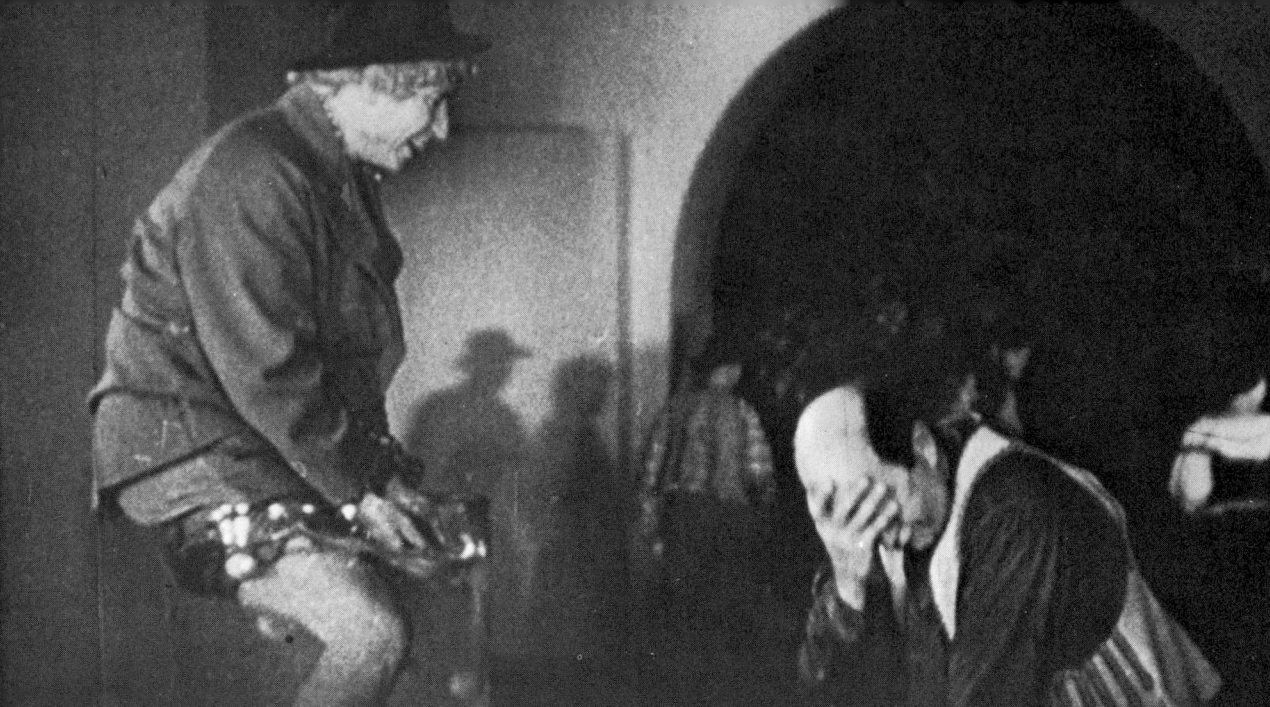

Harpo fiddles as Kennedy burns

well as dictatorial. In his first Cabinet meeting, he shows how *Robert's Rules of Order* can be twisted into a pretzel of personal politicking. He keeps his Cabinet waiting while he finishes a game of jacks. Then he asks: "Is there any old business?" "I wish to discuss the tariff," declares an overstuffed minister. "That's new business," reprimands Groucho. "Any old business? No? Then we'll take up new business." "I want to bring up the tariff," says the minister. "Sorry," says Groucho, "that's old business by now." The minister, disgusted, resigns. "I wash my hands of all this," he declares. "Fine" says Groucho, glad to have squeezed out the opposition. "Don't forget to wash your neck." Groucho is handed a document and asked if he finds it clear. "Clear?" he exclaims. "Why, a four-year-old child could understand this report." Then he mutters to secretary Zeppo, "Go out and get a four-year-old child. I can't make head or tail of it."

The relations between Fredonia and Sylvania are governed by inexorable historical forces. Every time Groucho and Trentino have a tiff, the two nations gear for war. Mrs. Teasdale acts as troubleshooter, always trying to patch up the differences between the two men. At first, she reconciles the pair. They joke until Groucho starts to recall the word Trentino used to insult him. "Was it swine?" asks Trentino in an air of lighthearted banter. "No, it was seven letters," Groucho remembers. "Idiot? Upstart?" "That's it," cries Groucho, and slaps Trentino across the face with his gloves. "This means war!" Groucho declares.

At this point, Trentino dispatches Chico and Harpo to Mrs. Teasdale's house to steal the Fredonian war plans. At the same time, Mrs. Teasdale calls Groucho away from a bedful of crackers to spend the night in her house as protection. Chico and Harpo, always masters of stealth, at tempt to sneak into the house by ringing the front doorbell. As the servant scours the area to determine who rang the bell, Harpo skips inside but shuts the door on Chico. Chico rings the bell. Harpo comes out to look. Chico shuts the door on Harpo. Finally Harpo rings, Chico comes out and the servant, returning, shuts the door on both of them.

Once guided inside by Trentino's accomplice, a Latin number named Vera Marcal, they are cautioned to be quiet. "If you are found, you are lost," Vera tells them. "How can-a we he be found, if-a we lost?" asks Chico. But Harpo takes the warning seriously. He doesn't make a sound, except for little things like setting all the clocks in the living room chiming, playing the inside of the piano like a harp, dancing a little jig to the clockwork music, turning over and triggering a music box. Chico finally stops the music and corners Groucho in the guest room, locking him in the toilet. "Let me out," screams Groucho. "Let me out, or at least throw me a magazine." Chico then paints a moustache under his nose, throws on a nightshirt, nightcap and glasses and heads for Mrs. Teasdale's room to get the plans. (His resemblance to Groucho is absolutely perfect, recalling boyhood pictures in which they looked like identical twins.)

Mrs. Teasdale notices Chico's "peculiar" accent immediately, but he passes it off as part of his training for a future espionage assignment in Italy. To confuse matters, however, Harpo has independently hit on the same plan and races into the bedroom, also looking the image of Groucho, as Chico ducks under the bed. Harpo struts and lopes awhile, puffing on a cigar and making faces. But with no accent at all, he can't hold out for very long. He exits and Mrs. Teasdale, believing herself alone, starts to disrobe. But there is Chico. "I thought you just left," she cries. Chico denies it. "But I saw you leave with my own eyes," she insists. "Who you gonna believe," challenges Chico, "me or you own eyes?" Succumbing to the pressure of so many Grouchos, she collapses on the bed, calling for water. But Chico takes off when he hears the real Groucho coming. Groucho enters to hear Mrs. Teasdale moan: "How about my glass of water?" "How about it?" replies an amused and puzzled Groucho.

Downstairs, Harpo fiddles with the wall safe, turning the dials furiously. Unfortunately, either the safe has a musical alarm system or Harpo has tuned in the radio because strains of the "Colonel Bogey March" explode all over the house. Harpo tries desperately to hush the radio, suffocating

"Sounds like mice"

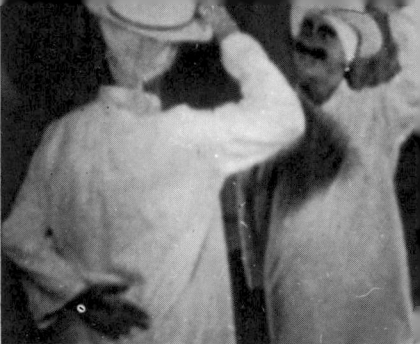

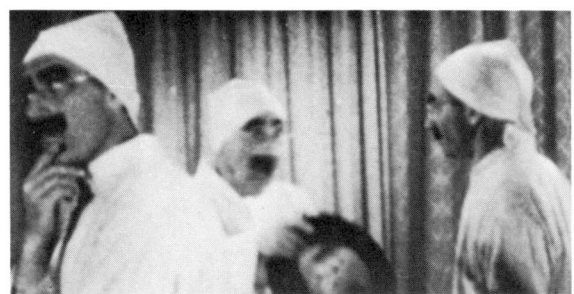

The celebrated mirror sequence: three Grouchos for the price of one

it with a pillow and finally beating it to death with a poker, but the music goes on. "What *is* that?" Mrs. Teasdale asks upstairs. "Sounds like mice," replies Groucho, who goes downstairs to locate the rodent band. Harpo finally solves his dilemma by dropping the entire wall safe-radio out the window. He dashes away, only to run directly into a wall mirror, smashing it and setting up the famous mirror scene. Harpo, still dressed as Groucho, is apprehended by the real Groucho and pretends to be ónly Groucho's mirror image. When Groucho strokes his chin, so does Harpo. When Groucho strides to the left, so does Harpo. Groucho crawls into the "mirror" view, only to find Harpo doing the same. He skips on by, as does his "image." In desperation, he breaks into a Charleston and spins around, arms outstretched, hoping to catch his reflection off guard. But Harpo merely waits for Groucho to spin full circle and casts his own arms out. Slowly the illusion breaks down. Groucho circles his reflection until the positions are reversed. They swap identical hats. But the jig is up when Chico blunders into the picture, one Groucho too many.

Chico is caught and brought to trial, where Groucho both attacks him and defends him, as he proposed to do for Helton in *Monkey Business*. The trial begins with the state's prosecutor demanding that Chico be shot to death. "I object," says Chico. "On what grounds?" roars the attorney. "I couldn't think of anything else to say," explains Chico, making more sense than is heard in most courtrooms. When Groucho calls him an "abject figure," Chico shifts his defense to "I abject." He tries to wriggle out by initiating a quiz game with the state's attorney. "What has a trunk," he asks, "weighs two thousand pounds and lives in a circus?" "That's irrelevant," cries the prosecutor. "That's-a right, an elephant," returns Chico. Groucho finally recommends that Chico receive "ten years in Leavenworth or eleven years in Twelveworth." "I take five and ten in Woolworth's," volunteers Chico. Before sentence can be passed, Mrs. Teasdale rushes in to announce that Trentino has consented to forget his quarrel with Groucho. "I'll be only too happy to meet Trentino," offers Groucho, sounding like every leader who professes to seek peace. Mrs. Teasdale assures him that Trentino will arrive soon, more than happy to extend "the right hand of friendship." "But what if he isn't?" muses Groucho, considering his vanity. And from there, he extrapolates the consequences of Trentino refusing to shake his hand, the embarrassment, the public humiliation. Soon it is not only possible but probable that Trentino will refuse to shake his hand. "Who does he think he is," screams Groucho, "that he can make a sap out of me in front of my own people?" At that moment, Trentino, followed by his retinue, enters. "So, you won't shake my hand," cries

Five and ten in Woolworth's

"To war! To war!"

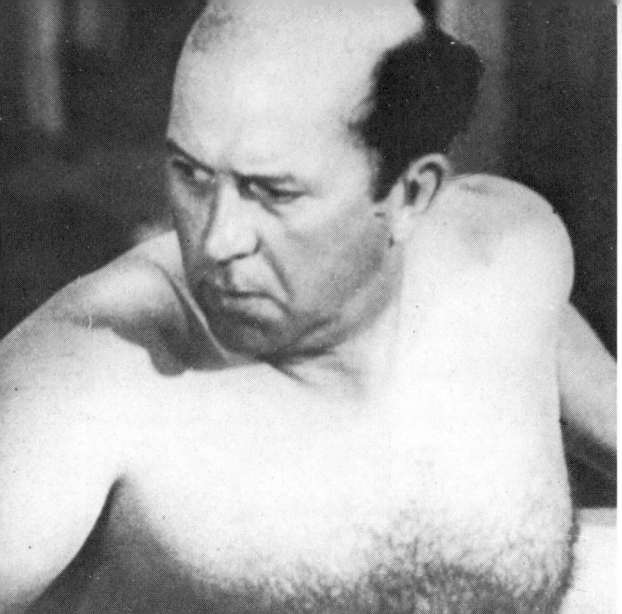

Tubful of surprises

Groucho automatically and slaps him again. WAR!!!

In "The Country's Going to War," the brothers do nothing less than set national hysteria to music. Minstrel show, Virginia reel, musical comedy, and the then popular Hall Johnson Choir are parodied in an extravaganza that lampoons the moaning, writhing, and mindless fever of patriotism that seizes a populace on the eve of war. The number includes a historical pastiche in which Harpo, as a mute Paul Revere rousing the citizens with a bugle, winds up deserting his mission the moment he spots a blonde undressing in a window. Once in her apartment, he is forced to seek refuge from her returning husband in the bottom of a full bathtub. Only when the husband unwittingly joins him in the bath and triggers the honk of his taxi horn does Harpo surface, blow a moist reveille and run, leaving the husband, Edgar Kennedy again,

to do his slow burn.

The war itself would do credit to the most disorganized Italian war games. Groucho sends telegrams to the front collect. "Isn't there ány answer to the message?" he asks. There isn't. "In that case," orders Groucho, "don't send it." A messenger rushes in, announcing that a general is undergoing a gas attack, and asks for advice. "Tell him to take a teaspoon of soda and half a glass of water." On the other side, the orders are equally ridiculous. Trentino tells Chico: "There's a machine-gun nest on hill twenty-two. I want it cleaned out." "Good," Chico replies, "I'll tell the janitor." Harpo, meanwhile, wanders about the front lines aimlessly, advertising on a sandwich sign the delights of military service: "JOIN THE ARMY AND SEE THE NAVY." Groucho gleefully mows down his own troops until Zeppo informs him of his mistake.

Finally Chico finds his way to the Fredonian headquarters, punching the time clock as he enters. The four brothers gather to select a volunteer for the dangerous mission of seeking aid. In a nice parody of the draft system, they select Harpo by lots—lots of rigging by Chico, who, following the playground rules of counting around a circle, keeps choosing himself by mistake, until he simply points to Harpo. Harpo marches off to cheers and into a closet full of fireworks, which detonate in a frenzy. (This foreshadows an identical scene years later in Jacques Tati's *Mr. Hulot's Holiday*.) At the same time, Chico telephones for help, sparking a sudden migration to the front of fire engine squadrons, battalions of motorcycle policemen, marathon runners,

long-distance swimmers, packs of baboons, herds of elephants and schools of porpoises. Mrs. Teasdale arrives at headquarters, and Groucho exhorts his brothers: "Remember, we're fighting for this woman's honor, which is probably more than she ever did." (After this scene was finished, Margaret Dumont, a true innocent, asked Groucho to explain the joke.)

The war is settled in much the same petty way it began. Trentino gets his head trapped in the door of Fredonian headquarters. When the brothers start pelting him with oranges like some target in a shooting gallery, he capitulates. Mrs. Teasdale breaks into glorious song—"Hail Fredonia." The brothers stop, slowly turn toward this intolerable advocate of patriotism and start pelting her with oranges as the film fades out.

The critics as a group were not enchanted by *Duck Soup,* though their

Wartime travelogue

reasons varied. For *Variety,* the jokes came too fast and furious. New York *Sun* critic John S. Cohen, Jr., felt they didn't come fast enough. "The Marx Brothers take something of a nosedive," he wrote after the film opened November 17, 1933. Even Richard Watts, the *Herald Tribune* critic and an admirer, felt that the brothers were "not at their best when mocking the frailties of dictatorship." The audience agreed. Why, then, has *Duck Soup* become a special favorite of later generations? Perhaps because its uncompromising view has been justified by the performance of govern-ments since. Perhaps because its wildness and abhorrence of moderation talk to a growing audience of alienated young people. If conventional patriotism is dead, *Duck Soup* provides a stylish requiem.

For Zeppo *Duck Soup* was the end of the line. In a letter to Groucho, he explained: "I'm sick and tired of being the stooge. You know that anybody else would have done as well as I did in the act. When the chance came for me to get into business, I jumped at it. I have only stayed in the act until now because I knew that you, Chico and Harpo wanted me to.

The Marxes at war

Trentino surrenders

"Hail, Freedonia"

But I am sure that you understand why I have joined Frank Orsatti and his theatrical agency and that you forgive my action. Wish me luck. Love, Zeppo." Groucho replied: "It's going to complicate things terribly for us, particularly on sleeper jumps. In the old days, we could split up peacefully, two to a berth. Now we're three and there's bound to be bad feelings." Actually, Zeppo's letter was painfully accurate and must stand as a rare document of honest self-appraisal. While handsome and blessed with a pleasant tenor, he had the ungrateful task of playing the romantic lead in films that didn't have one. He would appear in the first scene as a hanger-on and rush in at the end to remind the public that there were four Marx Brothers. But he lacked any real flare for performing and had the wisdom to recognize it.

Later, a friend asked the remaining three brothers whether they would accept a proportionately smaller salary with Zeppo gone. "After all," he argued, "you don't think three of you deserve quite as much money as four did, do you?" "What do you mean?" one of the brothers shot back. "Why, we're twice as good without Zeppo." And they were.

Harpo, Groucho, and Chico

Margaret Dumont

Allan Jones

Kitty Carlisle

Walter Wolf King

Siegfried Rumann

Otis B. Driftwood:	GROUCHO
Tomasso:	HARPO
Fiorello:	CHICO
Mrs. Claypool:	MARGARET DUMONT
Herman Gottlieb:	SIEGFRIED RUMANN
Rosa:	KITTY CARLISLE
Ricardo Baroni:	ALLAN JONES
Rodolpho Lassparri:	WALTER WOLF KING
The Captain:	EDWARD KEANE
Henderson:	ROBERT EMMET O'CONNOR

Also LORRAINE BRIDGES

* * *

Production: Irving G. Thalberg
Director: Sam Wood
Screenplay: George S. Kaufman and Morrie Ryskind
Additional Material: Al Boasberg
Story: James Kevin McGuinness
Photography: Merritt B. Gerstad
Art Direction: Cedric Gibbons, Ben Carre and Edwin B. Willis
Editing: William LeVanway
Musical Score: Herbert Stothart
Released by Metro-Goldwyn-Mayer, November 15, 1935. 92 minutes

Robert Emmet O'Co

7 A Night At The Opera (1935)

For a moment, the poor box office performance of *Duck Soup* threatened the Marx Brothers' film career. The Los Angeles *Times* in an article of April 24, 1934, described the quartet as "washed up." The New York *Times*, some nine months later, reported that movie studios looked on the brothers "with a degree of disinterest." And Paramount itself, having terminated its five-picture contract with the boys, was reluctant to renew it. Manny Cohen, who had replaced B. P. Schulberg as head of the studio, kept putting off the brothers with one excuse after another. "I'm just getting my feet under the desk here," he would tell the importuning Chico. Or, "Everything's all right, but give me a little time to get straightened out." Things smelled very bad. But by one of those curious coincidences that twist a career, Chico counted among his bridge-playing friends the slim, intense young genius of Metro-Goldwyn-Mayer, Irving Thalberg, who at thirty-seven was already head of production at the studio and later would serve as the model for F. Scott Fitzgerald's *The Last Tycoon*. Thalberg, had never talked business with Chico, but one day he asked him casually what the trio was up to. Trying to conceal its plight, Chico relied on the oldest line in the Hollywood book. The brothers, he told Thalberg, were between pictures, or at least between contracts.

The young producer suggested that Chico round up his brothers for a business lunch.

At the luncheon in the Beverly-Wilshire Hotel, the brothers quickly discovered that Thalberg had plans for them. He conceded that their pictures weren't bad. But he thought they could be great. "The trouble with your funny scenes is that they never help anybody," he told them. "If you had half the jokes, the picture would be twice as good and you'd gross three times as much." By the end of the lunch, Thalberg was pointing out errors in this scene or that from one or another of their pictures, and the brothers were as docile as lambs. "That's it, all right," Harpo would mumble. "We certainly were dumb there." But if the brothers were eating out of Thalberg's hand, he wound up feeding them well. Their new M-G-M contract called for a startling 15 percent of the gross receipts—not the net receipts, which is what is left over after the last press agent is paid, but 15 percent of each ticket. Part of the deal remained unwritten. "You get me the laughs," Thalberg promised, "and I'll get you the story." The story was *A Night at the Opera*.

Not all the ingredients that contribute to a great picture appear directly on the screen or among the credits. Certainly an intangible but critical part of the film's success can

Chico and Thalberg: a new career

be traced to the brothers' easy working rapport with Thalberg. While most actors cringed either inwardly or outwardly or both before the mogul, the Marxes reversed the process. Before their first conference, the boys found Thalberg's door closed to them briefly, so they all lit cigars, puffed them under the bottom crack and smoked the producer out. Another time, in the middle of the summer, Thalberg skipped out of a meeting momentarily to see Louis B. Mayer. When he returned, he found his fireplace ablaze and the Marxes camped around it, roasting potatoes. Thalberg never learned to cope with the brothers. Even after these warnings, he dared to keep them waiting again.

But when he finally wanted to open his door to them, he couldn't. The Marxes had barricaded it with file cabinets that took well over an hour to remove.

Thalberg contributed quite a number of tangibles as well. He assembled a fine cast that included Allan Jones and Kitty Carlisle and had the good judgment to retain their original singing voices even after the studio had gone to the expense of dubbing them with top stars from the Metropolitan Opera. He engaged the brothers' two finest foils, Margaret Dumont and Sig Rumann, a Viennese veteran of Ernst Lubitsch comedies. He also reunited the boys with their most successful writing team, Kaufman and Ryskind, and brought in the most talented one-line gagster of the day, a 300-pound giant of a man named Al Boasberg.

Boasberg had been hired by Jack Benny at $1,000 a week merely to look over and shore up his weekly radio script. He worked at his own pace and almost always in a hot tub. He didn't like to be rushed. Thalberg didn't like to be kept waiting. Finally, after the producer had hounded Boasberg for a particular scene, the gag man capitulated. "Okay, Mr. Thalberg," he told him over the phone. "I've got that material you wanted. But if you want it, you'll have to come over to my office and get it. I'm going home and leaving it here." Accompanied by the brothers, who were anxious to see it, Thalberg rushed to Boasberg's office. The script was nowhere to be found. But Groucho noticed something strange on the ceiling. On closer inspection it turned out to be the script. Boasberg had ripped it into a thousand tiny one-line strips and deliberately nailed each one to the ceiling. "It took us about five hours to piece it together," Groucho recalled in a biography by his son. "But it was worth it, for it turned out to be the nucleus of one of the most famous scenes we've ever done—the stateroom scene."

In one masterful stroke, Thalberg helped turn this and the other big scenes into surefire comic masterpieces. His brainstorm was a rather simple one on the surface, but it revealed a deep understanding of the essence of the team's comic gift. He proposed that the brothers take five big scenes on the road as a vaudeville show to put their jokes under the practical fire of a live audience. The Marxes embarked on a four-city tour—Salt Lake City, Seattle, Portland and Santa Barbara—playing four times a day. An article in the *Reader's Digest* outlined the mechanics of the tryout system: "When the patrons failed to laugh at a gag, that line came out. When they laughed late, the line was sharpened to take effect more quickly. When they laughed mildly, the line was sent back to the workshop. When they roared, the line was okayed for the film version. Morrie Ryskind and Al Boasberg sat in the theater, notebooks in hand, marking the responses of the audience from minute to minute. Every day they worked out new lines and gags to replace those that had failed. The first twelve pages of the script had seemed brilliant and witty, but eight of them were edited out by the audiences." One of the gags that went was an exchange between Groucho and a steward in which Groucho asks for French pastry. "But this is an Italian boat," the steward replies with ruffled vanity. "Well, then," Groucho shoots back and misses, "what's the rate of exchange?" The mighty stateroom scene was the greatest beneficiary of the tryout system. "They found out right from the beginning that the stateroom scene wasn't getting laughs

The brothers and Thalberg: an easy rapport

at all," recalls Allan Jones, who accompanied the brothers on the tour. "In a motion picture you could create the illusion of all those people packing into a little room. But on the full stage, it looked like just another scene." So the brothers compressed their crowding into a smaller space. As the tour continued, they increased the intruder ratio by several people per square foot. They also added ad libs whose success was timed by the writers on stopwatches. They returned from the tour boasting 175 surefire laughs.

Thalberg's most significant and lasting contribution to the brothers' films, however, was his wholly new conception of what a Marx Brothers' comedy should be. He replaced the wild, reckless terrain of the old films with a beautifully ordered garden of romance, music and recognizable plot. Music and comedy were wrenched apart; serious scenes set off comic ones. The brothers romped among sets far more splendid than any before and were treated to topflight supporting casts and costly costumes. The brothers themselves took on a more sympathetic complexion. They even helped the lovers. And while the seeds of this new formula grew to weaken their later picture, it worked like a charm in *A Night at the Opera*. It is generally considered their greatest film. No one has stopped howling long enough to verify whether it delivers its promised 175 surefire laughs.

The highly disciplined performances in *A Night at the Opera* reflect the firm hand of both Thalberg and his director, Sam Wood. Wood was a perfectionist who reshot scenes twenty or thirty times to get the one he wanted. Allan Jones believes that Wood shot so many takes because he really wasn't sure which was the best until he got the day's work into the cutting room. Unlike most directors, who supervise the cutting of the film after the entire picture is shot, Wood edited *A Night at the Opera* day by day. This tedious retake approach,

"Making love to Mrs. Claypool is my racket."

which often drove the brothers to distraction, endangered the spontaneity of the humor. But before each scene, Wood would exhort his cast to "go in there and sell 'em a load of clams" and always managed to pull out of the clam heap a take that was funny and fresh.

Kitty Carlisle remembers the atmosphere on the set as "deadly earnest." "Groucho," she says "would come up to me from time to time to ask me, 'Is this funny?' Then, totally deadpan, he'd try out a line. I'd say, 'No, I don't think it is funny,' and he'd go away absolutely crushed and try it out on everyone else in the cast. Chico was always playing cards in the back room and had to be called to the set. Harpo would work well until about eleven o'clock. Then he'd stretch out on the nearest piece of furniture and start calling at the top of his voice, 'Lunchie! Lunchie!' "

It was in this atmosphere of insanity off the set and strict control before the cameras that *A Night at the Opera* was made. As originally drawn up, the film was to start with the brothers popping through the M-G-M wreath to roar where Leo the Lion normally held sway. But M-G-M, more cautious than it had to be, feared that the gag would cheapen its trademark. Fortunately the film gets off to a fast start on its own. Margaret Dumont as Mrs. Claypool, once more a millionairess who seeks to make her place in high society, is being stood up for dinner at a restaurant in Milan by Otis P. Driftwood, penny-ante entrepreneur who has big plans for her. Groucho, of course, is Otis. When Mrs. Claypool has him paged, we find he has been dining with a comely blonde at the next table. "I've

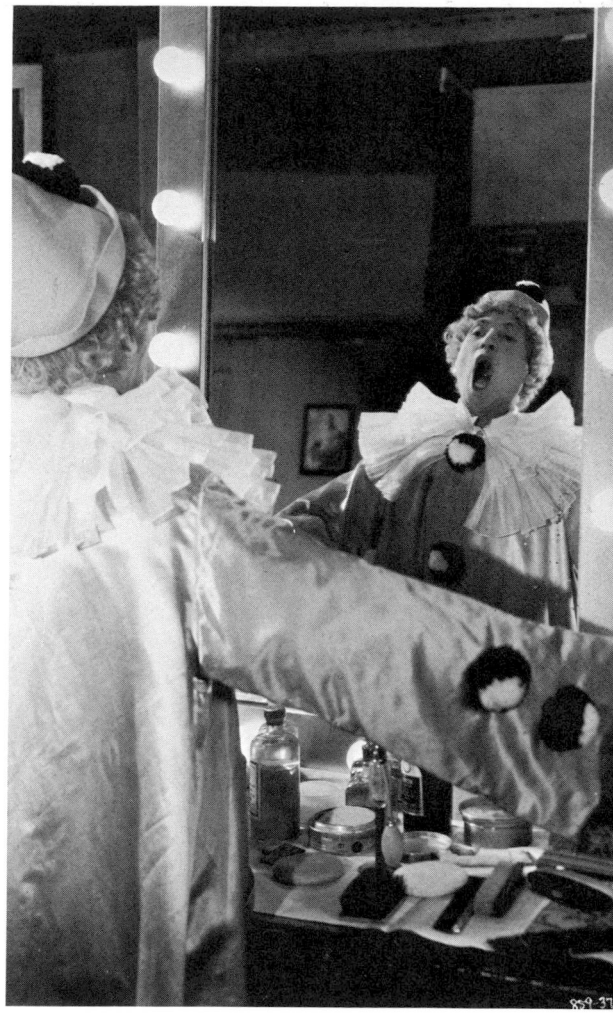

"_____!"

The romantic triangle
A. Jones, W. W. King, K. Carlisle

Harpo driving home a point

been sitting here since seven o'clock," Mrs. Claypool complains. "Yes, with your back to me," returns Groucho, once more wriggling free from an impossible dilemma. "When I invite a woman to dinner, I expect her to look at my face. That's the price she has to pay." He then receives the check, tosses it to his dinner companion and declares: "Nine forty! This is an outrage. If I were you, I wouldn't pay it."

Groucho sits down for a second dinner with Mrs. Claypool. "Have you got any milk-fed chicken?" he asks the waiter, who does. "Well, squeeze the milk out of one," he orders, "and bring me a glass." (This line, transported from another scene, was written to replace the dud about French pastry and rate of exchange.) Groucho has promised to put Mrs. Claypool in society, but in three months, she tells him, "You've done nothing but draw a very handsome salary." "You think that's nothing, huh?" Groucho retaliates. "How many men do you think are drawing

a handsome salary these days? Why, you can count them on the fingers of one hand, my good woman." "I'm not your good woman," exclaims the horrified Mrs. Claypool. "I don't care what your past has been," Groucho insists. "To me, you'll always be my good woman."

Groucho, tongue in cheek and foot in mouth, declares his undying love for the dowager. But Mrs. Claypool will have none of it, pointing to Groucho's rendezvous with the

The party of the first part—rip!

blonde. "That woman?" cries Groucho. "Do you know why I sat with her? Because she reminded me of you. That's why I'm sitting here with *you*. Because you remind me of you. Your eyes, your throat, your lips, everything about you reminds me of you, except you. How do you account for that?"

Groucho's plan for Mrs. Claypool is very simple. He will invest $200,000 of her money in the New York Opera. "Don't you see," he explains, "you'll get into society. Then you can marry me and they'll kick you out of society, and all you've lost is two hundred thousand dollars." Herman Gottlieb, impresario of the opera, is delighted to accept Mrs. Claypool's money. But when he starts romancing her, Groucho warns him off: "Look here, Gottlieb, making love to Mrs. Claypool is my racket. What you're after is two hundred thousand dollars. And you'd better make it sound plausible, because, as incredible as it may seem, Mrs. Claypool isn't as big a sap as she looks." Gottlieb, played with just the right balance of bluster and menace

by Sig Rumann, intends to spend Mrs. Claypool's money on hiring the celebrated Italian tenor Rodolpho Lassparri. He spirits the matron off to the opera to hear him. Lassparri is a very mean character, so mean, in fact, that he beats his valet, Harpo, when he catches the clown trying on one of his clown costumes in his dressing room. Lassparri whips him with a riding crop until Harpo rips off the costume and appears—in another costume, this one a naval outfit. Lassparri beats him again, and Harpo tears off his uniform, appearing—in another costume, a dirndl. Finally he sheds the dress and appears as he really is, in another costume.

Lassparri sings. Mrs. Claypool and Gottlieb listen. And Groucho keeps riding around the park in a carriage until the whole thing blows over. "Hey, you," he yells to the driver at one point, "I told you to slow down. Because of you, I almost heard the opera." He finally arrives at Gottlieb's box, cheering, "Bravo, bravo" just after the curtain has fallen. By then, the impresario and Mrs. Clay-

pool have decided to sign Lassparri to a $1,000-a-week contract. "Why, you can get a phonograph record of Minnie the Moocher for seventy-five cents," exclaims Groucho. "And for a buck and a quarter, you can get Minnie." Groucho hasn't the faintest idea who Lassparri is, but he heads backstage hoping to sign him himself and pocket a piece of the contract. Groucho runs into Lassparri, who is dressed as a clown, and asks him: "Can you sleep on your stomach with such big buttons on your pajamas?" Before Groucho can discover to whom he is talking, Lassparri is the victim of Harpo's revenge, a blow on the head with a large gavel. Harpo immediately applies the smelling salts to the tenor. "You're sorry for what you did," says Groucho. Harpo nods. "That shows a nice spirit," admires Groucho. And as Lassparri begins to come to, Harpo lets him have it again with the gavel. Groucho immediately takes credit for the knockout, placing a conquering foot on the victim's chest. "We had an argument. He pulled a knife on me, so I had to shoot him," he explains to Chico, who wanders by. Chico claims to represent the "greatest tenor in the world" and Groucho, without questioning, proceeds to sign him up in an insane parody of all contract negotiations. As it turns out, Chico manages Ricky Baroni, a little-known singer in the chorus, but the deal Groucho works out for himself is too attractive to complicate with such details. Of the $1,000 a night, Groucho takes only $990 and leaves Chico and his singer to split the rest. "Could he sail tomorrow?" asks Groucho. "You pay him enough money, he could sail yesterday," Chico replies, accepting the $10

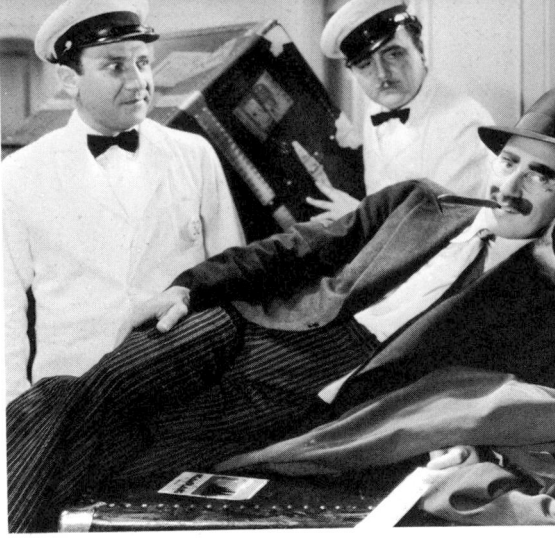

Groucho heading toward the celebrated stateroom

offer.

The contract scene is the greatest of the nonsensical exchanges between the fast-talking Groucho and the tenacious Chico. It starts with a baffling series of *non sequiturs* and, as it goes along, nothing becomes clear. Groucho produces a pair of contracts that run to the floor, hands one to Chico and volunteers to read aloud. "Can you hear?" he asks. "I haven't heard anything yet," replies Chico. "Well I haven't said anything worth hearing," explains Groucho. "That's-a why I didn't hear anything," counters Chico. "That's why I didn't say anything," concludes Groucho. Groucho starts threading his way through the gobbledygook of legal language, explaining that the "party of the first part in this contract shall be known as the party of the first part." But Chico doesn't like it. Groucho repeats it. Chico likes it a little better, but he wants to hear the first part over again—not the party of the first part but the first part of the party of the first part. "All right," says Groucho, happy to hang legalese with its own twisted rope, "it says, 'The

first part of the party of the first part shall be known in this contract . . .' Look," he finally concedes, "why should we quarrel about a thing like this? We'll take it right out." And they each rip the top of the contract off. Chico doesn't like the second party any more than the first. "You should have come to the first party," Groucho advises. "We didn't get home 'til around four in the morning. I was blind for three days." But they agree that the second party has to go. Rip! "Now I've got something you're bound to like," Groucho offers. "No, I don't like it," says Chico. "Don't like what?" "Whatever it is," says the always suspicious Chico, "I don't like it." Rip! "Now the next part," says Chico, "I don't think you're gonna like." Rip! "Well," says Groucho, "your word is good enough for me." Rip! "Is my word good enough for you?" "I should say not," says Chico. "Well," says Groucho, "that takes out two more clauses." Rip! Rip! By now, the contracts have shrunk to the size of envelopes. As the eighth and ninth parts go the way of the first part, the contract narrows to the dimensions of

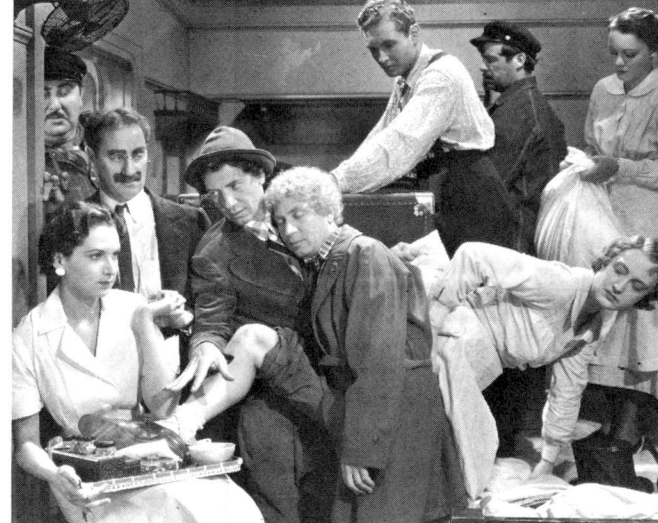

an African postage stamp. After everything is settled, Chico objects to one last provision. "That's in every contract," Groucho assures him. "That's what they call a sanity clause." "You can't fool me," laughs Chico. "There ain't no Santy Claus."

Once Lassparri has regained consciousness he is apparently signed, because he accompanies Gottlieb, Mrs. Claypool and Driftwood aboard ship to New York, selecting a beautiful young soprano, Rosa, to be his leading lady. Lassparri has designs on the singer, but she is in love with Ricky Baroni. Rosa, played by Kitty Carlisle, sings a dockside duet with Ricky, who seemingly is to be left behind. (Both Groucho and Chico objected to

the song, which was substituted during the tryouts, but Allan Jones pleaded for it. Thalberg made the final decision. "The Marx Brothers know comedy," he told the young tenor. "You know music. I'll leave it in." Thalberg's judgment was unerring. The song, "Alone," led the Lucky Strike Hit Parade for sixteen weeks and immeasurably broadened the film's appeal.) Before the ship pulls out, Chico kisses Rosa good-bye, and Harpo kisses everyone good-bye, including a startled little man with a beard.

But when Groucho arrives at his stateroom, a postage stamp with portholes, courtesy of Gottlieb, he discovers that his trunk not only con-

Three's a crowd

Chico and Harpo

caught in an extravaganza

tains a few shirts, but Chico, Baroni and Harpo wearing them. Harpo lies curled asleep like a dog in the bottom drawer of the chest. The stowaways are starving, so Groucho reluctantly steps into the hall and calls the steward. He is expecting a visit from Mrs. Claypool and would like to clear the room for romance. He orders two scrambled eggs, two boiled eggs, two fried eggs and two poached eggs. "And two hard-boiled eggs," Chico demands through the door. "And two hard-boiled eggs," echoes Groucho. "Honk" signals Harpo. "Make that three hard-boiled eggs." Groucho then orders some roast beef—rare, medium, well done and overdone. "And two hard-boiled eggs," says Chico. "And two hard-boiled eggs," says Groucho. Honk! "Make that three hard-boiled eggs," he amends. Two hard-boiled eggs — *HONK* — make that three hard-boiled eggs, are added on to orders of French pastry and black coffee (the coffee ordered to sober up some stewed prunes). Harpo

delivers a dozen more honks for a dozen more eggs to close out the order. Finally Groucho asks the steward, whom he calls Stu, if any tipping is allowed. When the steward eagerly replies that there is, Groucho asks him if he has two five-dollar bills. "Yes, sir," snaps the steward. "Well, then, you won't need the ten cents I was going to give you."

But all this, funny as it may be, is only to set up the celebrated stateroom scene. A succession of the ship's staff streams into Groucho's cubby— first two large chambermaids who must keep the sleeping Harpo afloat on their backs as they make the bed, followed by an engineer who has come to turn on the heat. A manicurist braves the crowd to trim Groucho's nails. "You better make 'em short. It's getting crowded in here," he comments. Like some subway nightmare at rush hour in which nobody gets off and hundreds pour in, the mass of tangled bodies is joined by the engineer's oversized assistant, a

Harpo clutching the plot line

Chicoski, Baronoff and Harpotski

woman in search of her Aunt Minnie, a gargantuan cleaning lady and a battalion of waiters loaded with hard-boiled eggs. Everyone manages to jam in when Mrs. Claypool arrives at her elegant best for her rendezvous with Groucho. She innocently opens the door and is suddenly overwhelmed by a torrent of human bodies.

The stowaways, deprived of their hard-boiled eggs, wander on deck that evening in search of food and immediately come across a beggar's paradise—an open buffet line that is part of the final-night celebration. (The crossing is accomplished in thirty-six hours, which must have been a record at the time, even for the movies.) Harpo staggers along the line from one sumptuous dish to the next, his eyes bugging, his mouth agape, walking in a dream as jolly Italian chefs heap food on him. One frame later, he is wiping his plate clean. Only Harpo can eat that fast. The Marxes and Allan Jones settle down for a little after-dinner music—a lavish production number with dancers and chorus here, a Chico special solo there, a bit of Harpo banging the piano top on his hands, which go as limp as two paintbrushes, and Jones singing "Cosi-Cosa," another song that became a popular hit. Wood's fine eye is especially apparent here as he cuts from time to time to beautifully shadowed portraits of the children who are listening. Even more apparent is Thalberg's money, which fairly drips from this number. It ends with Lassparri spotting the stowaways and sending the police after them.

The three are caught and confined to quarters. Chico paces while Harpo plays "Cosi-Cosa" on the kazoo and Allan Jones, as Baroni, does nothing.

"We can tear up the mayor's speech when we get there."

Jones has clearly taken the role normally assigned to Zeppo, which means that, like a phonograph, when he isn't making music, he isn't doing anything. Finally Chico grows tired of the kazoo and pitches it out the porthole. Like W. C. Fields jumping from an airplane after a fallen bottle of booze, Harpo leaps into the ocean after the kazoo. He is thrown a lifeline that turns out to be more of a plot line, for it lifts him into the quarters of three bearded Russian aviators taking an afternoon nap. Harpo seizes his scissors and . . .

We have three new Russian aviators — Chicoski, Harpotski and Baronoff—and their manager, Groucho, who are escorted from the ship by the mayor's official greeter and given a ticker-tape parade to a public ceremony at City Hall. There Chico is called on to deliver a speech. Stand-ing uneasily before the crowd of thousands at City Hall, he whispers to Groucho: "What do I say?" "Tell 'em you're not here," Groucho advises. "What if they don't believe me?" asks Chico. "They'll believe you when you start talking," assures Groucho.

"Friends," he begins, "we donna deserve this-a grand reception. And when I say we donna deserve it, believe me, I know what I'm talkin' about. So now I tell you how we fly to America. The first time we get halfway across when we run outta gasoline and we gotta go back. Then we take twice as much gasoline. This time we just about to land . . . maybe three feet . . . when whaddya think? We run outta gasoline again and back we go to get-a more gasoline. This time .we get plenty gas. Then I get a great idea. We no take gasoline. We take a steamship. And that, friends, is how we fly across the ocean."

It is Harpo's turn. He takes a glass of water, clears his throat, and takes another drink of water. Then, to clear his throat a bit, he takes another glass of water. He is about to "speak" but, feeling a little dry, he has a nice fresh drink of water. By now, his beard is showing signs of erosion and a detective in the crowd, one Henderson by name, challenges Harpo's identity. The brothers wax wroth as it were, and Henderson is forced to back down. Harpo, as indiscriminate as ever, kisses him on both cheeks, and suddenly Henderson is wearing a beard. The brothers disappear under the grandstand and flee to a nearby hotel.

Apparently safe, they sit down to a nice healthy breakfast — especially Harpo, who consumes a "cupcake" of one china cup between two flapjacks, one cigar nestled in a hot-dog roll and a hot necktie on toast. Then, suddenly turning dainty damsel, he lifts the top of the sugar bowl like a mirror and applies pancake makeup with a pancake, lipstick from a ketchup bottle and a few pinches of sauce behind the ears. Amid his antics, Chico comments, "I'm glad I didn't bring my vest." "I meant to tell you," says Groucho. "He ate your vest last night for dessert." The breakfast pageant is

"We donna deserve this grand-a reception."

ving eaten Chico's clothes,

disrupted by a knock on the door. The stowaways hide. It is Henderson, plainclothesman. "You look more like an old-clothes man to me," Groucho tells him. The detective notices the table is set for four. "And my alarm clock is set for eight," answers Groucho. Henderson wanders into the bedroom, still searching for the "aviators," and notices four beds. "You see those first three beds?" Groucho explains. "Last night I counted five thousand sheep in those three beds, so I had to have another bed to sleep in."

The brothers, hiding on the porch, start moving the furniture around. First there are three beds, then two, then one. Henderson staggers from room to room as the beds seem to skip about of their own volition. Finally he lists back into the bedroom, his sanity hanging by a thread, to find no beds. Instead an old lady with a doily on her head and a "Gookie" on her face is knitting in a rocker that resembles, to the trained eye, Chico under a sheet. Next to the senile stitcher is a man literally buried in a daily newspaper that appears to be smoking a cigar.

Harpo starts wearing his food

The opening night of the opera season arrives. Groucho strides in backstage to an obsequious chorus of "Good evening, Mr. Driftwood." Upstairs, however, he learns that Mrs. Claypool has fired him for associating with "riffraff." And Gottlieb has banned both Rosa and Ricky from singing. "All right, I'll go," he concedes as his name is being scraped off the door. "But I'm not making a nickel on it." His exit is a bit more rapid than his entrance. The elevator man pitches him down three flights of stairs. But Gottlieb has not yet seen the last of battling Groucho. When the opera master returns to his office that night, Harpo is lounging in his seat, pouring Scotch for Chico and Groucho with his feet. Gottlieb's objections are answered with Harpo's revenge, gavel to cranium, and the

hirsute impresario is hustled into the closet, leaving the brothers free to run wild at the opera.

Groucho in effect becomes Gottlieb for a night, which Groucho would consider one night too long. He replaces Gottlieb as Mrs. Claypool's escort and delivers Gottlieb's opening-night address—with a few amendments. Introducing the opera season as "made possible by the generous checks of Mrs. Claypool," Groucho adds: "I am sure the strains of Verdi's music will come back to you tonight, and Mrs. Claypool's checks will probably come back in the morning." He concludes: "Let joy be unconfined. Let there be dancing in the streets, drinking in the saloons and necking in the park." With this dignified beginning, the opera launches on its irreversible course

Sig Rumann making a short call

The beginning of the end

toward disaster. Harpo and Chico infiltrate the orchestra, Harpo playing first trombone with a violin bow (or first violin with a trombone). The overture to *Il Trovatore* moves along smoothly enough once Harpo has stopped fencing with the conductor. But when the orchestra turns to page two of its music, it breaks into "Take Me Out to the Ball Game," thanks to a little extra score Harpo and Chico have slipped into the program. Harpo bats with a violin, Chico pitches and Groucho, always quick to make a buck, appears at the rear, hawking peanuts. At last, the curtain rises. A hideous gypsy is warbling. Harpo throws her a Gookie and Groucho, back in his box, casts a curse on her, crying, "Boogie, boogie, boogie." A dance team toss each other about with Harpo stripping the distaff side of an item of clothing each time she prances by. The police close in from

the wings, joined by Gottlieb, who has finally worked his way out of the closet. Harpo takes the most direct route of escape by scampering up the scenery like a lizard up a wall, then turns Tarzan, swinging from the ropes that control the backdrops. As Lassparri sings, he finds himself holding forth from the back of a railroad train, then in front of a battleship, then suddenly in front of a fruit stand. Occasionally the fruit stand finds itself in front of Lassparri. Finally Harpo and Chico collaborate to kidnap and carry off the tenor to the roof of the stage. Gottlieb is stuck. He must have a tenor to satisfy the cries of the outraged audience. Baroni just happens to be handy, and he and Rosa sing an aria or two while Lassparri chews on his gag, ruminating on his fate. The crowd loves Baroni and Rosa. It tosses fruit at Lassparri when he finally wriggles free and at-

Lassparri hitting a high note

tempts to sing an encore. Baroni is signed on the condition that the police drop all charges against the brothers, a decision he may live to regret, for the last frames show Chico and Groucho quarreling over the party of the tenth part as they dismember Baroni's fame and fortune piece by piece.

At the time *A Night at the Opera* was made, no one dreamed it would become a classic. Its sneak preview at a Long Beach theater suggested at first that Thalberg's genius had deserted him completely. The audience laughed at the titles and that was that, not another laugh for the rest of the evening. But Thalberg would not take one no for an answer. He had the six reels of the film transferred immediately to a theater across the street in search of another verdict. The second audience howled at the titles and kept on laughing right to "The End." *A Night at the Opera* was a hit. Virtually every reviewer in America exhausted the superlatives of the English language in endorsing the latest Marx lunacy. Thorton Delehanty spoke for them all when he wrote in the New York *Post*: "It is a dangerous thing to rate any Marx

Curtain call

few quick scene changes

Brothers picture as their 'best,' yet even at the risk of having to eat my own words I would say that none of their previous films is as consistently and exhaustingly funny or as rich in comic invention and satire as 'A Night at the Opera.'" If box office returns are a measure of excellence, which they aren't, the film was the finest Marx movie to date, answering Thalberg's trust with a $3 million profit.

Amid all their success, the Marx Brothers did not forget the trick that writer Al Boasberg had played on them with the strips of the stateroom scene. As was probably prearranged, the gag specialist did not get his name on the final product, which gave the brothers an opening. They sent Boasberg an autographed picture of themselves with the following inscription. "To our pal, Sorry, but we couldn't get your name on this picture either."

Reprise: The brothers and Dumont

Margaret Dumont

Harpo, Groucho, and Chico

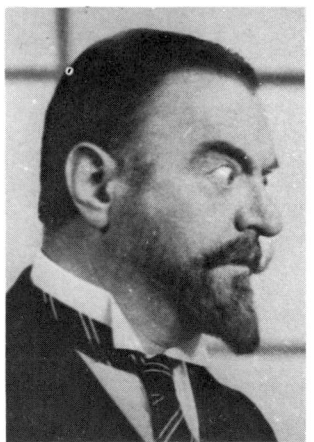

Siegfried Rumann

Esther Muir

Douglas Dumbrille

Dr. Hugo Z. Hackenbush:	GROUCHO
Stuffy:	HARPO
Toni:	CHICO
Mrs. Emily Upjohn:	MARGARET DUMONT
Dr. Leopold X. Steinberg:	SIEGFRIED RUMANN
Gil Stewart:	ALLAN JONES
Judy Standish:	MAUREEN O'SULLIVAN
Morgan:	DOUGLAS DUMBRILLE
Whitmore:	LEONARD CEELEY
Miss Nora:	ESTHER MUIR
The Sheriff:	ROBERT MIDDLEMASS

Also VIVIEN FAY, IVIE ANDERSON and THE CRINOLINE CHOIR

Maureen O'Sullivan and Allan

* * *

Production: Irving G. Thalberg and Sam Wood
Associate Producer: Max Siegel
Director: Sam Wood
Screenplay: George Seaton, Robert Pirosh and George Oppenheimer
Story: George Seaton and Robert Pirosh
Photography: Joseph Ruttenberg
Art Direction: Cedric Gibbons, Stan Rogers and Edwin B. Willis
Editing: Frank E. Hull
Music Direction: Franz Waxman
Released by Metro-Goldwyn-Mayer, June 11, 1937. 109 minutes

Leonard Ceeley

8 A Day At The Races (1937)

As is so often the case in Hollywood, the formula of one successful film is automatically applied to the next. So it was with *A Day at the Races,* which followed the Thalberg format to the letter—but with several key differences. The most important of these was the absence of Thalberg himself. Three weeks into the shooting of the film, the frail, intense, overworked young producer contracted pneumonia in both lungs and died. He was thirty-seven. Before he fell ill, he had laid all the groundwork for *Races,* but his presence during its filming and his uncanny judgment on the dozens of small choices that influence a comedy during production were lost. Not that the picture was anything like a failure. It survived, in fact, as one of the brothers' best. But *A Day at the Races* is a clear step down from *A Night at the Opera,* and part of the slippage must be attributed to Thalberg's passing. Also, George S. Kaufman had left California, depriving the brothers of one of their finest writers and a leading wit of the day.

The writing chores were turned over to three men who had never worked for the brothers before—George Seaton, Robert Pirosh and George Oppenheimer, with an assist from Al Boasberg. "Ordinarily, when we were working out their scenes," explained Pirosh, "I impersonated Groucho and Seaton impersonated Chico." Then he added, tongue in cheek, "It took two of us to impersonate Harpo: one to wear the wig, the other to chase the blondes." Fortunately Pirosh wrote funnier jokes for the script than this one. Even so, it points up what is felt throughout the picture—that the writers, new to the team, were looking over their shoulders at earlier films for inspiration. In *A Day at the Races,* the routines hold up well indeed. But the script does not venture beyond the established limits of the previous films. The mold had been set by men like Kaufman, Ryskind, Perelman and Johnstone. The new writers were not about to break it.

Finally, *A Night at the Opera* had furnished the Marxes with perfect settings—the familiar, hemmed-in, decorous precincts of an Atlantic crossing and the highbrow, black-tie background of the opera itself. "Hit a fellow in old clothes with a snowball and it won't mean a thing," Thalberg once explained. "But dress a man up in tails and a silk hat and then knock his hat off, and you'll get a laugh." Or, perhaps, 175 of them. The sanitorium setting in *A Day at the Races,* dominated as it was by the majestic Margaret Dumont, worked well enough. But the racetrack was in many ways as wild and disreputable as the brothers themselves. While the Marxes seemed delightfully out of place at the opera, there was nothing incongruous about Chico at the track.

Despite these minor deficiencies, *A Day at the Races* was funny enough to earn $4 million, a record for a Marx Brothers film. Sam Wood, who shared the production work, also directed. We may assume that he followed Thalberg's blueprint assiduously. Like his boss, Wood believed that music and romance were essential to a successful comedy. "There is as much need for relief from comedy as from the starkest tragedy," he, argued. "Audiences may think that they'd like to laugh every minute, but they wouldn't. The emotional demands are just too great. That's why, in *A Day at the Races,* the romance and music are included as interludes." This theory is violently disputed by devotees of the early films. But M-G-M was out to make money, not classics. As it turned out, they managed to make both. But the theory was a risky one. In the later Marx Brothers films, as the scripts grew weaker, the comedy at times seemed to provide relief from the music and romance.

The tryout system instituted under Thalberg was so helpful that the brothers undertook a 6,000-mile road-show tour before shooting *A Day at the Races.* They enlisted the active help of the audience as they traveled through Duluth, Minneapolis, Chicago, Cleveland, Detroit and Pittsburgh, passing out more than 30,000 cards that asked for comment on the funny lines, the bad ones and the general level of performance. With the aid of these cards, stopwatches and their own instincts, the team and their writers selected what they advertised as "The 175 laughs which the

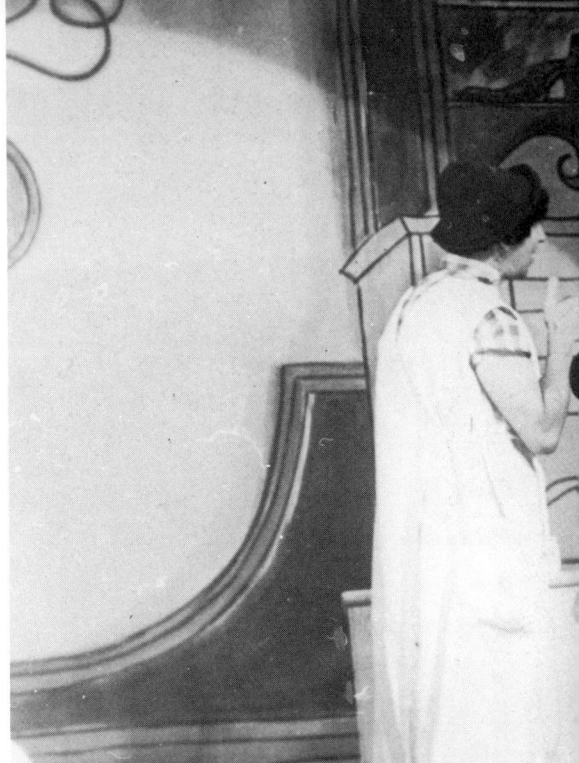

Trying it out on tour

audience enjoyed most." "The 75 of those with the highest laugh rating," the news release went on, "will be used in the picture." Whether they really had a fixed number is highly doubtful, if not ridiculous, but there is little question that their material benefited greatly from head-on collisions with live audiences. "That was the trouble with being a Marx Brother," Groucho confirmed in a conversation with his son, Arthur. "We weren't like other comedians. We had to try everything out first. If we had shot *Opera* with the material we opened with in Seattle, it would have been the end of all of us."

In *A Day at the Races,* Groucho plays Dr. Hugo Z. Hackenbush, veteran veterinarian, or longtime horse doctor to you. The writers originally titled him Dr. Quackenbush, de-

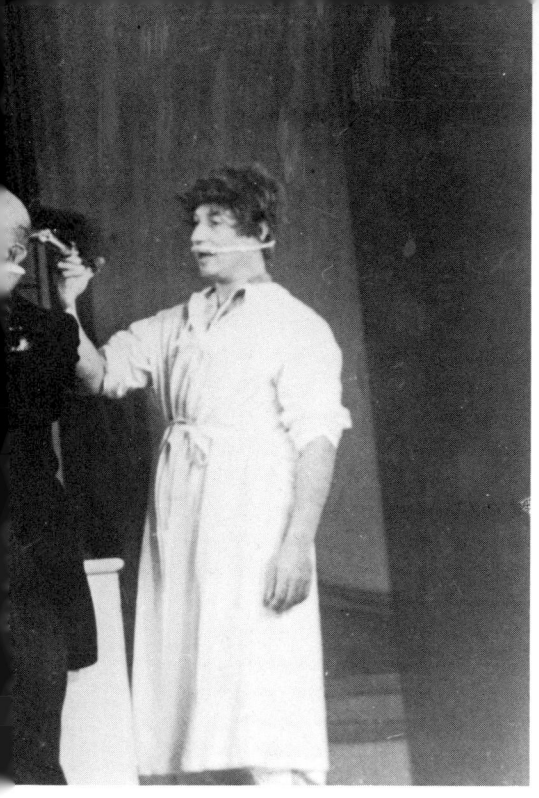

none too good for their patients, who are vain hypochondriacs suffering mainly from water on the brain. Hospitals and sanitoriums are hotels for the chronically rich. Mrs. Upjohn compresses this vision into one line when she defends Hackenbush: "I didn't know there was anything wrong with me until I met him." As Mrs. Upjohn, Margaret Dumont is at her finest—fretful, haughty, and unbendingly stoic in the face of Marxian harassment. Her performance won her the Screen Actors Guild award for Best Supporting Actress.

Save the Standish Sanitorium is the theme of the film—not particularly stirring, but a serviceable skeleton on which to hang comic clothes. Standish's owner, Judy Standish, played by Maureen O'Sullivan in a change from her Tarzan pictures, faces liquidation unless she can meet her mortgages. Otherwise she will have to sell to mean Mr. Morgan, the owner of the nearby racetrack, who wants to convert the sagging structure into a casino. His man, Whitmore, the sanitorium's business manager, is boring at the operation's financial foundations from within. Only Mrs. Upjohn and her millions can save the hospital, and she, it turns out, is about to leave because the doctors refuse to find anything wrong with her. But Chico, Judy's friend and sanitorium chauffeur, summons Hackenbush to the rescue in the hope that the dowager's romantic attachment to him will convince her to stay.

Hackenbush jumps at the offer to desert his middling trade as veterinarian. He packs his bags and tosses a huge pill to an ailing equine patient. "Take one of these every half mile," he counsels the horse, "and call me if

lighted with all the name implied and confident that no one in real life with the power to sue possessed such an outlandish name—or if he did, that he would certainly be too ashamed of it to bring it into court. But at the last minute, the M-G-M legal department announced that not only were there Quackenbushes in America, but Dr. Quackenbushes. The writers deferred, content to let a bird in the hand be worth a quack in the bush.

Even as Hackenbush, the horse doctor remains Groucho's favorite role. "I liked the role," he explained, "because it tickled up the medical profession, and I think it could stand a bit of lampooning now and then." As usual, the satire is sufficiently broad to take in most everything in view. Doctors are depicted as senile, incompetent and self-serving, but

"You look like a pretty big pill yourself"

there's any change." He arrives at the sanitorium seemingly even before Chico telegrams him, confirming Chico's longstanding confidence that "if you pay him enough, he could come yesterday." Groucho takes an immediate dislike to Whitmore, whom he finds not only boring from within, but boring from any angle. He hands him his bags and tips him a dime. "This is Mr. Whitmore, our business manager," he is told. "Oh, I'm sorry," Groucho apologizes. "Here's a quarter." Groucho is then introduced to the doctors on the staff. "Johns Hopkins, '17," says one of the bearded fogies. "Mayo Brothers, '28," says another. "Dodge Brothers, '29," counters Groucho. This disreputable reference could hardly have sold many cars, but the Chrysler Company was so delighted by the mention that it gave each of the brothers a new Dodge.

As in each of the films where Groucho takes over a new job, he immediately presents his moth-eaten credentials. "At the age of fifteen I filled prescriptions in a drugstore," he announces proudly. "But don't you have to be twenty-one to fill prescriptions?" one of the doctors asks. "That's for adult prescriptions," explains Groucho. "I only filled prescriptions for children." To show off his expertise, he gets to work immediately by handing Mrs. Upjohn a horse pill the size of a ping-pong ball. "That looks like a pretty big pill," snipes Whitmore. "Say, you look like a pretty big pill yourself," Groucho snaps back. Unnerved by the new doctor, Whitmore tries to call Florida to check up on his medical background. But Groucho gets wind of this and intercepts the call in his office next door to Whitmore's. "Colonel Hawkins talkin'," he tells Whitmore over the phone. Then he places a sheet of paper in the desk fan and says: "Sorry, you'll have to talk loudah. There's a hurricane blowin'." Each time Whitmore screams into the phone, Groucho buzzes him on the intercom to tell him to keep his voice down. By the time the business manager returns to the phone, "Colonel Hawkins" is just finishing his report on Hackenbush. Groucho has his victim caught in a vise and slowly tightens it. "I'm sorry, Colonel," says Whitmore, returning to the phone from the intercom, "but what's that you said about Hackenbush?" "You mean, Dr. Hackenbush?" returns Hawkins. "He's not here." "I know he's not there, he's *here*," screams Whitmore. "Then what are you botherin' me for?" asks the colonel. Whitmore struggles to regain his composure, but his effort is doomed. "Are you sure you're speaking about Hugo Z. Hackenbush?" he asks. "Who?" asks hard-of-hearing Hawkins. "Doctor Hugo Z. Hackenbush! ! ! ! ! !" screams Whitmore. "Who's calling him?" asks Hawkins. "Standish Sanitorium! ! ! ! ! !" "Yes," replies helpful Hawkins. "That's where he works. I understand he's doing a mighty fine job up there."

Whitmore is teetering at the breaking point, but Groucho wants to play with him a bit longer before pushing him over the edge. "I want to get some information regarding his qualifications for the job," begs the desperate Whitmore. "What job?" Hawkins asks. "As head of the sanitorium!" whines Whitmore. "Who?" Whitmore flips his lid. "Hackenbush ! ! ! ! ! !" Groucho buzzes Whitmore on the intercom. "Whitmore," he asks, "are you calling me?" "No,

you sap !" he screams, then turns back to the phone, only to hear Hawkins once more ask, "Now what was that name?" "Hackenbush!" Whitmore bellows in despair. "Hackenbush! ! ! ! ! !" "Well," concludes the unruffled colonel, applying the finishing touch, "as soon as he comes in, I'll have him get in touch with you." "No!" Whitmore shrieks slamming down the phone, his bureaucratic nightmare having driven him thoroughly mad.

Harpo, as usual, is unemployed in several jobs. He is fired as Morgan's jockey when he wins a race he was supposed to throw. "Oh, you been fired," exclaims Chico as Harpo tells him the news by striking a match. Harpo also takes care of High Hat, the slow racehorse purchased by Gil Stewart, Judy Standish's fiance, with the last $1,500 the couple owns. That leaves $00.00 with which to pay the feed bill. The sheriff arrives at the stable, ready to foreclose on the horse, but Harpo and Chico manage to convert their last $5 into $15 this way: Chico hands the sheriff a $5 bill. The sheriff pockets it. Harpo picks it and returns it to Chico, who pays another $5. The pair manages this ruse three

The fruits of victory

$5 will get you $15

"tutsi frutsi ice cream"

9 jockey's guides, $1 each

times until Harpo, a bit too eager, reaches through the man's pocket all the way down his leg. He leans there for a minute like a fallen tree, his eyes twinkling as the sheriff stares down at him. Suddenly Harpo pulls away, triumphantly brandishing the sheriff's sock. The constable takes chase, and High Hat is reprieved.

Chico also has two jobs. When he has no money, he works as a chauffeur. When he really has no money, he works the track, posing as an ice cream vendor whose cart contains hot racing tips instead of cool refreshment. Chico knows he can win a bundle betting on Sun Up, the favorite, but he hasn't the ready cash. Groucho arrives, ripe for the kill, and Chico moves in. "Tutsi-frutsi ice cream," he cries, intercepting Groucho before he can reach the parimutuel window. "Get you tutsie-frutsi ice cream." Groucho wants to bet on Sun Up also, but Chico cautions him against it, offering instead a surefire tout book for only $1. "One dollar," he says, "and you remember me for the rest of you life." Groucho is impressed. "That's the most nauseating proposition I ever heard," he comments. His greed overcomes his skepticism, as it always does in suckers, and he buys the pamphlet which Chico produces from his cart. "ZBXYRL" will win the next race, it says. A free code book will unravel the mystery, Chico explains, free "except for a one-dollar printing charge." The con game grows. To understand the code book, Groucho must pay two more dollars for the free master code book. The two dollars is for the cost of delivery. "But I'm standing right next to you," Groucho complains. "All right, then, one dollar," concedes

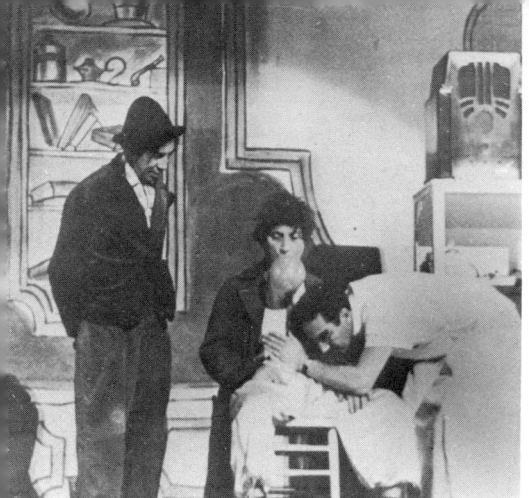

Harpo's examination as it appeared on tour

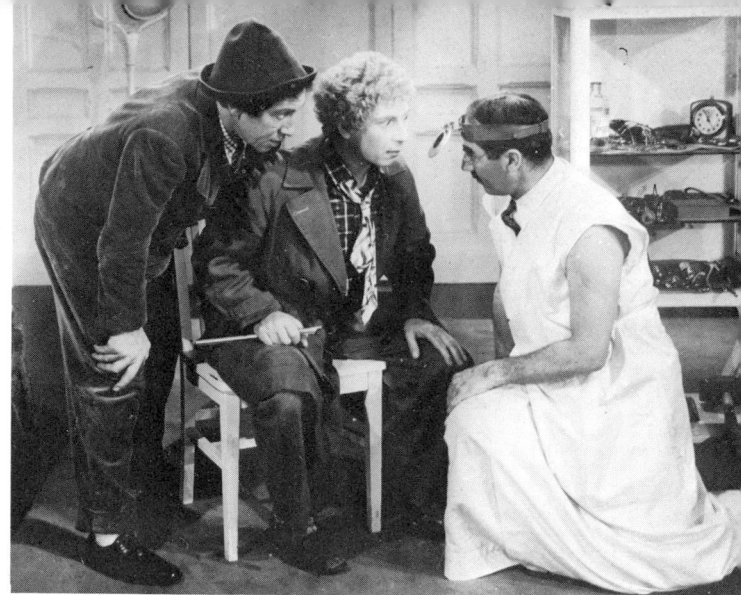

and on film

Chico. Groucho still isn't satisfied. "Couldn't I move a little closer and pay fifty cents?" he bargains. Chico is too quick. "Then I'd move over here," he says, "and charge one dollar again."

Before the skinning is over, Groucho has purchased a $4 set of breeder's guides to decipher the master code book, nine jockey's guides at $1 apiece to puzzle out the breeder's guides and a dozen other volumes to make sense of the whole mess. Chico quickly cashes in his take on a ticket on Sun Up. He comes back to help Groucho, who has become a human bookcase, clutching a stack of volumes in his arms, others between his knees and balancing still others on his stomach as he leafs through his secret information to find his "sure winner." Chico cuts through the red tape to explain that Roses, a 50–1 shot, is the horse to bet on. Groucho drags his sucker's treasury over to the window just as the race ends. Sun Up has won. Chico turns in his ticket and takes off. But all is not lost. Groucho reflects for a moment, dumps the books back into the ice cream cart, and waits for the next sucker, crying, "Tutsie-frutsie ice cream. Get your tutsi-frutsi ice cream."

Groucho is far more masterful as an incompetent doctor than as an incompetent horse player. He performs two superb medical examinations which reflect his thorough training at Dodge Brothers. Whether he is phoning the steam room to find if his frankfurters are done or rebutting the challenges of his colleagues, he is always in command. "The X rays show nothing wrong with her," cry the M.D.'s as he is about to examine Mrs. Upjohn. "Who are you going to believe," he shoots back, "me or those crooked X rays?"

As a warm-up for his diagnosis of Mrs. Upjohn's fantasies, he examines Harpo. First, the great Hackenbush takes his pulse. "Either you're dead," he proclaims, "or my watch has stopped." To clear up the mystery, Groucho pops a thermometer in his patient's mouth. Harpo savors it for a second, judges it good, and munches and swallows it. "Your temperature certainly went down fast," Groucho remarks. Harpo is thirsty after his snack and bats down the nearest bottle from the medicine cabinet. "Don't drink that poison," Groucho cries. "It costs four dollars an ounce." Next come the reflexes. Groucho gets down on all fours to test them. Harpo's reflexes are as good as ever, as he instantly mounts the doctor and gives him the spurs. Finally Groucho delivers his diagnosis: "He's got about a fifteen percent metabolism, an overactive thyroid and a glandular affectation of about two percent, with a one percent mentality." Harpo radiates pride at his fine showing. But his smile collapses into a frown when Groucho concludes. "He's what we designate as the crummy moron type. All in all, this is the most gruesome piece of blubber I've ever peered at." It turns out, however, that Groucho has his auriscope turned backward

and has been examining himself in the mirror. Chico points this out, but Groucho has a ready answer. "I knew it all the time," he whines, like a six-year-old. "That was a good joke on all of us, wasn't it?"

Admittedly, Groucho's destruction of medical lingo is neither as sharp nor as devastating as his destruction of legalese in *A Night at the Opera*. But his thorough working over of Mrs. Upjohn, with help from his brothers, atones for anything left standing after the examination of Harpo. Whitmore has called in Dr. Leopold X. Steinberg to defrock Groucho. Steinberg is an Austrian specialist, played by Sig Rumann, while Groucho is a horstrian specialist. Under the critical eye of Stein-

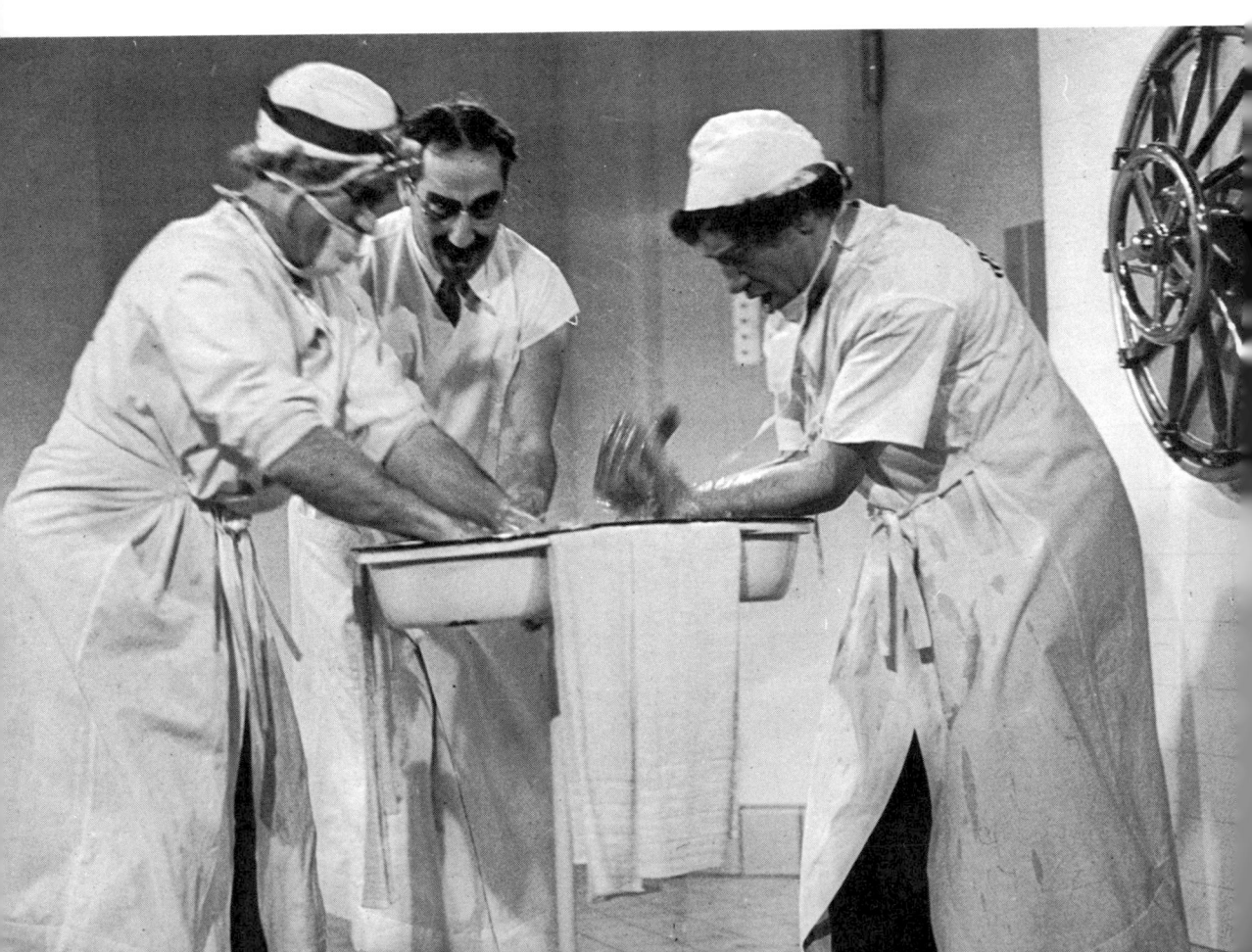

berg, Groucho draws on every weapon in his arsenal. First he softens up Mrs. Upjohn with flattery. "It's the old story," he says, declaring his love. "Boy meets girl. Romeo and Juliet. Minneapolis and St. Paul." On the other hand, he fends off Steinberg with a hail of insults. His diagnosis of Mrs. Upjohn is "high blood pressure on the right side and low blood pressure on the left side." "There is no such thing," fumes Steinberg. "She looks like the healthiest woman I ever met." "You look like you never *met* a healthy woman," returns Groucho. But words cannot delay Groucho's ultimate test—the examination itself. He proceeds to the operating room, then washes his hands several hundred times to buy time. Eyeing Stein-

berg, he drops his watch in the water. "I'd rather have it rusty than stolen," he says pointedly at the specialist.

The examination begins, Groucho aided by Chico and Harpo, whose uniforms read in block letters JOE's SERVICE STATION and BRAKES RELINED. Chico hears Groucho mention Dr. Steinberg's name and takes it for his own. Harpo thinks it is *his* name. So, when Groucho introduces his assistants to the Viennese, it goes like this: "Dr. Steinberg, by a strange coincidence, this is another Dr. Steinberg." Then, looking at Harpo, "May I introduce my colleague and good friend, another Dr. Steinberg. [The three brothers and Steinberg all start bowing, like buoys on a rough sea.] This is a Dr. Steinberg, that's a Stein-

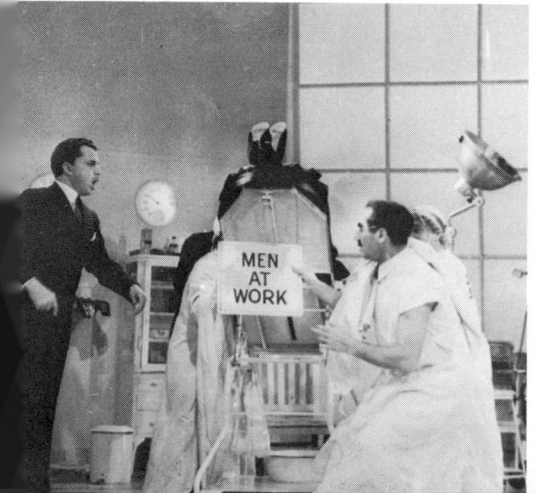

Margaret Dumont gets a thorough medical extermination

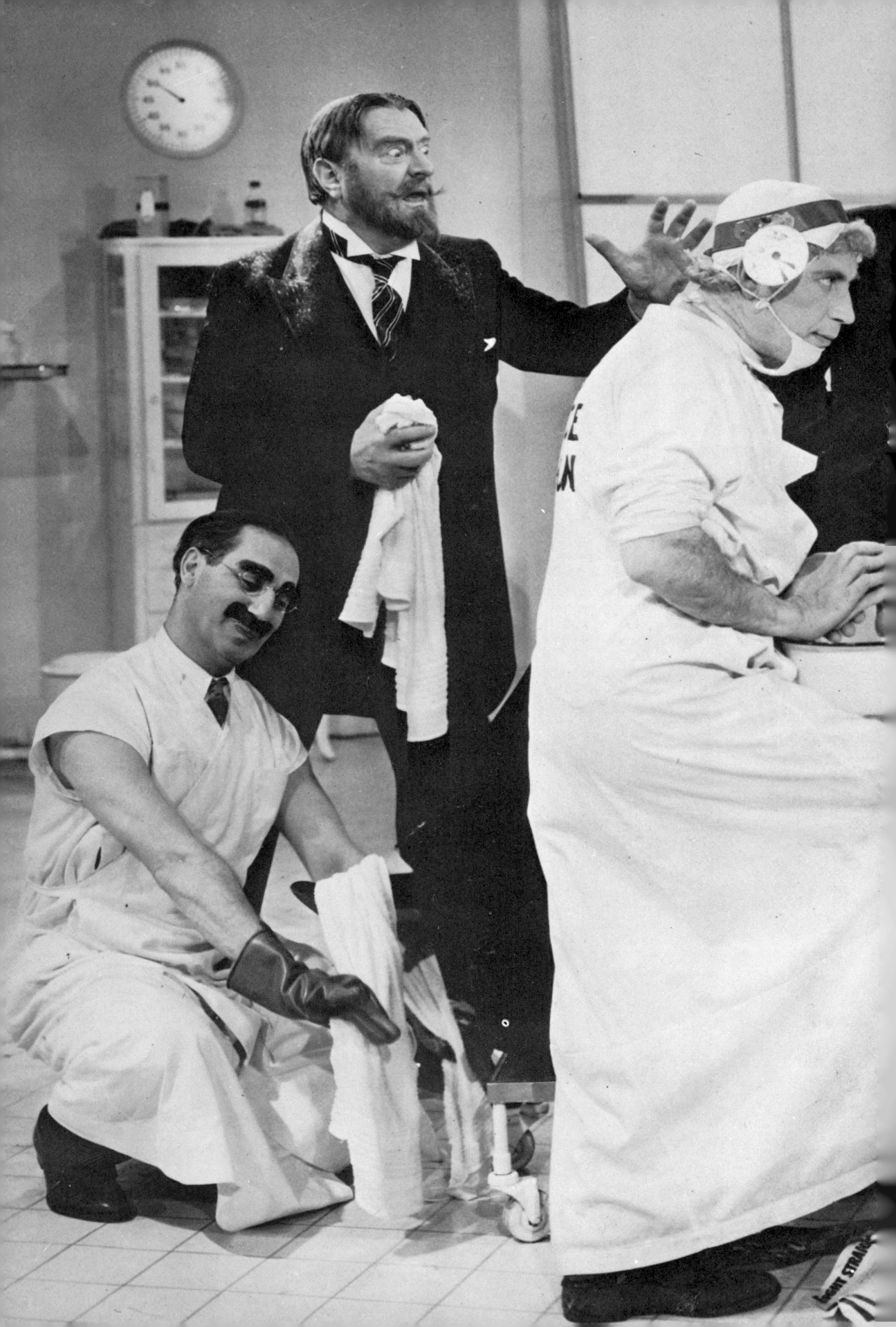

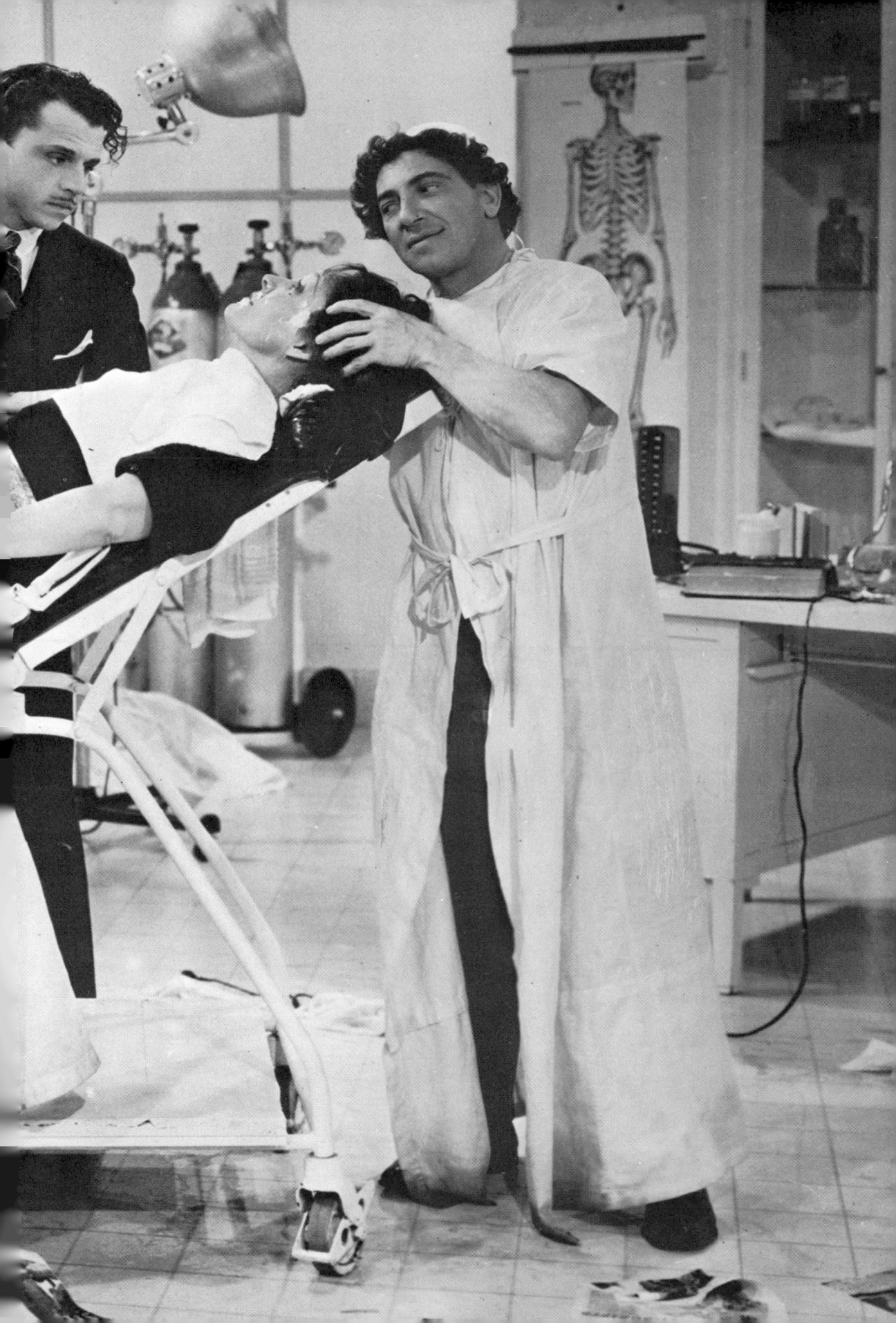

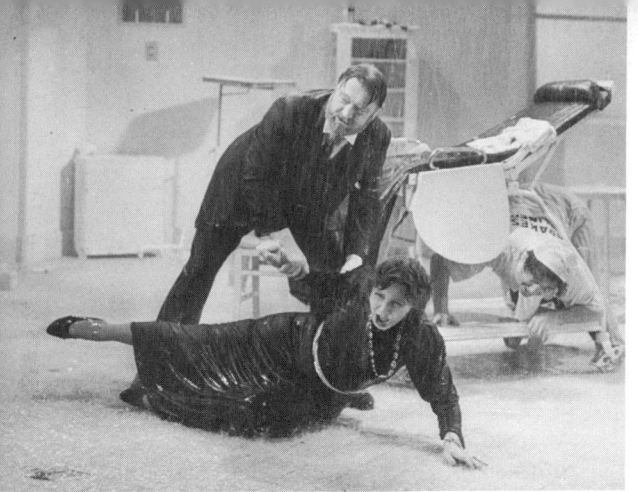

Examination successful—patient demolished

"Not for me, three men on a horse."

berg. Dr. Steinberg and [pointing to Mrs. Upjohn] Mrs. Steinberg. [Groucho drifts over to an anatomical drawing.] Doctor, I'd like you to meet *another* Dr. Steinberg. [Then, pointing to a smaller skeleton.] That's Steinberg junior."

Steinberg—the real Steinberg, that is—is furious at being suckered into all this bowing. "In all my years of medicine—" he growls. "Don't point that beard at me," snaps Groucho. "It might go off." At last, the brothers get to the subject at hand, Mrs. Upjohn. They lay her out on the half-cranked operating table, rush to wash their hands again, and then let her have it. Harpo lathers her face while Chico gives her a shave. Groucho hangs a MEN AT WORK sign on her feet and polishes her shoes. Chico finishes the treatment with a vigorous shampoo. But X rays are necessary. Harpo immediately turns newsboy, shouting a silent "Ex ray, ex ray" as he peddles invisible papers. Then, for no reason at all, which is the reason that motivates most of what Harpo does, he pulls the sprinkler system. The operating room becomes a rain forest. Before the staff can apprehend the "Hackenbush team," High Hat races through the chamber and rescues them.

The brothers have accomplished what Whitmore and Morgan have been trying to do throughout the film—discredit Groucho. At one point, the villains even unleash a call girl named Miss Nora to seduce Groucho, which would appear on the face of it to be the easiest job of the century. But Harpo and Chico get wind of the plan and save Groucho before he can be discovered by Mrs. Upjohn in an uncompromising position. The scene is the highlight of the film and one of the brothers' very best. Miss Nora, played by Esther Muir, who seems a dead ringer for Thelma Todd, arrives on time for the rendezvous. "Do you like roses?" asks Groucho, meeting her at the door. "How did you know?" replies the delighted Nora. "I didn't," says Groucho, "so I got you forget-me-nots." He hands her a great beaten-up sunflower. She sits. He pushes in her chair. "Thenk you," she says. "Thenk *kiyew*," replies Groucho, more British than the king, in the first of a volley of *thenk kiyew*s that bounce about the scene. Groucho takes her stole, remarking, "I always take the wrap." Just as the couple are settling down for a little betrayal, Chico and Harpo rush in and pounce on Nora. They invite Groucho to join them. "Not for me," he says, "three

"If I were any closer, I'd be in back of you."

Esther Muir disappears into the decor . . .

men on a horse." Nora recovers, sputtering: "I've never been so insulted in my life." "It's still early in the evening," warns Groucho prophetically. Groucho chases his saviours out. But undaunted, they return, Chico behind a moustache and Harpo behind a pack of bulldogs. "If you're looking for fingerprints," Groucho tells Chico, turned detective, "you're a little early." Nora, putting on some pancake makeup, tells Harpo to "blow." He obliges, and the room explodes with powder. Once more Groucho banishes his bodyguards. It is getting late. Mrs. Upjohn is scheduled to arrive. So Nora snuggles up to Groucho. "Closer," she coos, "closer." "If I were any closer," Groucho remarks, his hands full of Nora, "I'd be in back of you."

The loathing couple retires to the couch when Chico and Harpo return once more, carrying pails, paint and paper. "We came to hang the papers," declares Chico, the wall paperer. "Why don't you start by hanging yourself?" offers Groucho. For once in their lives, Harpo and Chico take their work seriously. By the time they finish papering the walls, the couch has disappeared. Mrs. Upjohn and Whitmore burst into the room. Groucho pops out of the wall to explain to the dowager that he was having the room fixed up for their honeymoon suite. Whitmore is foiled. But what about Miss Nora? She emerges from under the couch pillows several minutes later, after Mrs. Upjohn has left. Only the limits of the censorship code keep her from speaking her mind. "I'll get even with you, you dirty, low-down, rotten, cheap,

. . Groucho claims to be feathering a love nest for Margaret Dumont

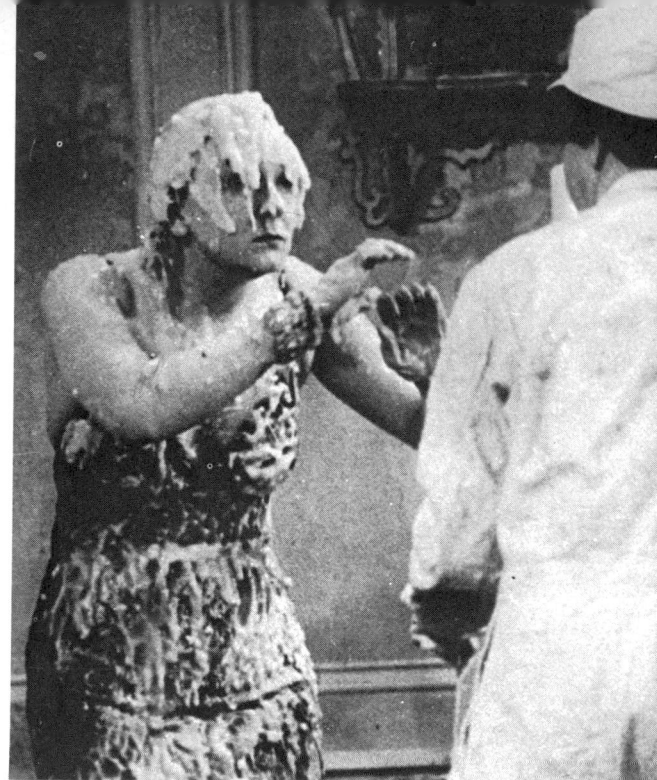

Emerge Miss Muir: "You dirty, low-down, rotten, cheap double crosser."

double crosser," she yells, exhausting all the "nice" bad words. Harpo replies by papering her bottom.

If there must be musical scenes and romance, they are tolerable and strategically placed in this picture. One of the key stratagems of the Thalberg formula is the "low point," that moment at which all seems dark for the brothers, their plans dashed, their hopes blank, the prospects of the romantic couple equally barren. The so-called logic behind this is to allow the brothers to rise to even greater heights by comparison. So these low points invariably fall as the movie rounds the backstretch before heading into its triumphant finale. Such a moment occurs after the operating scene in *A Day at the Races* when the brothers are in disgrace, the lovers have little prospect of saving the sani-

torium and even the horse, High Hat, risks being corralled by the sheriff. At this point, however, the music serves a specific function, smoothing the transition from doldrums to delirium. Judy and Gil sing the hopeful "Tomorrow Is Another Day" and Harpo dances like Pan through a Negro shanty town in a number that includes brilliantly athletic jitterbug sequences, vigorous choral singing and the exquisite voice of Ivy Anderson. In the light of the present, the sequence, for all its musicality, is embarrassing in its clear-cut segregation and stereotypes. Only Harpo breaks the color line as the townsfolk cry the famous "Who Dat Man?" The musicale is interrupted by the sheriff and his men, who have come to seize High Hat. The big horse leaps past them and over small buildings with a single

Off to the races

Harpo and Ivy: "Who Dat Man?"

bound, showing himself a great steeplechase horse.

The film closes, of course, at the track, where Gil enters his steed in the steeplechase. The brothers help his cause, blowing the spectators' hats onto the course, rerouting the track into the countryside and generally fouling up things while Gil and Judy try to sneak High Hat past Morgan's men. In the end, Harpo rides him to defeat—until it turns out that, after a fall, Morgan's jockey and Harpo had switched horses. High Hat wins after all. Merriment reigns. Swept off his feet by the joy of the moment, Groucho promises Mrs. Upjohn: "Marry me and I'll never look at another horse."

With *A Day at the Races,* the

united front of friendly reviewers that had hastily formed to applaud *A Night at the Opera* started to dissolve. The New York *Times* critic called it "comparatively bad Marx," although he hastened to add that bad Marx was better than good most anything else. Others praised the film, while recommending it to "Marx fans only." But generally, even those who thought it a step down from their best liked the film well enough. One, Robert Garland, liked it too well, perhaps, because he tried to write his review in Marxian style, with disastrous results: "Now that the four of them, like ancient Gaul, are divided into three parts," he wrote for the New York *American,* "they work harder than ever at their monkey business. At the races and at their wit's

As the race ends, Groucho loses . . .

end, they're besides themselves with their catch-as-catch-can comicalities."

Many stories emerged from the shooting of *A Day at the Races,* among them that the brothers kept a racehorse in their apartment during the shooting and barnyard animals in their dresser drawers. But probably the most imaginative of them appears in the book by Groucho's son. It concerns the final racetrack sequence shot at Santa Anita. Small Wonder, Morgan's horse, and High Hat battle down to the wire. Chico had read the script, like everyone else. But when the race was to be filmed, Groucho discovered him making a little bet on the side with one of the extras. Chico's money, it turned out, was on the sure loser, Small Wonder. "I always thought you were crazy," said Groucho. "Now I'm sure of it." "What's crazy?" defended Chico, pointing at the tote board. "The odds on Small Wonder are fifteen to one."

but High Hat wins

Groucho, Lucille Ball, Chico, Ann Miller, and Harpo

Philip Wood and Donald MacBride

Frank Albertson

Gordon Miller:	GROUCHO
Faker Englund:	HARPO
Harry Binelli:	CHICO
Christine:	LUCILLE BALL
Hilda Manney:	ANN MILLER
Leo Davis:	FRANK ALBERTSON
Wagner:	DONALD MacBRIDE
Gribble:	CLIFF DUNSTAN
Timothy Hogarth:	PHILIP LOEB
Sasha:	ALEXANDER ASRO
Dr. Glass:	CHARLES HALTON
Simon Jenkins:	PHILIP WOOD

Cliff Dunstan

Alexander Asro

* * *

Production: Pandro S. Berman
Assistant to Producer: Philip Loeb
Director: William A. Seiter
Screenplay: Morrie Ryskind
Based on Stage Play by: John Murray and Allen Boretz
Photography: J. Roy Hunt
Art Direction: Van Nest Polglase and Al Herman
Set Decoration: Darrell Silvera
Editing: George Crone
Music Director: Roy Webb
Released by R.K.O., September 30, 1938. 78 minutes

9 Room Service (1938)

The excerpt in the *World Telegram* of June 28, 1938, seemed to explain it: "Harpo said the Marxes long have wanted to try a proven play instead of manufacturing their own out of gagging conferences and vaudeville tryouts. They were handicapped by lack of good stories." The proven play was *Room Service,* which ran sixty-one weeks on Broadway and was purchased for the screen by RKO at the then record price of $225,000. But there was likely more behind the new venture than the natural ambition of tested comedians to try something new. For one thing, the excursion from their M-G-M contract meant a little extra money. Chico, the perennial gambler, surely must have welcomed the offer. Groucho must have looked on it as a hedge against the poverty that, in his mind, was always just around the corner. "I've always been terrified of dying broke or of being a failure," he once confessed. "I've never taken a bit of success for granted. When it came, I was always sure it wasn't going to last." By Chico's account, Harpo always agreed with the brother who had his ear last. With Chico and Groucho both for the new film, amiable Harpo surely went along. Add to this the probable uncertainty at M-G-M over what to do with the brothers—an uncertainty that ended with the worst possible decisions—and *Room Service* appears to have been a logical solution to a lot of the Marxes' problems at the time.

That it turned out to be a disaster is their fault only insomuch as they chose to do it. For *Room Service,* as adapted by Morrie Ryskind, was ill-fated from the start. A pleasant hotel farce, it never got out of the hotel, except for the briefest sequence in a theater at the end. Its pace under director William Seiter was virtually funereal next to the furious drive of a true Marx Brothers picture. And the brothers themselves were miserably miscast. Groucho, as Gordon Miller, the producer who tries to keep his play going with one hand and his creditors away with the other, is a pleasantly desperate character. But he is a toothless shadow of the old Groucho. Chico takes the role of Binion, changed in the film to Binelli in deference to his fraudulent nationality. Chico is supposed to be the play's director, but this role stretches even the credulity of a Marx fan. We cannot imagine him staging a hit. We know that any play under Chico's direction would surely begin with two intermissions for the merchandising of everything from tutsi-frutsi ice cream to tout books and would conclude with the first act, followed by the third at Belmont. We never see Chico in action as director, which is perhaps a blessing. Harpo, as Faker Englund, is a man without a function. He tries to squeeze his private routines into the brief breathing

"This is Mr. Englund, the brains of the organization." (Lucille Ball, seated far right)

Wearing everything they own

spaces of the original play without success. The script worked splendidly on the stage, supported by George Abbott's brisk direction and the staccato slamming of doors by characters coming and going. But on the screen it is pretty close to living death. Lines hang in the air long enough to dry laundry on them.

Perhaps, however, in the end, it is just as well *Room Service* was made, if only as a kind of negative object lesson. It answers for all time any questions about the brothers' ability to survive outside their own world. We need never wonder how the Marxes would have fared with a screenplay not specifically tailored for them. *Room Service* tells all.

The brothers retain their traditional costumes, if not their traditional characters: Groucho in swallow-tailed coat, Harpo in baggy pants and plaid shirt, Chico in dunce cap. Morrie Ryskind's contribution in adapting the play appears minimal, a line here, a structural change there, but not the drastic overhaul the play required to make it a viable Marx Brothers vehicle. The film opens in the lobby of the White Way Hotel,

supposedly located off Times Square, but as tranquil and seemingly rustic as a lodge in the Adirondacks. Groucho has conned his brother-in-law, Gribble, the hotel manager, to extend him and his cast of twenty-two actors $1,200 in credit in return for a 10 percent interest in the show, *Hail and Farewell*. The play was entitled *Godspeed* in the Broadway version but was changed in the film to conform to the infantile Hollywood production code. Lines from the stage play like "God damn it" and "Go to hell" were similarly disinfected to read "Jumping butterballs" and "Go to blazes." Gribble is nervous because the hotel supervisor, Wagner, will soon arrive to check the books. Groucho would like to find a backer and settle his account but, he explains, "You can't shake suckers out of your sleeve." He looks up his sleeve for some suckers and, finding none, adds, "At least, I can't."

The film shifts to Groucho's hotel room, where it remains like a prisoner on death row until its release for bad behavior at the very end. Chico enters, declaring: "The rehearsal, she's-a wonderful. Yes siree, it's-a wonderful.

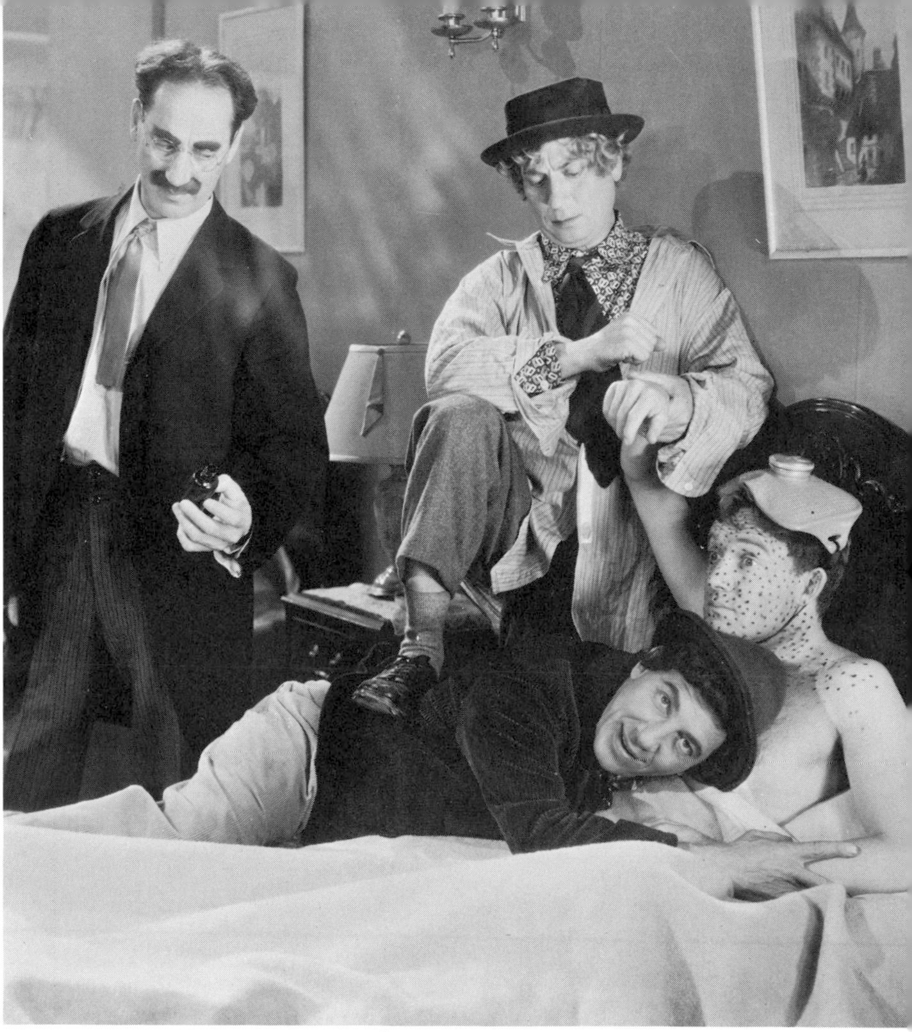

Albertson as Davis with localized case of measles

I still think it's a terrible play, but it makes a wonderful rehearsal." The boys decide to skip out on their bill and forget the whole thing. Since they can't be seen leaving with their bags, they try wearing everything they own—three pairs of pants, three shirts, three jackets. Harpo arrives shirtless, leaving himself room for an extra garment. "I see he came prepared," says Groucho appreciatively. "No," corrects Chico. "He don't believe in shirts." "Oh, an atheist, eh?"

Most Marx Brothers films are relatively free of plot. But this one works by plot alone. It is a situation comedy.

SITUATION I—Lucille Ball, one of the actresses, rushes in to announce that she has found the show a backer, a Mr. Jenkins, who will arrive shortly with a fat check. The brothers cannot leave now, but Wagner will arrive soon, and they won't be allowed to stay, either. (Miss Ball, here a tall, raw-boned, broad-shouldered girl in her twenties, was allotted a tiny part that allowed her no comic opportunities.)

SITUATION II—The playwright, a completely naive idealist named Leo Davis, suddenly shows up, having run away from home. He believes everything is going well with the show. At

Sasha's dinner entrances Harpo

Putting the pressure on Jenkins . . .

. . . yields a contract

first, the brothers try to get him to go back to Oswego, whence he came. Groucho does everything to discourage him, even introducing him to Harpo. "This is Mr. Englund, the brains of the organization. That'll give you some idea of the organization." But Davis, played with perfect simplicity of mind by Frank Albertson, refuses to leave. "I've burned my bridges behind me," he declares. Harpo lifts the back of his jacket to check for burned breeches. Groucho invokes the image of the lad's mother, weeping and waiting for him by the family fireside. "But we have no fireside," protests the young author. "You have no fireside?" returns Groucho, a little shocked. "How do you listen to the President's speeches?"

SITUATION III—Jenkins arrives. He represents "a very wealthy man," one Zachary Fisk, who is willing to bankroll the show to the tune of $15,000 for a small consideration. "You see," says Jenkins, "there's a young lady involved." "And she would like to play a small part," adds Groucho, completing the condition. "How did you know?" "It came to me in a dream, Mr. Jenkins," replies Groucho. Not exactly a dream. The brothers' first Broadway show, *I'll Say She Is,* was financed on exactly these terms. A Hackensack, New Jersey, pretzel manufacturer named Herman Broody agreed to back the show if the producer Joseph "Minimum" Gates could find a spot in it for his girl friend. Gates, as his nickname implies, hired the brothers because they cost the minimum, four for the price of one.

Here Jenkins finds the brothers willing to meet his conditions. He announces that he will return the next morning at 10 A.M. with the check in hand. This creates SITUATION IV. Wagner, the hotel supervisor, played with the fury of a mad dog by dough-faced Donald MacBride, tells the brothers they have twenty minutes to pay their $1,200 bill or out they go. The Marxes must figure out a way of staying in the room until Jenkins arrives the next morning with the money. "Don't try the old trick of staying in the room," warns Wagner. "I'll drive you out. I'll send in painters, fumigators." "You should have sent in fumigators weeks ago," Groucho remarks weakly.

The brothers cook up a little variation on the suggestion by Wagner. They decide to stay in the room. They also give Davis the measles, hoping the hotel help will refuse to cross their threshold. Harpo administers the measles by blowing iodine through a spaghetti strainer onto Davis. But the plan has its drawbacks. Chico and Groucho can't get out. There is nothing for them to do cooped up but think about how hungry they are growing. "I'm so hungry," says Groucho, who passes the time cheating at solitaire, "I see spots before my eyes." "Mine are beginning to look like hamburgers," adds Chico. "When you get one with onions," Groucho says, "give it to me." Groucho tries faking a woman's voice and calling room service, requesting some food for a guest who has developed tapeworm. No luck. "They say the tapeworm has to register," he explains. The odds on a free meal for the brothers (the only kind they can afford) continue to skyrocket. Harpo rushes in with a turkey dinner, but the bird takes wing and exits by the window. "Well, there

's a very rare case. He's got-a red tapeworm."

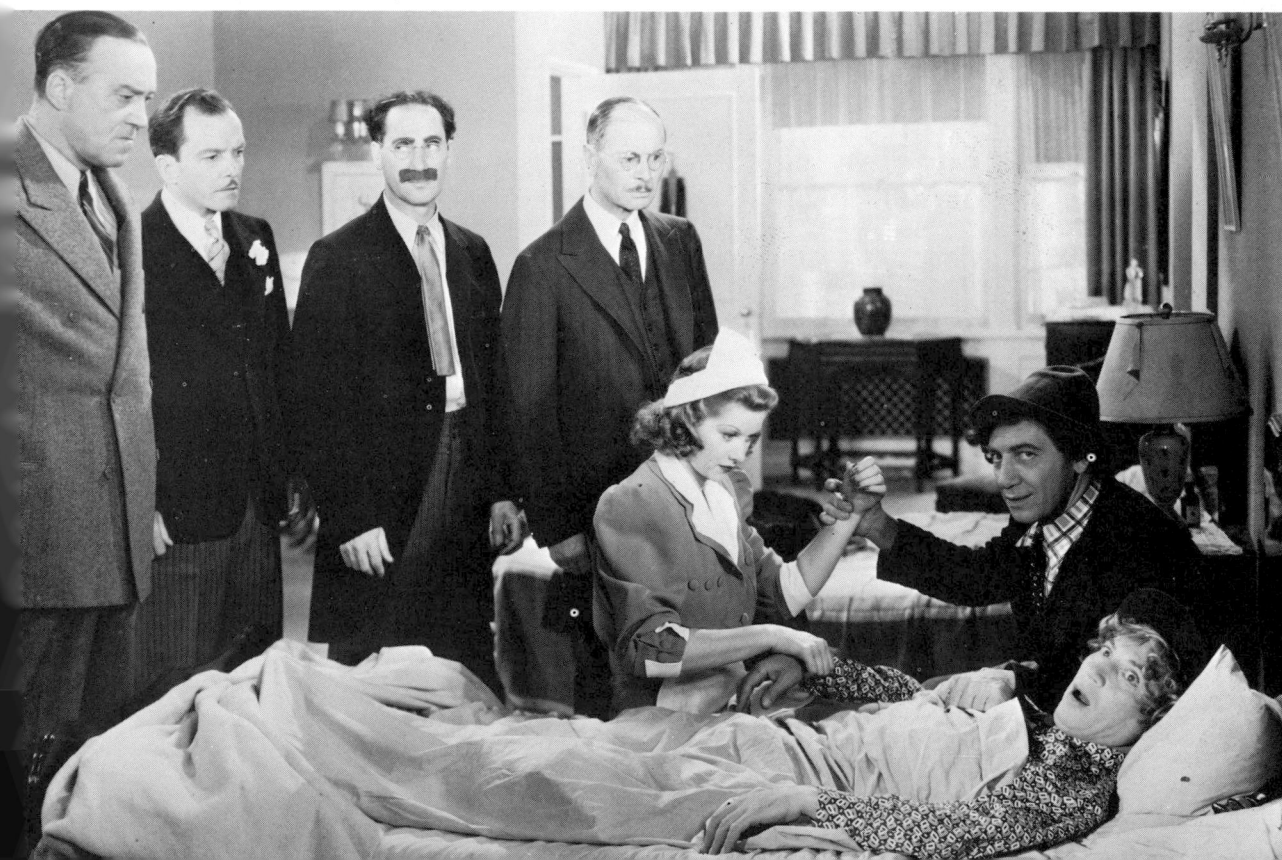

were no cranberries anyhow," Groucho notes mournfully, trying to console himself. The brothers finally find their way out of this forest of hunger pains by bribing Sasha, the hotel waiter. If he will deliver dinner to their room, Groucho proposes, they will find a part for him in *Hail and Farewell*. "What do you think, Binelli?" Groucho asks as Sasha strikes a dramatic pose. "Looks just right to me," approves Chico, a demented glint in his eye. "I could eat him raw."

A beaten Jenkins . . .

The deal is signed, and Sasha comes through with the victuals, affording Harpo his one sustained moment of comedy: the salad scene. Deadly serious, he downs the greens like a crazed robot, never pausing to chew or swallow as his hand carries a steady, methodical procession of forkfuls mouthward. He interrupts the conveyor belt only once, to shoot out a hand and catch a handful of salt Chico has tossed over his shoulder. He nearly devours his own hand licking the salt clean.

Davis breaks quarantine to meet his girl friend, Hilda Manney, portrayed by the fine musical comedy dancer Ann Miller. In this film, she does no dancing, just as the Marx Brothers do no gagging and Lucille Ball no mugging. She merely looks unaccountably unpretty, as if the camera, following a malicious streak in its nature, set out to catch her at all the wrong angles. "There's a time and a place for love," contends Groucho, trying vainly to stop Davis. "I like it anytime," says Chico. Chico wants to know if Harpo has ever been in love. Harpo smiles shyly and shows the brothers his girl friend, a two-inch rubber Kewpie doll that squeaks

when squeezed. Chico nods understandingly, adding, "Of course, I like them a little bigger." The doll serves Harpo well when he has to replace Davis as the patient during an examination by the hotel doctor. The doctor wants him to open wide and say "Ahhhh." "Peeeeep," replies gapemouthed Harpo, squeezing the doll. "Ahhhhhh," says the doctor. "Peeeeeeep." "Ahhhhhhhhhhhh." "Peeeeeeeeeeeeep!"

The doctor is vanquished in the battle of the ahhs and peeps. But he's a sore loser. He threatens to reveal Harpo's illness as a fraud. So the brothers lock Doc in the john. Wagner is also skeptical. "This man isn't Davis," he declares. "I met Davis yesterday, and he didn't look anything like *that*." "Certainly," shoots back Groucho. "The man's aged ten years on account of the service in this hotel." "His hair wasn't red yesterday," counters Wagner. "It's a very rare case," explains Chico. "He's got-a red tapeworm." This is one of several references to Harpo as a redhead. In *Go West* one of the girls in the back room warns another, "That redhead's a terror." Marx fans think of Harpo

that knocks Harpo's eyes out

as a check . . .

as blond. Maxine Marx, Chico's daughter, explains the discrepancy this way: "On the stage, Harpo wore a red wig, but when he went to pictures he found that the red wig photographed black. Since he wanted to keep the impression of its being red, he lightened it. As he kept lightening it, however, people began calling him blondie, once again because of the black and white photography."

The brothers manage to hold Wagner off until the timid Jenkins arrives. He is obsessed with keeping his patron's name secret. "You have my word," says Groucho, pledging silence, "and you know how much that's worth." Just as Jenkins is to sign, he's besieged by a cyclone of events. Wagner marches in and starts throwing Groucho out of the hotel. Harpo runs about, chasing the runaway turkey with a baseball bat, felling every piece of crockery in sight. The doctor, bound and gagged, tumbles out of the closet, then discloses the name of the secret backer. Jenkins, his nerves shot, signs the $15,000 check just to escape, dashing madly through the door and into the closet, where he is assaulted by an avalanche of pots and pans.

As soon as he finds his way out, we learn, he cancels the check. But Wagner, ignorant of this, allows Groucho the run of the hotel and all the credit he can squander. Wagner doesn't discover until the show's opening night that he's being taken. He threatens to call the police and to seize the sets and props of the play. This leads to the FINAL SITUATION. The brothers must find a way of keeping Wagner away from the theater and themselves out of the clink until the opening-night rave reviews assure them enough money to pay all their bills. "I guess they'll take our fingerprints," says Davis, as the brothers ponder their predicament. "They got mine," replies Chico, who has done a turn in jail. "It's not bad," he assures Davis about prison. "You behave yourself, they make you a trustee."

Davis mentions that he once faked dying while in high school. The Marxes seize on the remark and then on Davis, whom they thrust in bed once again. He is to spend the evening dying. "You mustn't die before eleven o'clock," Chico warns him. "Good

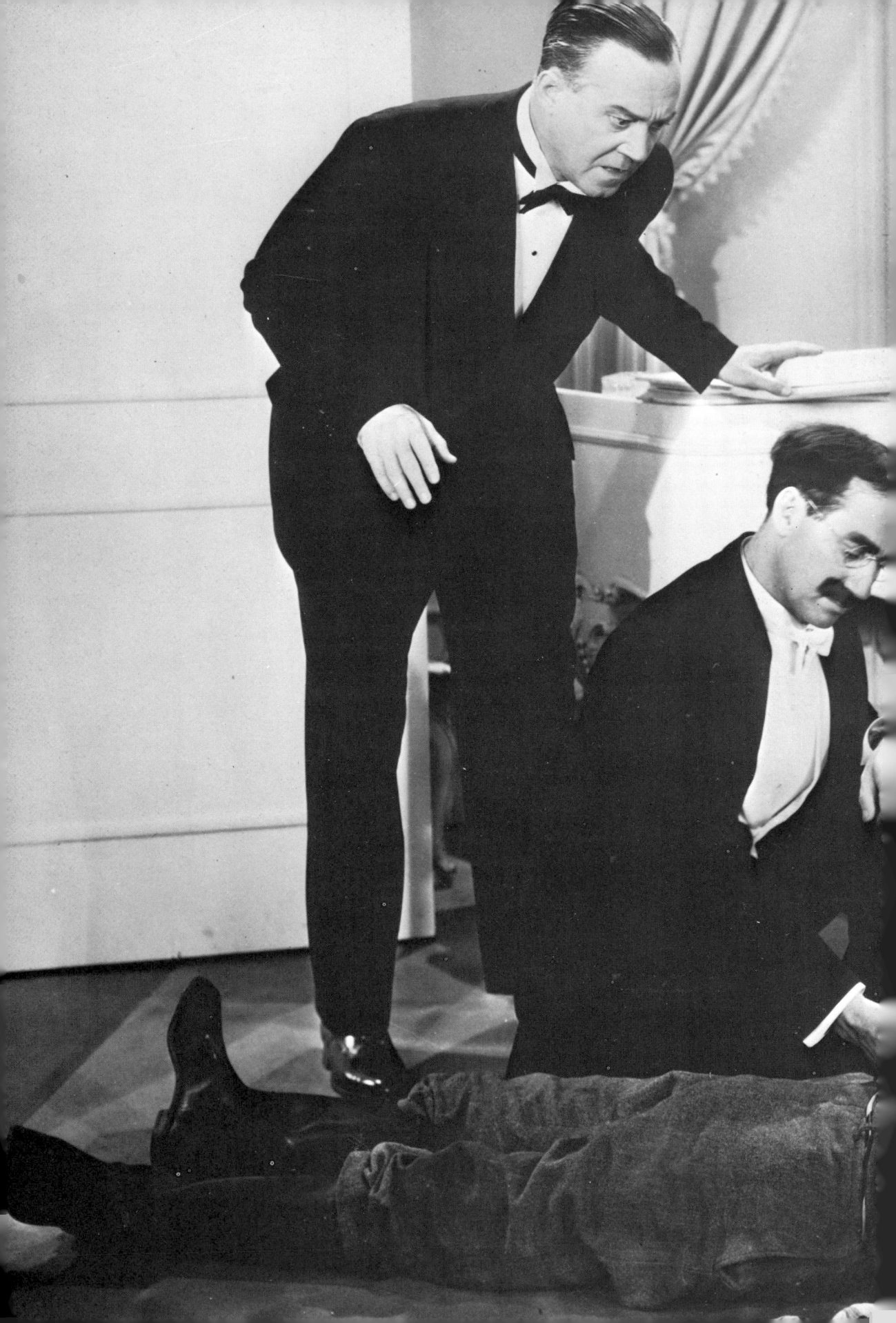

Question: How to keep Wagner from the theater?

luck, Davis," adds Groucho. "Drop dead." The playwright starts perishing on cue, a bottle of poison at his side. Wagner is contrite, feeling he has driven Davis to it. Harpo administers relief. He bolts in with glassfuls of milk for the dying man, then downs them himself. Davis, contrary to orders, expires. "Too soon, too soon," grieves Groucho. "He died too soon." "An hour too soon," adds Chico.

Wagner wants to notify the police, but the brothers stall him. They invite him to join them in several hundred choruses of "Swing Low, Sweet Chariot," while Harpo, a memorial candle burning in his hat, accompanies them on the harmonica. Weeping a bit too profusely, Harpo lays a wreath over the fallen playwright. A few moments later, Wagner leaves to call the police. As he opens the door, Harpo falls through, a knife pinning a note to his chest. "WAGNER DROVE ME TO MY DEATH," it reads, "JUST AS HE DROVE LEO DAVIS." Wagner is so worried about what multiple suicides will do to the reputation of the hotel that he agrees to dump Harpo in the alley outside the theater.

Inside, the play is a roaring success as we see by a stock shot of an audience applauding feverishly. Davis is busy yelling, "Author, author," and Sasha, the waiter, is exhorting a mob onstage to honor their fallen comrade. Who is this gallant worker who has sacrificed his life for the cause? Harpo tumbles onstage, the same knife stuck in his chest.

There is nothing like time to change one's critical perspective. *Duck Soup,* today considered a classic, was rudely treated by the critics of the day. *Room Service,* by contrast, received almost nothing but rave reviews. Rose Pelswick of the *Journal American* called it "fast, loud and funny," and Archer Winsten of the New York *Post* thought it "hilarious entertainment." The rest of the New York critical corps seconded their superlatives. There were a few mild dissenters. Frank Nugent of the New York *Times* gave it a qualified pan, calling it "not good Marx and not nearly so effective as the play." And the *New Yorker* reviewer regretted that the brothers had "tried to adapt themselves to the framework of a situation instead of dragging the framework after them. Once can even be

disappointed that so much is left of the original play." This was certainly one of the problems. Five members of the Broadway cast were recruited for the film—Donald MacBride, Charles Halton, Phillip Loeb, Alexander Asro and Clifford Dunstan. They all felt that to be effective, they had to project their bodies virtually through the camera lens.

But the real problem lay elsewhere. And Groucho, clear-eyed in the face of all the flattering reviews, put his finger on the trouble. "It was the first time we had tried doing a play we hadn't created ourselves," he said. "And we were no good. We can't do that. We've got to originate the characters and the situations ourselves. Then we can do them. Then they're us. But we can't do gags or play characters that aren't ours. We tried it, and we'll never do it again." The brothers returned to autobiography.

Answer: Invent another illness for Davis

Harpo, Groucho, Harry Gamorra (Gorilla), and Chico

Margaret Dumont

Eve Arden

Nat Pendleton

Florence Rice and Kenny Baker

J. Cheever Loophole:	GROUCHO
Punchy:	HARPO
Antonio Pirelli:	CHICO
Mrs. Dukesbury:	MARGARET DUMONT
Julie Randall:	FLORENCE RICE
Jeff Wilson:	KENNY BAKER
Peerless Pauline:	EVE ARDEN
Goliath:	NAT PENDLETON
Jardinet:	FRITZ FELD
John Carter:	JAMES BURKE
Little Professor Atom:	JERRY MARENGHI
Whitcomb:	BARNETT PARKER

Fritz Feld   Jerry Marenghi

* * *

Producer: Mervyn LeRoy
Director: Edward Buzzell
Screenplay: Irving Brecher
Photography: Leonard M. Smith
Art Direction: Cedric Gibbons and Stan Rogers
Set Decoration: Edwin B. Willis
Editing: William H. Terhune
Music Direction: Franz Waxman
Music: Harold Arlen
Lyrics: E. Y. Harburg
Released by Metro-Goldwyn-Mayer, October 20, 1939. 87 minutes

James Burke

10 At The Circus (1939)

Even if *Room Service* had turned out to be the roaring success the Marx Brothers hoped of it, the team would have been obliged by contract to return to M-G-M. When they did come back to Metro, a bit more tarnished than triumphant, they discovered that their stock had fallen a bit. Instead of the customary team of writers, the studio delegated the screenplay to one man, Irving Brecher, who had never worked with the Marxes before. The tryout system, always an expensive way of sharpening material, was canceled. And the studio, they found, was content to let their old routines carry the load. The three Marx Brothers movies after *Room Service* might be called "the tired trio." The relentless drive that characterized the team's films here begins to sputter. All three pictures are splendid off and on. But the scripts start their gradual decline here. And for the first time, the Marxes start repeating themselves—not in a way that ruins the fun, but in a way that makes these films more familiar than unpredictable. The pleasure in the late M-G-M movies, and there's plenty, lies in the solid fulfillment of expectations. By now, the audience had come to expect an insult sequence between Groucho and Margaret Dumont or some other matron or moll, a piano routine from Chico, a harp solo from Harpo, a translation scene between the two of them, a villain, a romantic couple, a

few songs, a low point and a rousing finale. The Marx Brothers delivered, but the freshness was gone. The films are wonderful but worn, like beautiful, battered antiques.

But M-G-M should not take all the blame. Every comedy team, like the human organism itself, passes its prime. Age was just beginning to sap the brothers of their energies. Doubtless less sentimental, sharper scripts and generally better attention from the studio would have produced better films. But the brothers had mellowed. "After Thalberg's death, my interest in the movies waned," Groucho writes in his autobiography. "I continued to appear in them, but my heart was in the Highlands. The fun had gone out of picture-making. I was like an old pug, still going through the motions, but now doing it solely for the money." Groucho was never happy with the motion picture regimen that obliged him to be funny at eight in the morning. But it would be wrong to accept this disclaimer of interest at face value. In a letter to Arthur Sheekman, he sounds tired all right, but behind his fatigue burns a flicker of enthusiasm in what he is doing. "Our picture, 'A Day at the Circus,' is progressing rather rapidly considering that it's our picture," he writes Sheekman, "and we'll almost finish on schedule. I believe it will be better than I thought . . . although I must admit, in establishing an alibi, that I have seen very little of the rushes."

Then he turns off the enthusiasm. "I'm getting too old for rushes," he complains. "The projection rooms, or at least the ones they give us, are either a long climb or in an air-conditioned cellar, and I've decided to wait until the picture plays the Marquis before seeing it. At least, if I don't like it, I might win the Chevrolet. There's some talk of the Ritz Theater raffling off a Buick and, if they do, I might not see the picture at all."

Groucho was right in one respect. *At the Circus,* if not a masterpiece, was better than he feared it might be. In the career of almost any other comedy team, this middling Marx Brothers film would be considered a classic.

At the Circus is essentially *A Day at the Races* with sawdust instead of turf. Groucho once again comes to the rescue of a concern that is sinking fast. In this case, Jeff Wilson must pay off the debt on his circus or a character named John Carter will buy him out. It is not exactly clear who Carter is, except that he's no good, rotten, mean, callous, rude, unsympathetic, untrustworthy, dishonest, bad-tempered, ruthless. God knows what will happen to the nice circus animals if he ever gets hold of them. Jeff Wilson, on the other hand, is sweet Kenny Baker, the man with the choir boy tenor, naive, generous, good and in love with the bareback rider, Julie Randall. Julie, as played by willowy Florence Rice, is all glucose and glycogen, goodness dripping from every pore. This couple has to be the most repulsively saccharine all of the romantic leads the brothers played against. Their cozy little ballad,

"Nobody gets onna the train unless they gotta the

"Two Blind Loves," in which Jeff is so in love he can't distinguish between a rancid doughnut and a wedding cake, haunts the film like a recurrent headache. It is incredible that the Marxes should side with such an intolerable couple. W. C. Fields would have reduced Jeff to penury in an instant and dispatched Julie into white slavery, just for the fun of it.

But the brothers as allies of the nice people is part of the Thalberg formula. Fortunately Marx fans have been trained by the team to suspend their disbelief at the drop of a kazoo, so they merely ignore Jeff and Julie, who are after all, only part of something as superfluous as the plot, and enjoy the brothers. As in *A Day at the Races*, Chico, friend of the failing enterprise, calls in Groucho, who travels under the name J. Cheever Loophole, professional shyster. Drawn by the fragrance of a fee, Groucho arrives just as the circus train is about to pull out amid a torrential downpour. But when he tries to mount the iron horse, Chico stops him. "Nobody gets on-a the train unless they got-a the badge," he explains. "You mean my Lone Ranger badge?" returns Groucho. "Sorry, they took it back because I stopped eating the cereal." "You ain't gotta the badge?" asks the shocked Chico. "Quiet," cautions Groucho. "The engineer might be eavesdropping, you old badger, you." Chico suggests that Groucho get a badge from Jeff Wilson, except that Jeff is on the train, and nobody gets on the train without a badge. "You know," says Groucho, "if you hadn't sent for me, I'd probably be home right now in a nice warm bedroom in a comfortable bed with a hot toddy . . . that's a drink." "That's-a too bad," consoles Chico. "You know, if it was up-a to me, I'd let you on the train, like that." "Oh?" says a delighted Groucho. "Yeah, but it's not up-a to me," says Chico. "No," replies Groucho, checking his wet feet, "but it's up to my ankles. If I were any drier, I'd drown." Harpo arrives, led by a seal on a leash. He shows Chico a whole raft of badges inside his coat (left over from *Horse Feathers*). The seal raises its tail, displaying its

Harpo and Chico "redestruct" the crim

Goliath and Little Professor Atom rob Jeff.

badge. Harpo is the assistant to the circus strong man, Goliath. He sets off the cannonballs that Goliath catches in his bare hands. As is always the case, he and his boss cordially despise each other. Chico finally takes pity on Groucho and gives him a badge. But when Groucho tries to mount the train, Chico pushes him back onto the platform. "That's last year's badge," he explains.

On board, the three brothers get acquainted. Groucho, always mistaking someone for someone else, takes Harpo to be the circus owner. "You're the greatest owner since P. T. Barnum," he tells Harpo in flattery that with Groucho is never idle. "It's a P. T. we haven't met before." Harpo replies by flashing a dragon's tongue noisemaker in his face. "I'll teach you to keep a civil tongue in your mouth and out of mine," chides Groucho. The shy old shyster is introduced to the circus company and launches into

one of his most delightful musical numbers, "Lydia, the Tattooed Lady," while Harpo swings on the ceiling lamp. Lydia's epidermis, Groucho tells us, is a geography and history lesson in one. "Here is Captain Spaulding exploring the Amazon," he sings, pointing out parts of the lady's anatomy. "Here's Godiva but with her pajamas on."

Suddenly crime strikes. Jeff is about to retrieve the $10,000 he has hidden in the gorilla cage—the money that will return him to solvency—when Goliath and the midget, Little Professor Atom, bop him over the head and steal it, apparently both in the employ of Carter. Chico and Harpo rush to the rescue too late, but Chico suggests they "redestruct" the crime. "You ever been to the police station?" asks Chico, checking out Harpo's credentials. The silent one grins, nods, and flashes a sign bearing his picture: WANTED FOR JAYWALKING, 50 CENTS.

"Fifty cents?" cries Chico. "See, crime doesn't pay." The two brothers alternately assume the roles of Jeff and his attacker, but the "redestruction" always finishes with Harpo bashing Chico over the head. "I better break-a dis case before you break-a my head," Chico concludes. But Chico and Harpo are rank amateurs compared to a rank professional like Groucho. "Let's not jump to concussions," advises the self-styled legal eagle. "Watch the eagle swoop down."

With this courageous pledge, Groucho swoops into Goliath's room, gets a look at his muscles, and instantly turns tail. "I'm just a little nobody who wears glasses," he tells a belligerent Goliath, pulling out his glasses to prove his point. Goliath suggests, "How should you like I should break you in two?" "Could I file separate income taxes?" Groucho asks. The legal eagle quickly revises his strategy. He doesn't dare pick on someone his own size, so he heads directly for Little Professor Atom's compartment. A cigar has been left at the scene of the crime. Does the midget smoke the same rotten brand? "If we compare smells and they're alike," cries Groucho triumphantly, raising the cigar butt in the air, "this is the rope that will hang him." *"Adieu,"* cries Groucho, off to the midget's cabin to sample his cigars. *"Adieu,"* cries Chico, following Groucho. "———," cries Harpo, waving farewell to an invisible crowd.

On the face of it, the task seems

How should you like I should break you in two?"

simple enough even for Groucho. But his foe is tougher than expected, resourceful, energetic, capable of foiling the detective at every turn, the one man Groucho can never conquer—Chico. "We just wanted to trap you into a confession," Chico tells the midget by way of explaining their visit. Then, turning proudly to Groucho, he says, "I know my stuff, eh?" Groucho quickly offers another reason for their intrusion. "We just happened to be passing by," he says, "and saw a firefly burning in your window." Pretending to be out of cigars, Groucho asks the midget for one. But each time he does, overobliging Chico offers Groucho one of his own. "Why don't you trade your head in on a bowling ball?" Groucho suggests. Groucho tries again. Chico steps in with a cigar. The midget lights it. Chico lifts the midget to him and takes a light from him, then passes the little fellow to Groucho, who is waiting with an unlit stogie. "Bad luck," says Groucho. "Three on a midget." Then he turns an accusing finger down toward Atom. "Do you know if you had hit Jeff a little harder the charge would have been moider—pronounced *moider*. Eeeeeyoooo hoooo haaaarrhaaarrr." "Yeah," adds Chico. "How would you like to go to Sing Sing and get the high chair?" Groucho feigns running out of cigars again, hoping to be offered one by the midget. But, sure enough, Chico intercedes with one of his own. "I thought this cigar was in my other suit," he explains. "I wish you were in your other suit," replies Groucho, "and your other suit was being pressed." "These cigars are imported," argues Chico, "They're hard to get." "I haven't had any trouble,"

"The charge would have been moider—pronounced moider"

answers Groucho. "Not with that plantation under your vest." The scene ends with the moment Marx fans have been waiting for; Harpo finally speaks. Throwing back his head, he utters his first and only word on screen—"Aachooo." His sneeze wracks the midget's furniture into a heap in the corner.

Undaunted, Groucho presses his investigation, even if he can't press Chico's suit with Chico in it. When the circus sets up again, Loophole visits the dressing room of Peerless Pauline, the human fly. Pauline is Carter's girl friend and may be holding the ten grand. Eve Arden plays Pauline. Here, she is young, pretty and talented enough to deserve better than her eventual fate on television. She is hanging upside down from the ceiling when Groucho arrives. "If this is a spirit reading," he says, "I'd like

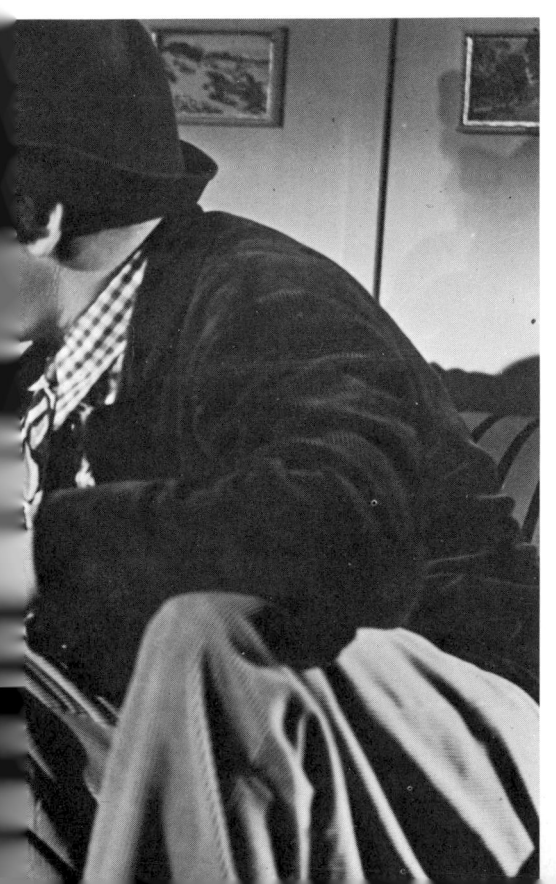

something good in the fourth at Belmont." Prowling about her effects, he discovers the $10,000 and salts it away in his vest. Pauline quickly unsticks herself and steers her victim to the couch to peck and pick his pocket. But he is wary. As a diversionary action, he whips out his cigarette case, flips it open and offers: "Peanut brittle?" She will have none of it, grabs him, and wrestles him down. "Your father wasn't by any chance an octopus, was he?" Groucho asks, still struggling. Pauline manages in the clinch to retrieve the money and slips it down the front of her costume. Groucho is stumped. Approaching the camera, he says, "There must be some way of getting that money without getting in trouble with the Hays office." He hits on the idea of coaxing Pauline to walk upside down in the hope that gravity will do its work on the billfold. But Pauline will only walk the ceiling if Groucho joins her. "No, I'd rather not," he defers. "I have an agreement with the houseflies. The flies don't practice law, and I don't walk on the ceiling." Finally, desperate, he agrees and retreats behind a screen to change, popping out momentarily to whine like a naughty virgin, "I know I'm gonna hate myself in the morning." Strolling about the ceiling at last in a ridiculous pair of tights, Groucho tells Pauline, "I never thought we'd be hanging around together." His ploy works. The money falls. But Pauline jumps down, picks it up, and leaves Groucho hanging like a stalactite. Harpo rushes in. He immediately solves Groucho's dilemma, cutting all the laces to his suction boots. Groucho falls like a stone.

Chico and Harpo haven't given up

Eve Arden stashes the loot

on Goliath, however, only proving that fools rush in where eagles fear to tread. As soon as the circus takes to the rails, the two self-appointed detectives sneak into the strong man's room while he is sleeping. "He's asleep like a baby," Chico announces. Harpo immediately whips out a baby bottle, smiling, then rushes toward the giant with the bottle for a club. Chico restrains him. Goliath stirs, but each time he does, Chico puts him back to sleep with a lullaby. They figure Goliath has stashed the cash somewhere around his double-decker bed. They have hardly begun their search when Chico steps on Harpo's hand, which goes limp. Hollering sweet nothings, Harpo rushes to the sink, bathes his dead hand in iodine and then uses it to paint the wall. The brothers want to lift Goliath's blanket but he is clutching the top, so Harpo merely cuts across the cover just below his hands, leaving the giant holding the fringe. More noise. More lullabies. Chico has another idea. Perhaps the money is in the pillow. While he slashes it open, Harpo accidentally turns on the fan.

Suddenly, in one of those miraculous transformations that spring from Harpo's genius, he has become a sidewalk Santa Claus in a feather snowstorm, a pillow under his shirt, a slab of cotton for a beard, a nightcap gracing his beautiful, shining face. In one hand he holds a spittoon for a charity pot. In the other, he rings a bell heartily, careless of the consequences, lost in his world of make-believe. But Chico has learned that "if we're found, we're lost" and produces a lullaby just in time. If the

Groucho, pondering a way of retrieving the money without offending the Hays office, hits on a plan (r). Harpo rescues him

money is not in the pillow or under the blankets, the mattresses must be searched, and searched thoroughly. The only way to conduct a really thorough search, Harpo figures, is to crawl inside the mattress. He slits it open and disappears under the sleeping Goliath, an occasional honk the only sign of life. A honk, however, is no lullaby. Goliath sleepily lifts the mattress to the top berth, winding up in a Marx Brothers' sandwich: Harpo on top, lucky Goliath in the middle and Chico buried underneath. When the strong man finally comes to his senses, he does what any sane man would do on awakening from a sound sleep amid Marxes. He runs, screaming, out of the cabin. Harpo emerges from the mattress, then systematically disgorges the entire contents of the bed in a huge solid burp of feathers.

But all is not lost, not as long as Loophole is on the job. By some odd coincidence written into the script, Jeff's aunt is the wealthy Mrs. Dewksbury of Newport's 400. She is throwing a party. If Groucho can only set up the circus silently outside her house (absurd?) and delight her guests, the old battle-ax might fork over the $10,000 and save the day. Groucho doesn't know Mrs. Dewksbury. On the other hand, Mrs. Dewksbury doesn't know Groucho. But Groucho simply takes the situation and Mrs. Dewksbury in hand. "What's this?" cries the butler, grabbing Groucho by the coat as the legal eagle swoops into the Dewksbury mansion. "It's English tweed," shoots back Groucho, who introduces himself as "Mr. Dewksbury." "I understood Mr. Dewksbury passed away," says the

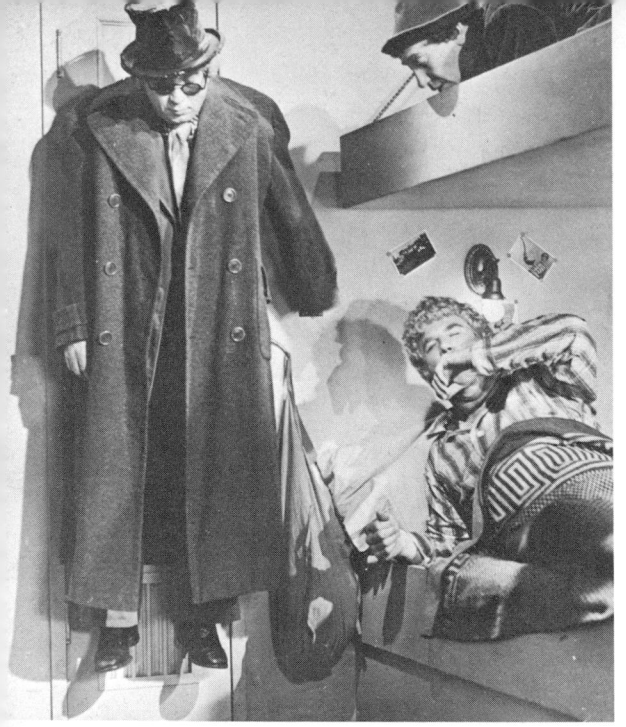

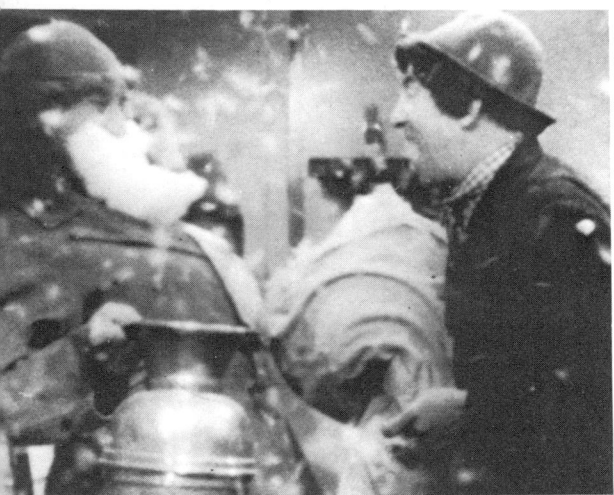

butler. "Oh, yes," replies Groucho, "a typographical error. Passed out was more like it. What a brawl that was. Well, here I am, after the brawl is over."

Groucho, showing more cheek than Fatty Arbuckle, bolts upstairs and into Mrs. Dewksbury's arms, crying, "Snookums." Mrs. Dewksbury doesn't know him. "You mean you've forgotten?" cries Groucho. "Those June nights on the Riviera when we sat beneath the shivering skies, bathing in the Mediterranean. We were young, gay, reckless. That night I drank champagne from your slipper. Two quarts. It would have been more, but you were wearing inner soles. Ah, Hildegarde." "My name is Susannah," huffs the ruffled Mrs. Dewksbury. "Let's not quibble," implores Groucho. "It's enough you've killed something fine and beautiful. Oh, Susannah. Oh, Susannah." Suddenly he starts playing an invisible bango and singing, "Oh, Susannah, Oh, won't you fly with me?/For I need ten thousand dollars, for the sheriff's

Featherbrains at work

after me." Mrs. Dewksbury threatens to call the servants. "Let the servants know," proclaims Groucho, who is as brazen with women as he is cowardly with men, especially when he has nothing to lose. "Let the whole world know!"

Groucho swings into action. Jardinet and his orchestra are to entertain at the Dewksbury party. He slips to a phone and calls the captain of the ship that Jardinet has taken from France. "His real name," Groucho tells the captain, "is DT's O'Connor. It's the biggest dope ring in years, and Jardinet is the head dope. Now keep him in the brig until I can find some more dope." Groucho then telegraphs Jeff and instructs him to detour to Dewksbury's. (If you're wondering what happened to the low point before we head into the finale, it occurred a little early in this film, but it was so low it was hardly worth reporting. Jeff finds he has been disinherited for running a circus. Julie and he are about to split up. Then the good news about Mrs. Dewksbury's relation to Jeff pops up. The low point was there, all right. It was just so low you could miss it without a minesweeper.)

The final banquet begins with Groucho counting the house. "It looks like they all showed up," he reports, counting 400. "There'll be no second helpings." As in *A Night at the Opera,* Groucho attributes the fine evening to "Mrs. Dewksbury and her checkbook." "I suggest we give the kid a great big hand," he tells a sea of stuffy faces. "I'm sure Marie Antoinette would like to say a few boring words." Each time Mrs. Dewksbury opens her mouth, she produces the trumpet of an elephant.

"Well, here I am, after the brawl is over"

"You've killed something fine and beautiful"

while Harpo erases the opposition

Groucho plays for time by insulting Margaret Dumont

(The circus has arrived.) "You should cut out starches," Groucho advises her. Groucho must stall until the circus is set up. Mrs. Dewksbury announces, "If no one cares for more coffee, we'll be going." The whole assembly stands, but Groucho pipes up, "I want another cup of coffee." The assembly sits. Groucho will do anything to kill time, even declare his love to Mrs. Dewksbury. "I love you feverishly," he tells her. "Have you got a thermometer on you?" Outside the banquet hall, Harpo kills time too, by playing tic-tac-toe on a giraffe's behind.

Just as things look fine, Jardinet arrives. Groucho hustles him into the hall. "You look tired," he tells him. "Why don't you go back to Paris and sit down?" Instead, Jardinet and his orchestra set up on a floating bandstand by the ocean. Harpo and Chico cut him loose, and the orchestra, briskly rendering the Prelude to Act Three of *Lohengrin,* floats merrily off to sea, serenading the waves. Carter—remember him?—represents the final obstacle. He tries to burn down the circus. Imagine that? But in the film's most brilliant and memorable moment, Harpo rides to the rescue on an ostrich, bopping out Carter's men

with one end of his taxi horn, extinguishing the fire with the other.

The show goes on. The stuffy 400 are delighted. But the best act is unexpected. The gorilla breaks loose, chasing Carter onto the high wire. Harpo joins the scramble. In the confusion, Mrs. Dewksbury gets stuck in a cannon which shoots her into the bizarre trapeze act, Marx Brothers and gorillas hanging all over her. Finally the gorilla catches up with Carter and retrieves the money. The final shot shows him licking his thumb and carefully counting out the loot.

The sequence involved a fair amount of stand-ins and trick shots. But not enough of them as far as Margaret Dumont was concerned. "For the benefit of those who wonder if I actually did perform on the trapeze," she said, after the film was made, "tell them yes. Most people accuse me of using a stand-in. But I hung head down while the Marx boys clutched my legs. I had to see it through." But the experience was enough to make her pause before joining the team again. "Never again," she vowed, "even if they try to write a part for me." They did, in

The Big Store, and she played it.

Charitable is the best that can be said of the reviews of *At the Circus.* Some critics championed the film, but without great conviction. Others, like Howard Barnes of the New York *Herald Tribune,* were candid. "Between them," he wrote of the brothers, "they whip up some passages of high hilarity, but there is no sustained comic note in their new offering.... What is chiefly wrong with 'At the Circus' is that the brothers Marx have almost none of the split-second timing which marked their great films of the past." Frank S. Nugent of the *Times* went to the heart of the matter, calling the picture "a rather dispirited imitation of former Marx successes." A critic today might be more generous, especially in the light of what generally dismal stuff has passed for comedy in the past two decades. But next to the films that preceded it, *At the Circus* is a considerable drop down.

One funny sequence never made the picture. It involved a dispute between Harry Gamorra, the great gorilla imitator, and the agent who owned the gorilla skin, an item worth $5,000. Incarcerated in this cage of hair, Gamorra fainted twice during the shooting, but the agent refused to provide ventilation. During a lunchtime break, Gamorra settled the argument on his own. He borrowed an ice pick from the kitchen, hung the skin up, and belted a number of holes into it. The story, as reported by Groucho in his biography, ends this way: The agent notices something strange after lunch when Gamorra doesn't faint. "He's been in that skin for almost three hours and hasn't fainted yet," cries the agent. "My experience has been that the man inside the skin always faints inside of two hours." After a few minutes' investigation, the agent emerges, a ludicrous figure indeed, the skin slung over his shoulder, crying, "Somebody stuck holes in my gorilla!"

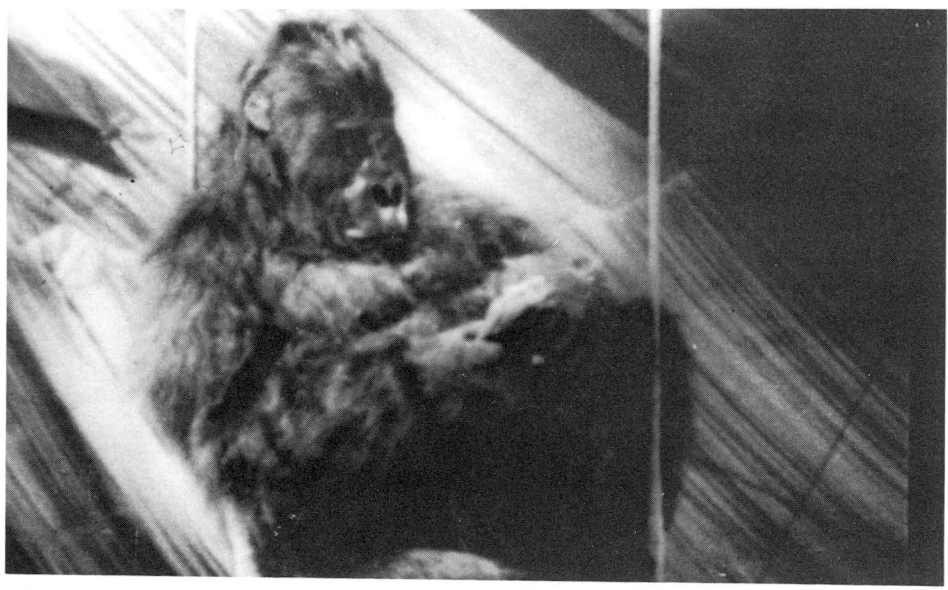

The daring young ape on the flying trapeze

Groucho, Harpo, and Chico

John Carroll and Diana Lewis

Walter Wolf King

Robert Barrat

S. Quentin Quale:	GROUCHO
Rusty Panello:	HARPO
Joseph Panello:	CHICO
Terry Turner:	JOHN CARROLL
Eve Wilson:	DIANA LEWIS
Red Baxter:	ROBERT BARRAT
Mr. Beecher:	WALTER WOLF KING
Lulubelle:	JUNE MacCLOY
Railroad President:	GEORGE LESSEY
Halfbreed:	MITCHELL LEWIS
Dan Wilson:	TULLY MARSHALL

Also LEE BOWMAN, CLEM BEVANS and JOE YULE

* * *

Producer: Jack Cummings
Director: Edward Buzzell
Original Screenplay: Irving Brecher
Photography: Leonard Smith
Art Direction: Cedric Gibbons and Stan Rogers
Set Decoration: Edwin B. Willis
Music Direction: Georgie Stoll
Editing: Blanche Sewell
Music: Roger Edens
Lyrics: Gus Kahn
Released by Metro-Goldwyn-Mayer, December 6, 1940. 80 minutes

11 Go West (1940)

"The boys at the studio have lined up another turkey for us," Groucho wrote his friend Arthur Sheekman in the fall of 1939, "and there's a strong likelihood that we'll be shooting in about three or four weeks. I'm not looking forward to it, but I guess it's just as well to get it over with. I saw the present one the other day [*At the Circus*] and didn't much care for it. I realize I'm not much of a judge but I'm kind of sick of the whole thing and, on leaving the theater, vowed that I'd never see it again. I don't feel this way about all of our pictures: 'A Night at the Opera,' for example, I always enjoyed lookng at and, to a lesser degree, 'A Day at the Races,' but the rest sicken me and I'll stay clear of them in the future."

By July of 1940, the picture was still being lined up. " 'Go West' is being constantly postponed," Groucho wrote Sheekman. "I read the script and I don't blame them. If they were smart they'd pay us off and get three other fellows or take all that money and open up a big, gaudy cat house." The postponements suggested to Groucho that the studio was "afraid to make it." The delays also caused him special problems. "All I get is a weekly announcement to come to the wardrobe department and be fitted for a pair of early American pants," he complained to Sheekman in one of a number of missives collected in *The Groucho Letters*. "I

had my hair darkened to match my greasepaint moustache, but it has been so long since the scheduled starting date that the dye has faded, and I will have to have it done all over again. So you see, my theatrical career has dwindled to being fitted once a week for a pair of early American pants and having my hair dyed every three weeks. This is a fine comedown for a man who used to be the Toast of Broadway."

Groucho's pessimism about his films shouldn't be taken too seriously. While certainly honest and deeply felt at the time, it had a way of turning around. Groucho did not "stay clear" of his films as he vowed. In 1966 he attended a Marx Brothers festival in Vienna, where all of his films were shown. He damned *At the Circus* while it was being shot, reversed himself when it was over, and then condemned it again later on. The same is true of *Go West*. For all his misgivings about the picture before and during production, he concluded in a letter to Sheekman: "I haven't seen it hooked up but I imagine it's pretty good."

Grouch was no stranger to the badlands. As a youth he had survived an adventure a good deal less probable than anything that happened in *Go West* itself. One of Groucho's earliest show business stints took him to Colorado as part of a singing trio. Unfortunately his mentor, an unscrupulous vaudevillian, deserted the lad in a town named Cripple Creek. To earn his considerable fare home, this product of the pavement was forced to take a job driving a grocery wagon over the mountains between Cripple Creek and a hamlet named Victor, negotiating precipitous roads that skirted a gorge two thousand feet below. Somehow Groucho, who had barely ever seen a horse before, let alone driven one, survived the ordeal.

The impulse behind *Go West* was just the reverse: to make the improbable seem real. As director Eddie Buzzell explained it at the time: "On the surface, most people believe that the Marx Brothers participate wholly in insane, nonsensical comedy. That is far from true. They do wild, mad things. But most of our story con-

ferences are spent making things plausible. Perhaps these things *don't* happen in real life, but they *can* happen, and that allows people to laugh."

After the mediocre reception of *At the Circus,* the studio allowed the brothers to test the material for their new picture before live audiences.

As in their other pretested films, the ordeal of live fire paid off, most notably in the opening sequence. As originally written by Irving Brecher, Groucho fleeces his brothers by selling them a farrago of inessential sagebrush supplies—a coonskin cap, cake of ice, bear trap. The audience chuckled, but less and less as the scene progressed. Audience sympathy, it turned out, was with the suckers. So Brecher added a comic complication. As finally shot, Groucho winds up losing

Groucho, out to fleece the tenderfeet,

winds up noticing "something corrupt

everything but his shirt. And that is left to him, apparently, only because Harpo, having stolen his money, pants leg and hat, isn't interested in adding to his wardrobe.

In its attitude toward plot, *Go West* combines the worst of both the early and the later films. Unlike the wild Paramount pictures, the film makes a concession to popular taste in following a deliberate story line. But the story is so clumsy and loosely structured that it offers none of the compensating discipline and form of the Thalberg creations. The supporting cast is weak. Margaret Dumont is conspicuous by her absence, especially in a scene where Groucho pitches woo to a derelict. The villains display neither the comic gifts nor the

menace of the better Marx heavies, although Walter Wolf King, who was so beautifully vain and vicious as Lassparri in *A Night at the Opera*, plays Beecher, the fat-cat swindler. The five intervening years have puffed King from a classically lean, dark agent of evil to a portly, somewhat mellowed chiseler. And the romantic leads, Diana Lewis and John Carroll, are little more than pieces of studio driftwood, stiff, unconvincing, sometimes embarrassing.

Despite all this, *Go West* is full of great fun, fine sequences, and sustained moments of comic foolishness that compare favorably with some of the best the brothers did. The opening scene is a masterpiece of counterpointed visual and verbal comedy. Groucho as S. Quentin Quayle (the S.

going on around my pants"

stands for San) arrives at the train station ready to follow Horace Greeley's great dictum. He turns to the clutch of porters who have toted his bags. "Do any of you fellows have a dime?" he asks, outfitted in a slicker's top hat. "No? Then keep the baggage." He hands the ticket vendor money for a trip out West, adding, "Don't bother counting it." "Hey," says the man, "there's only sixty dollars here." "I told you not to count it," answers Groucho. The ticket seller tells him he's ten dollars short. "That's highway robbery," returns Groucho. "No wonder you're behind bars."

Enter Chico and Harpo, looking like a true tatterdemalion. Groucho hears the word "money," which provokes a Pavlovian response. He moves in. "All we want to know is, where's the train," Chico asks. "It's on the tracks," Groucho replies, sizing up his prey. "It seldom comes in here." Chico and Harpo are in worse shape than Groucho. Harpo has squandered sixty of the seventy dollars needed for the trip on a curvaceous number. He tells Chico so with his hands. "Oh, you buy a snake," says Chico. But the pair still owns the difference between Groucho and his fare—ten dollars. And nothing stands between Groucho and ten bucks. Gold is lying all over the streets, Chico tells him, and Harpo, whipping out a shovel, starts collecting the imaginary nuggets into his sack. "The way he's dressed," observes Groucho, looking at Harpo, "it looks like *he* was lying all over the streets. Of course there's gold lying all over the street, but they won't let him take any. He's a tenderfoot." "You wear those shoes and you gotta tender feet too," defends Chico. Groucho

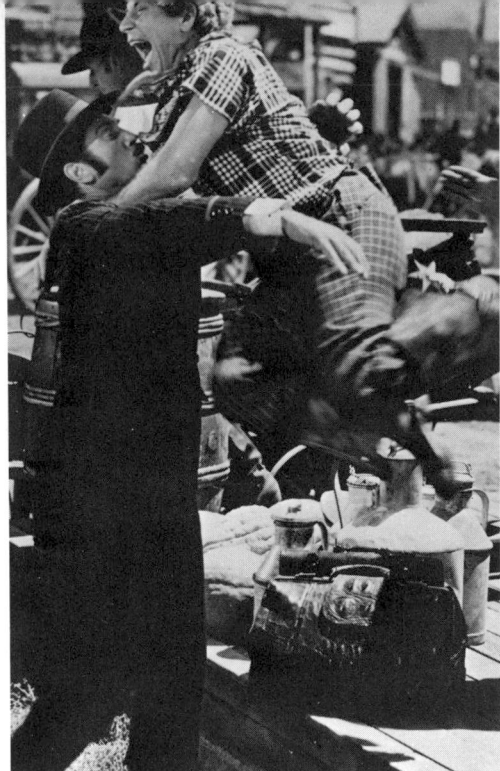

"Mr. Beecha!"

looks down at Harpo's grubby boots. "Oh, those are shoes," he exclaims. "I thought that was fungus with buttons." True con man that he is, Groucho conjures up images of Harpo being shot immediately by Western badmen, dressed as he is. "What's the matter with that hat?" Chico objects. "That hat cost a lot of money." "How much did it cost him?" Groucho asks. "I dunno," says Chico, "He stole it." "You love your brother, don't you?" Groucho says. "No," replies Chico, "but I'm used to him." Groucho then produces a coonskin cap, which he plunks on Harpo's head backward. "Isn't the tail supposed to be in the back?" Chico asks. "Not on him," answers Groucho.

The double swindle begins like a

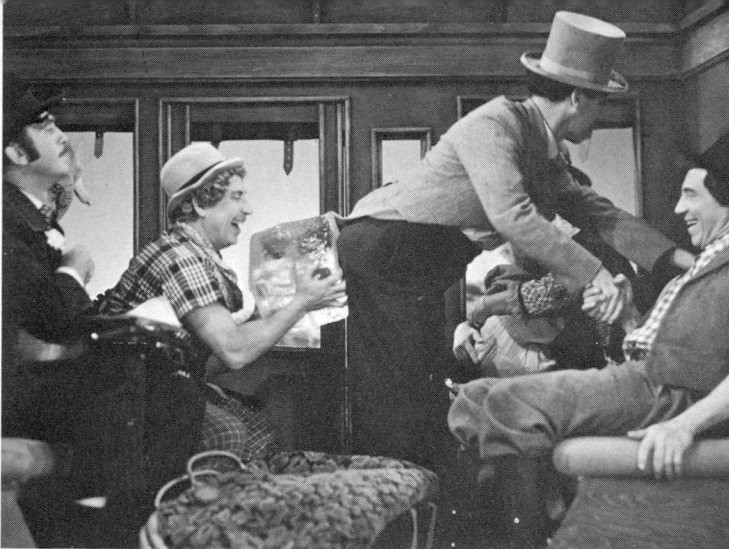

The great stagecoach fiasco

double fugue. Groucho asks one dollar for a succession of useless items, even though, as he puts it, "I'm only making a dollar on it." Chico keeps paying him with a ten-dollar bill attached to a string. Each time Groucho pockets it, flies back to Chico, who also receives nine dollars change. After the fourth flight of the sawbuck, Groucho asks whether Chico has noticed anything zooming past them. "It must have been a pigeon," answers Chico. "No, it wasn't a pigeon," Groucho says. "It must have been a frog," offers Chico. Groucho disagrees: "It had numbers on it." "Those were the license plates," Chico explains. After a while, Groucho runs out of things to sell. But Chico and Harpo like the rate of exchange—nothing gets you nine dollars—so they volunteer to pay Groucho a one-dollar sales tax, one dollar to prove that they're honest, one dollar for anything as long as they get nine dollars change. And they don't care in what denomination. "He take a four and a five," explains Chico about Harpo. But Groucho, who has noticed "something corrupt going on around my pants," is wary of making any more one-dollar profits. "I couldn't afford it," he explains. He finally traps the ten-dollar bill in his pocket so all the yanking in the world won't free it. But Harpo, always adept with his scissors, simply cuts away Groucho's pants leg and snips off the pocket. "You know," Groucho remarks, "it's suddenly got-

*Groucho mixes pleasure with business and suffers
the consequences*

ten very chilly in here." In a last desperate move, he tucks his remaining money in his hat. As he bids his "suckers" farewell, Harpo switches hats on him.

The strict rules of the M-G-M formula forbid the brothers to victimize the romantic couple in any way. Ridiculous as it seems in many of the films, the brothers risk life and limb for characters who in the early films belonged to the world of the enemy. In *Go West,* however, Buzzell helps the brothers express what must have been their attitude toward these stiff sweethearts. When Terry Turner and Eve Wilson meet for the first time and embrace, a horse cranes his neck across the screen, blocking the lovers from view. They carry on their inane chatter while the horse stares out at the audience, a look of boredom twenty feet high stamped across his long face.

The lovers are central to the plot, but to little else. Old man Wilson owns a deed to land that is barren of gold. But Terry convinces the railroad to build its new line across Wilson's territory, turning the claim into a gold mine. Terry has bothered to arrange all this in the hope that Wilson will call off the longstanding feud between the Turners and Wilsons and allow him to marry Eve. Once these ponderous facts have been established, the picture concerns itself with the efforts of the villains to wrest the deed away from Chico and Harpo, who have acquired it, and the efforts of all three brothers to get it back.

Harpo and Chico realize the importance of the deed immediately. They guard it so closely that in five minutes they manage to give it away.

In the town saloon, Harpo is so dry he could light a match on his tongue—and does. But when he intercepts and downs a beer intended for another customer farther down the bar, he and Chico must write out an I O U to pay for it. Chico, always careful not to think every minute, hands the saloon owner, Red Baxter, an "I O ME ten cents," written on the back of the valuable deed. In typical Marxian logic, they rush out of the saloon to deliver the deed they have just given away. But on their way down the street, they intercept a telegram intended for Dan Wilson, the original owner.

Chico explains to Harpo that they won't open it because it isn't addressed to them. Then he relents. "Okay, we open it, but we don't read it." He eyes Harpo, who is grinning a bit too broadly. "Hey, I don't think I can trust you and I know you can't trust me, so I tell-a you what we do. I read it, but we no listen. Put-a you fingers up." They both stand there, plugging their ears with their fingers, while Chico reads the telegram aloud. It explains that a representative of the railroad, a Mr. Beecher, will be arriving on the next train to purchase the deed. When they are through, they both play dumb—that is, Chico plays dumb; Harpo doesn't have to. "Hey, Rusty," he confesses to Harpo, "I cheated. I listened." Harpo leers. "You listened too, eh?" Harpo nods furiously and, chuckling, they head out of town to meet Beecher.

Duel in the saloon

A characteristic display of Marxian courage

As the train unloads, Chico cries, "Hey, Mista Beecha, we're here to meetcha. Mista Beecha, we're supposed to meetcha." Beecher introduces himself. "That's funny," says Chico. "We don't recognize you. Do we, Rusty?" Harpo shakes his head gravely. "Naturally you don't recognize me," answers Beecher, actually trying to reason with Chico. "We've never met." "Yeah?" says the ever-suspicious Chico. "Then how do I know it's you? If I don't know what Mr. Beecher looks like, the only way I can tell is if he wears a white carnation." Harpo plucks one from the hat of a lady passing by and sticks it in Beecher's buttonhole. The two of them then walk away from Beecher, leaving him to puzzle out what's going on. A moment later, they return, strutting arm in arm, Harpo whistling and rolling his eyes toward the heavens. Suddenly Chico spots the carnation and screams, "Mr. Beecha," rushing over to him. Just as Beecher is shaking Chico's hand again, a bit dazed by the nonsense, Harpo leaps into his arms and hugs him.

Beecher wants to see the deed, but Harpo explains in sign language that they have left it back in town. So they all pile into a stagecoach, already occupied by a woman and baby. Chico is furious at Harpo. "You talk-a too much," he whispers to him. "Next time you keep-a you hands *shut*." The stage picks up a hitchhiker named Quayle. "Say, where did I see your face before?" Groucho asks Chico, vaguely remembering the fleecing he took at the station. "Right where it is now," Chico replies. What follows is a cross between the stateroom scene and a takeoff on the popular film *Stagecoach*. Beecher starts bidding for the deed. Groucho matches him, raising the price ultimately to $15,000. Beecher insults Groucho, who replies threateningly: "If you weren't smaller than me, I'd beat the daylights out of you." Beecher rises. "I'm bigger than you," he says. "Well," counters Groucho, "that's *another* reason." Meanwhile Harpo starts lounging all over the passengers. He knocks Beecher's hat into his satchel every time the railroad man reaches for the contract, then closes the satchel on his hand. He launches joyfully into a game of musical hats with all the passengers, then shovels them a huge block of ice to cool the compartment off. He lolls on their laps, puts his feet up, ricochets and tumbles about the cabin, always mashing or jostling the trapped travelers. Just as the compartment looks as if it's going to burst at the seams, the woman passenger produces triplets. (Unfortunately the television version slices this sequence to ribbons, robbing it of any kind of comic climax.)

When they all reach town, Groucho goes upstairs in the saloon to negotiate the deal with saloonkeeper Baxter and Beecher. "I give you my

Chico and Groucho light up in the front while Harpo blows up the rear

solemn word as an embezzler that I'll be back in two minutes," he promises. Sure enough, two minutes later, the villains toss him down a flight of stairs, without deed or cash. This tumble is not merely a two-story drop, but a visible symbol of Grouchos' fall from grace since the early pictures. A similar drubbing would have been unthinkable in the Paramount films. Groucho may have taken a fall in *A Night at the Opera,* but he recovered quickly and eventually more than repaid Gottlieb. Here he is simply the victim of a sight gag. The man who once "licked his weight in wild caterpillars" has fallen a long way. He manages a rejoinder—"I was going to thrash them within an inch of their lives, but I didn't have a tape measure"—but slinks away to lick his wounds at a nearby table, finding himself face-to-face with a drunken cowpoke. "Didn't we meet at Monte Carlo the night you blew your brains out?" he asks, launching into an ab-

surd routine normally directed at Margaret Dumont. "How we laughed. Ha, ha, ha. Foolish, foolish child, this can never be, this thing that's happened between us." "Burp," says the cowhand. "Supposing I brought you to my country place at Drooling-on-the-Lapel? What would people say?"

With one brother as cowardly as Groucho and the other as devious as Chico, all the dangerous assignments fall to Harpo. He has to avenge Groucho's honor. He and Baxter square off, hands clutching the six shooters at their sides. They stride toward each other, closer . . . closer. Harpo pulls and . . . produces a whisk broom. The bystanders and Baxter laugh as Harpo brushes him off until —BANG!!!! The whisk broom fires, nearly blowing Baxter's head off. Harpo also recovers the deed. While the other brothers are being pampered and boozed by the saloon's floozies, Harpo sets a stick of dynamite under the safe in the back room.

Two giant intellects get together

It fizzles. He pulls off the wick and pulls out a party hat, then stomps about merrily like a birthday boy. The next time, he tries a real dynamite stick instead of a party favor, with improved results. The safe swings open, and Harpo snatches the deed. Baxter rushes in, but Harpo has disappeared, having wedged himself into the wooden dome of a rolltop desk. The sequence ends with a nice parody of the theatrics of the classic Western. Baxter orders the brothers to put their hands up. Eve enters behind him and tells him to put his hands up. One of Baxter's pals sneaks up behind Eve and orders her to put her hands up. An Indian buddy of Eve's marches in and tells the bad guy to put his hands up. Another heavy enters, ordering the Indian to put his hands up. Finally Terry rushes in and commands the bad guy to put *his* hands up. Terry gets the deed, and the brothers flee.

They head for the railroad station, which must have been originally planned by the brothers themselves, located as it is miles from the town it serves. On their way to the station, the brothers stop off at an Indian reservation. The chief won't talk to Groucho, who bears a striking resemblance to the ugliest face on the tribe's totem pole. Chico steps in, offering to act as translator. He speaks Indian, he explains, because he was born in Indianapolis. But it is Harpo who learns to converse with the chief, honking an animated chat as the Indian grunts away. "You know," Groucho comments to the audience, "it's stimulating when two giant intellects get together."

The finale belongs to the best tradition of comedy in that it is almost entirely stolen from another comedian—in this case from Buster Keaton's masterpiece, *The General*. The brothers grab the controls of the train East, racing away from Baxter and Beecher and toward the railroad office, where they will cash in the deed for Eve and Terry. The railroading expertise of the brothers could be written on the small end of a mosquito's egg, so they consult an instruction booklet. "Maybe that book's a-no good," Chico suggests. "Of course it's good," Groucho assures him. "It's an engineer's manual." "But a-supposing the engineer's name ain't Manuel?" "Then he's got to change his name," Groucho explains. "He can't make a fool of this book." Actually the engineer is in no shape to change anything, gagged and bound on top of the wood car. Groucho points to the cloth stuffed in his mouth and remarks: "This is the best gag in the picture." The engineer disappears with the rest of the wood when Harpo

Harpo Marx, the missing link

The duel of the oilcans

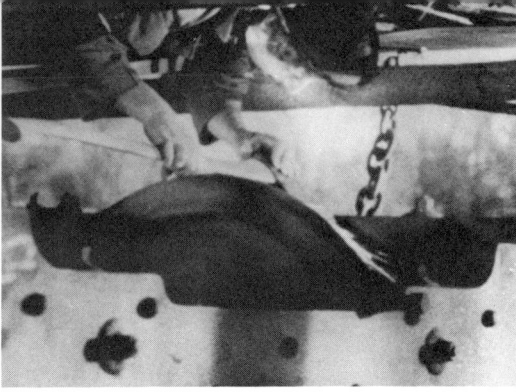

Harpo with an ax to grind (above) turns Pullm[an] into flatcar

accidentally triggers the dump mechanism. To make matters worse, Chico yells to Harpo, "Brake! The brake!" and Harpo, always the literalist, breaks the brake. Now the train can't stop when it must and won't move once it runs out of wood. Harpo tries to slow it by throwing kerosene by mistake instead of water into the firebox. Later he experiments with a new form of propulsion—popcorn—which does very little to advance the train but manages to flood the cabin with enough goodies to serve a movie theater for a month. When Baxter and Beecher try to disconnect the cars, Harpo redeems himself by serving as the missing link, grabbing one car with his hands, the other with his feet and holding them together as he stretches like a human garter.

The Marxes steal all kinds of Keaton gags. They swing on the directional signals, which turn 360 degrees and place them far down the top of the train just as the heavies are about to catch up to them. The train leaps the track, picks up a house on its cowcatcher and comes bearing down on Harpo. As in Keaton's *Steamboat Bill,* Harpo passes through the front door of the onrushing house and out

the back without being hurt.

Beecher and Baxter grab a wagon and chase the train, which is fast running out of fuel. Harpo saves the day. Wielding an ax like a maniac, he systematically chops up the cars and feeds them into the fire. By the time he has finished, the elegant express has been reduced to a long, rickety string of open flatcars carrying a cargo of bewildered passengers. The Marxes win the race. In the last sequence, Harpo is rewarded for his heroics by being allowed to drive the first spike on the new railroad. Taking an overgenerous backswing, he drives the nearest railroad executive through the ground instead.

The critics generally welcomed *Go West* as an improvement over *Room Service* and *At the Circus.* And so it is, if only in the ferocity of its pace and the lunacy of its conception. Archer Winsten of the New York *Post,* noting that *Room Service* was "the worst they ever did," lavishes praise on their sagebrush epic: "From the foreword which quotes Horace Greeley's dictum of 'Go west, young man, go west' and asserts that the Marx Brothers made him sorry he ever said it, to an insane train ride for climax, the Marxes are in their own peculiar groove. They are nuts, professionally and profitably." Another New York reviewer ranked *Go West* as "up to and often above the Marx par."

But it required more than good reviews to convince Groucho that he wasn't tiring of the film business. "*Go West,*" he told a reporter, "is probably our next to last picture together. I've been acting for a long time and it's been fun, but now we fell like we'd like to do something on our own. Harpo may go on a lecture tour and Chico may take out a band. I hope to keep occupied in various ways." One way Groucho kept himself occupied was by making three more movies.

Driving the first spike

Groucho, Chico, Marion Martin, and Harpo

Margaret Dumont

Douglas Dumbrille

Wolf J. Flywheel:	GROUCHO
Wacky:	HARPO
Ravelli:	CHICO
Martha Phelps:	MARGARET DUMONT
Mr. Grover:	DOUGLAS DUMBRILLE
Tommy Rogers:	TONY MARTIN
Joan Sutton:	VIRGINIA GREY
Fred Sutton:	WILLIAM TANNEN
Peggy Arden:	MARION MARTIN
Kitty:	VIRGINIA O'BRIEN
Guiseppi:	HENRY ARMETTA
Maria:	ANNA DEMETRIO
George Hastings:	PAUL STANTON
Arthur Hastings:	RUSSELL HICKS
Duke:	BRADLEY PAGE

Also CHARLES HOLLAND

* * *

Producer: Louis K. Sidney
Director: Charles Reisner
Screenplay: Sid Kuller, Hal Fimberg and Ray Golden
Story: Nat Perrin
Photography: Charles Lawton
Art Direction: Cedric Gibbons and Stan Rogers
Set Decoration: Edwin B. Willis
Editing: Conrad A. Nervig
Music Direction: Georgie Stoll
Music: Hal Borne
Lyrics: Sid Kuller and Hal Fimberg
Released by Metro-Goldwyn-Mayer, June 20, 1941. 83 minutes

Tony Martin and Virginia Grey

Henry Armetta

12 The Big Store (1941)

While *Go West* was well received, letters of complaint poured into M-G-M lamenting the absence of Margaret Dumont. The great dowager had served the brothers well in eight films to that point. Her aristocratic bearing, her brilliant sense of timing, her infinite patience and boundless good humor had gradually established her in the public mind as the fifth Marx Brother. Once Zeppo departed, she become an indispensable asset as the only member of the family to play it straight. "I'm not a stooge, I'm the best straight woman in Hollywood," she would proclaim. "There's an art to playing straight. You must build up your man, but never top him, never steal the laughs from him."

But Miss Dumont was more than a fine foil. Without aid of decor or props, she embodied in her statuesque figure all the pomp and pretension of high society itself and, as such, provided the brothers with a kind of portable target. Miss Dumont came by her role honestly. The woman who played Mrs. Claypool, Mrs. Teasdale and Mrs. Dewksbury of Newport's 400 was herself a member of high society, wife of sugar heir John Moller, Jr. By the time she joined the Marx Brothers in *The Cocoanuts* in 1928, she had already enjoyed a successful stage career playing blueblooded matrons. She had a fine comic gift but, right from the beginning, the brothers wanted her to play it serious. "I was playing a small-town social climber in *The Fourflushers* when George S. Kaufman saw me and asked me if I'd be the society leader who had the part opposite Groucho Marx in *The Cocoanuts*," she once recalled. "I was amused and said yes. I thought the society leader funny, but whenever I tried to clown her, Groucho would say, 'I like you dignified.' "

Miss Dumont didn't realize what she was letting herself in for, but she soon found out. "After three weeks as leading lady," she reported, "Groucho had pushed me out of windows, pulled chairs out from under me, broiled steaks in the fireplace of my apartment, put frogs in my bathtub and made my life miserable in general, on the stage and off." Harpo also loved teasing her. Once, when they were shooting a sequence from *At the Circus*, Harpo playfully mauled the matron, then whispered in her ear, "Hey, babe, don't play so rough." Miss Dumont broke up, and the scene had to be done again.

Miss Dumont was at her best in her romantic tilts with Groucho, where she would suffer his puns and indignities and still manage to carry the scene and keep it credible. Groucho proposed to her so often in the course of their twelve-year screen courtship that one newspaper reported that she was his wife. "I told Groucho that the story was embarrassing," she said afterward. "He said, 'Embarrassing? I've just written an article about my wife, and the magazine is running her picture. When the article comes out, I'll be arrested for bigamy.' " As far as the public was concerned, Groucho and Miss Dumont were an inseparable screen couple. When M-G-M made *The Big Store,* there was no doubt who would play the dowager. "I was afraid I was being taken for granted," the pleased Miss Dumont said at the time. "Missing *Go West* was the best thing that could happen to me."

Margaret Dumont's presence all but saves *The Big Store* from oblivion. Without her and the splendid badinage she affords Groucho, this last M-G-M picture wouldn't have amounted to a row of haberdasheries. The story, as usual, is foolish and the musical numbers—aside from satiric ditties by the brothers—more boring than ever before. If George S. Kaufman considered *The Cocoanuts* a musical comedy without music, he

might very well have called *The Big Store* a musical comedy without comedy. But the exchanges between Groucho and his trusty inamorata redeem the whole messy business. In *Go West* Groucho played third fiddle to Chico and Harpo. But with the return of Margaret Dumont, he reclaims his identity as the world's mangiest lover and appropriates center stage.

Groucho is Wolf J. Flywheel, attorney at leisure, who lives in a one-room office with his obedient houseboy, Harpo. Business is so bad that he spends the morning reading the newspaper and Harpo spends the afternoon selling it. Margaret Dumont carries the name Martha Phelps, a dowager who is heir to her nephew's fortune. She seeks out Flywheel to protect her nephew, Tommy Rodgers, who has developed an unfortunate inclination for being knocked unconscious. The culprit, unknown to Mrs. Phelps, is Glover, the manager of Phelps' Department Store, who plans

Breakfast is served

How to turn a pigpen into a detective office

to kill Tommy, marry Mrs. Phelps and thus gain 100 percent ownership of the operation. So much for the plot.

Mrs. Phelps' arrival at Flywheel's office triggers an instant transformation of the premises. Groucho's bed folds into the wall, forming a cabinet marked "Liabilities." Harpo reels in a network of drying laundry, revealing the sleuth's shingle: "Bloodhounds transfused, fingerprints manicured, gin rummy." The stove on which Harpo is cooking his boss' breakfast collapses into a desk. And Groucho sets up a one-man hum of activity to impress his new—perhaps only—client. A hand attached to the back of a door delivers urgent telegrams at periodic intervals. The dictaphone and telephone are never still, both triggered by buttons that Groucho steps on under his desk. The moment Mrs. Phelps attempts to tell her

troubles, Groucho calls himself on the dictaphone. "Hello, Winthrop," he instructs his imaginary secretary in an imaginary back room. "Get me the district attorney." Then he picks up the phone and tells the imaginary district attorney: "That's ridiculous. I've been in constant touch with Scotland Yard." Buzzzzzz. "Winthrop? Get me Trinidad. Hello, Dad? I won't be home for dinner." Mrs. Phelps lamely tries again. "Just a minute," barks Groucho. Buzzzzz. "Winthrop? Get me Gangbusters. Hello, Gangbusters? Who caught the crook last night? Sheriff Hawkins?" Buzzzzz. "Winthrop, get me Sheriff Hawkins. Hello, Hawkins? Congratulations."

Harpo composes himself at the typewriter, ready to take down Mrs. Phelps' story. As she begins, he puts on a brilliant display of frantic cross-handed, whirlwind typing, his hands blurring like those of a concert

"This man's a cad, a yellow cad!"

Harpo holds the door for Margaret Dumont

pianist, his eyes popping. Mrs. Phelps carries on bravely, but her words are lost in the burps and chugs and clatter of this improvised riveting machine. She repeats her story, but Harpo redoubles his feverish pounding. The carriage flies off the typewriter. Harpo replaces it with the base of the telephone and keeps on going. His performance ends with an explosion of hot buttered toast, intended for Groucho's breakfast. Mrs. Phelps wants to know what Groucho charges to handle the case. The sleuth puts his fee at $20,000 but concedes, "Only a cheap chiseler would ask that much." Mrs. Phelps is prepared to pay $500. "Oddly enough," says Groucho, "I'm prepared to take it. Shall we bind the deal with a kiss or five dollars in cash? You lose either way."

Groucho might as well accept. He has nothing else cooking—except his breakfast, which, neglected in his desk, starts smoking up the room.

Groucho passes the smoke off as camouflage and whisks his client toward the door. Harpo whisks Groucho's moth-eaten coat at the door. Under the pressure of the brush, the coat sheds a pile of hair on the floor. "That's funny," says Groucho, viewing the hirsute heap. "I thought I shaved this morning." The trio piles into Groucho's sleek sedan, whose vintage can be divined by the sign it carries on its rear fender: WELCOME HOME, ADMIRAL DEWEY, HERO OF MANILA.

At the department store, Mrs. Phelps introduces Groucho to Grover. Groucho hates him immediately. To a simple how-do-you-do, Groucho tells the oily executive: "That's a rather personal question, isn't it, old man? What I do and how I do it is my concern." Then, turning to Mrs. Phelps: "If you marry me, your concern will be my concern." Mrs. Phelps wants Grover to take Groucho on as store detective, but Grover questions Groucho's experience in the field. "I was a shoplifter for three years," Groucho assures him. But Grover wants to know how he will react under battle conditions. "We will assume I am a customer returning a baby carriage," poses the executive, played by Douglas Dumbrille, who was the racetrack owner, Morgan, in *A Day at the Races.* "Are you married?" Groucho asks. "No, of course not," shoots back Grover. "Then what are you doing with a baby carriage? This man's a cad. A yellow cad," Groucho concludes. Grover tries another example. "A woman faints. What do you do?" Groucho wants to know how old she is. "What difference does that make?" cries Grover. "Do you hear that?" Groucho responds. "A woman's life is in danger, and he asks, what difference does it make? And that charla-

Harpo, hustled into the department store . . .

pays a brief visit to the crockery department

"If you marry me, your concern will be my concern."

tan is running your store? Martha, I'm firing him immediately." Later he tells Mrs. Phelps: "You mean that a woman of your culture and money and beauty and money would marry this impostor?"

Groucho has designs on Mrs. Phelps. His courtship of the department store dowager inspires some of screenwriter Brecher's best dialogue. "Martha, dear," Groucho intones, "there are many bonds that will hold us together through eternity." "Really, Wolf? What are they?" "Your government bonds," replies Groucho, "your savings bonds, your Liberty bonds. And maybe, in a year or two after we're married, who knows, there may be a little baby bond." "Oh, that would be wonderful," squeals Mrs. Phelps. "Tell me, Wolfie dear, will we have a beautiful home?" Groucho is puzzled. "Of course," he says. "You're not planning to move, are you?" "No," she answers, "but I'm afraid after we've been married awhile, a beautiful young girl will come along and you'll forget all about

me." "Don't be silly," assures Groucho. "I'll write you twice a week." Groucho will go to any lengths to woo his future pen pal. He even recites romantic poetry. "Why, that's Byron," exclaims Mrs. Phelps. "Yes," Groucho says wistfully. "He was thinking of you when he wrote it." Mrs. Phelps is touched by the sentiment. Groucho pours it on, inventing a few atrocious verses of his own. "I worked five years for Burma Shave," he says, citing the source of his inspiration.

Up to now, Chico has served Tommy Rodgers as bodyguard, sticking to him like the gum on his shoes. "From now on," he has pledged to Tommy, "you and me are going to be insufferable." But Tommy, played and sung with charm by Tony Martin, has been bopped so often his skull is beginning to resemble a balloon with warts. He needs professional help—from Wolf J. Flywheel. Before Groucho will step in, he exacts his fee in debasing flattery. "I'm afraid I wouldn't be happy here," he says petulantly. "I'm not appreciated." "I think you're great," says Tommy. Great isn't good enough. Groucho wants something more. "What do you *really* think of me?" he asks. "Well," Tommy stammers, "I, I, I think you're wonderful." Still not good enough. "Do you think I'm any good?" Groucho coaxes. "Man, you're terrific." Well, not bad, but Groucho wants something with a little more zing. "How am I?" he wheedles. "All right?" Tommy is virtually driven to his knees. "Wanna know?" he asks Groucho, in what must remain as the superfluous question of the century. "You're terrific." Satisfied, Groucho turns to the audience: "I could listen to this man all day."

While all this has been going on, Harpo has been doing what he does best—getting into trouble. As Groucho's chauffeur, neatly decked out in underwater goggles and rags, he carries a portable fire hydrant with him. He used it to attract stray dogs in *Horse Feathers* and apparently has carried it in his trench coat for the past nine years. As chauffeur, he plants the plug in front of parked cars, calls a cop and, when the cop forces the cars to move on, drives his own wreck into the empty space, pulling the plug back into the front seat. He is a little closer to his old self in *The Big Store* than in the other M-G-M films. When he discovers Mrs. Phelps' purse in the car, he does what any honest man does. He steals the money, then returns the purse to her. Later, in the store, he helps an arrogant customer find some material for a hat that will match her dress. We discover where he got the material when the woman stalks away from the counter with her bottom bare.

Groucho is also more self-seeking and less sentimental here. Grover sends paid killers into the store to bump off Tommy. A friend of Tommy's rushes to Groucho, who is sleeping in the bed department. "Get up," the messenger yells. "The killers are in the store." "Well, then," remarks Groucho, "why doesn't somebody wait on them?" Groucho spends a good deal of his time in the bed department, but Grover undermines his sleep by declaring a sale there. Families representing every ethnic group in America invade the showroom—Chinese kids, American Indian children, Nordic tots, and black babies

Ethnic cavalcade

Groucho looks the merchandise ove[r]

"Remember when I gave you lessons?"

mount the beds and disappear into the walls. The sequence, for all its activity, is labored—not only because the ethnic conception is out of date and of dubious taste, but because the humor belongs to the machines, not to the Marxes. The brothers are reduced to pushing the buttons, worthy task for the Three Stooges perhaps, but the brothers are no stooges.

On the other hand, the musical numbers performed by the brothers in *The Big Store* contribute to rather than retard the comedy. Chico and Harpo perform their first and only piano duet on screen. "Remember when I gave you lessons?" Chico reminds Harpo, who is providing the oompah accompaniment as his elbow regularly slips off the ledge of the piano and onto the keys. Actually Chico was supposed to give Harpo lessons when the two were boys on 93d Street, since their mother couldn't afford the extra twenty-five cents for Harpo's instruction. But while he was unusually diligent in practicing him-

self, Chico never found time to teach Harpo. "What piano I learned," Harpo once wrote, "I learned by myself." This amounted to a repertoire of two tunes—"Waltz Me Around Again, Willie" and "Love Me and the World Is Mine." Often, because he looked exactly like Chico, Harpo would substitute for him at jobs, varying his two tunes by playing them at different speeds and different octaves—until the proprietor of the saloon or movie house caught on to him. But Harpo was destined to be a fine musician right from the beginning. His first job: playing a whorehouse piano at the Happy Times Tavern.

In *The Big Store* he performs his most imaginative and delightful harp routine. He wanders into an eighteenth-century salon mocked up by the department store, clothes himself in satins and wig, and sits at the harp between two mirrors. As he embarks on the Mozart C Major Sonata, all three images of Harpo agree. Suddenly, he is flanked by himself on bass

and himself on violin. The bass player is twirling his instrument and the violinist is fiddling hot jazz. The Harpo Marx Trio, featuring Harpo Marx, Harpo Marx and Harpo Marx, plays merrily on.

Time is growing short for Grover to do away with Tommy Rodgers, for the young singer-stockholder is about to sell his interest in the store to a rival concern. A picture-taking ceremony is planned. Desperate, Grover loads one press camera with a pistol while the store staff is distracted by the last-minute party they have to whip up in honor of the sale. The party turns out to be one of those little Hollywood diversions, simple, innocent, amateur, pulled together at the spur of the moment: Tony Martin, backed by a full symphony orchestra and thoroughly rehearsed boys' choir, in a ten-minute pseudo-cantata entitled "Tenement Symphony."

All this, of course, is prologue to the chase finale, triggered when Grover kidnaps Tommy's girl friend, Joan, just as the brothers take a picture of her. Once developed, the snapshot will show who abducted Joan when the lights went out. Grover and

The merchandise looks Groucho over

a pair of store detectives set out in hot pursuit of the Marxes, who roller skate out of reach along the counters, seek refuge in the elevators, and finally motor about the store on bicycles. The bicycles break in half. Undaunted, the brothers take flight on the workable halves. They toss rugs and barrels before their pursuers, mowing them down like mobile tenpins. In the end, however, Grover corners them at gunpoint, extracts the photo and rips it into bitsy pieces. All appears lost. The brothers are arrested. But when a press photographer innocently focuses his lethally loaded camera on Grover for a news photo, the dastardly villain is forced to stop him and, in so doing, admit his guilt. Groucho is not surprised. He reminds Mrs. Phelps, "I told you in the first reel he was a crook."

The finale of *The Big Store,* for all its frantic energy, fails for much the same reason as the bed department scene—the Marx Brothers were no longer up to performing their own sight gags. While cleverly put together, the final chase is executed almost exclusively by doubles and, as such, has little relation to the special comic attributes of the brothers. In the last M-G-M films, Groucho could still gab; Chico was still master of the malapropism; and Harpo's silence was as pregnant as ever with comic invention. But as a trio, the team was no longer capable of the old agile, high-powered horseplay. Like Chaplin, Keaton and Fields, the Marxes depended on their bodies as well as their words to get laughs. When those bodies lost their athletic zip, a major dimension of their humor vanished.

The film was roundly panned by

The brothers develop the mug shot; the mug appears and demands it, but Harpo rolls off with it

the critics. One suggested that "the world of films and film fun has moved on, and has left the Marx Brothers far behind. Which is a strange and sad thing." Most reviewers, however, were less sweeping in their judgment. But noting that *The Big Store* was billed as the Marxes' screen farewell, they grudgingly admitted that the time for retirement had come. Wrote Leo Mishkin in the New York *Morning Telegraph*: "This swan song of the Marx Brothers is just a hodge-podge knockabout farce, bearing little relation, either actual or spiritual, to the past." Still, even those who disliked the picture were saddened to see the brothers go. "It will be a pity if the rumors are confirmed," wrote Gilbert Kanour of the Baltimore *Sun*, "for while the Brothers have had their ups and downs, they would definitely be missed."

Groucho reaffirmed his vow to quit. "When I say we're sick of movies," he told a reporter, "what I mean is that the people are about to get sick of us. By getting out now, we're just anticipating public demand and by a very short margin. Our stuff is stale, and so are we. The fake moustache, the dumb harp player who chases the ladies, and the little Italian were funny at first, but it became harder and harder with each picture to top the one before. To get out of the groove, we have to get out of the movies." Privately he confided to Sheekman: "I'm happy to escape from this kind of picture, for the character I'm playing now I find wholly repulsive. Acting in the movies no longer interests me."

Groucho was right about the team's decline. But he was wrong about its popularity. Groucho always worried that one day he would be dumped by the public. Instead, public demand twice more summoned him to the screen.

Chico suggests who dunnit

Lisette Verea

Siegfried Rumann

Charles Drake and Lois Collier

Dan Seymour

Chico, Groucho, and Harpo

Ronald Kornblow:	GROUCHO
Rusty:	HARPO
Corbaccio:	CHICO
Count Pfefferman alias Heinrich Stubel:	SIEGFRIED RUMANN
Beatrice Rheiner:	LISETTE VEREA
Lt. Pierre Delmar:	CHARLES DRAKE
Annette:	LOIS COLLIER
Captain Brizzard:	DAN SEYMOUR
Galoux:	LEWIS RUSSELL
Kurt:	FREDERICK GIERMAN
Emile:	HARRO MELLOR
Spy:	DAVID HOFFMAN
Smythe:	HALL HARVEY

* * *

Production: David L. Loew
Director: Archie L. Mayo
Original Screenplay: Joseph Fields and Roland Kibbee
Additional Material: Frank Tashlin
Photography: James van Trees
Production Designer: Duncan Cramer
Set Decoration: Edward Boyle
Editing: Gregg G. Tallas
Music: Werner Janssen
Music and Lyrics: Ted Snyder, Bert Kalmar and Harry Ruby
Released by United Artists, May 10, 1946. 85 minutes

Frederick Gierman

13 A Night In Casablanca (1946)

The brothers held to their vow of retirement throughout the war. Harpo toured Army camps. Groucho concentrated on radio work. And Chico played the night club circuit with his own band. But in 1946 public demand and the promise of making an independent picture in which they would own part of the profits lured the Marxes back to the film-making grind. Warner Brothers' saga *Casablanca* had been one of the most successful movies of the war. Taking their cue from this Bogart-Bergman romance with its background of espionage and intrigue in North Africa, the Marxes set out to make a parody entitled *Adventures in Casablanca,* ultimately changed to *A Night in Casablanca.* Just as the film went into production, the brothers received a letter from Warner's legal department threatening to sue. In a series of strokes from his lethal pen, Groucho slew the enemy.

"I just don't understand your attitude," he wrote Warners in one of a number of missives canonized in *The Grouch Letters.* "Even if you plan on re-releasing your picture, I am sure that the average movie fan could learn in time to distinguish between Ingrid Bergman and Harpo. I don't know whether I could, but I certainly would like to try. You claim you own Casablanca and that no one else can use that name without your permission. What about 'Warner Brothers'? Do you own that too? You probably have the right to use the name Warner, but what about Brothers? Professionally, we were brothers long before you were . . . even before us there had been other brothers—the Smith Brothers; the Brother Karamazov; Dan Brothers, an outfielder with Detroit; and 'Brother, Can You Spare a Dime?' This all seems to add up to a pretty bitter tirade, but I assure you it's not meant to. I love Warner's. Some of my best friends are Warner Brothers."

Dazed, the legal department wrote back asking for an outline of the plot. "I play a Doctor of Divinity," Groucho replied, "who ministers to the natives and, as a sideline, hawks can openers and pea jackets to the savages along the Gold Coast of Africa. When I first meet Chico, he is working in a saloon, selling sponges to barflies who are unable to carry their liquor. Harpo is an Arabian caddie who lives in a small Grecian urn on the outskirts of the city." Warners wanted more details. Groucho wrote them to say that the plot had been revised. "In the new version," he explained, "I play Bordello, the sweet-heart of Humphrey Bogart. Harpo and Chico are itinerant rug peddlers who are weary of laying rugs and enter a monastery just for a lark. This is a good joke on them as there hasn't been a lark in the place for fifteen years. . . . Harpo marries a hotel detective; Chico operates an ostrich farm. Humphrey Bogart's girl, Bordello, spends her last years in a Bacall house." Warners dropped the matter.

Actually, Warners had little to fear. Aside from the setting, the recruitment of Dan Seymour to play the role of police chief and a handful of lines, *A Night in Casablanca* owes nothing to the Warner Brothers epic, and vice versa. That, however, is not the film's weakness. The brothers had great fun in *Go West* without doing in the classic Western. *A Night in Casablanca* suffers from a far more common screen malady—bad script. Like all comedians, Groucho could rise just so far above his material, as he knew better than anyone. He once put it this way: "Writers thought because they wrote long speeches for me and had me talking fast and using a lot of *non sequiturs* and silly puns, that was all there was to it. That's my style all right. The trouble is, a lot of writers forgot to be funny along with it." In *A Night in Casablanca,* all of them forgot.

Their task was not made easier by the retirement of Margaret Dumont. Instead, a Rumanian beauty named Lisette Verea played opposite Groucho. She possessed few of Miss Dumont's comic gifts, and, worse, as a young beauty she offered fewer comic possibilities than the endlessly insultable dowager. Her initiation by the brothers, however, as recorded by Earl Wilson, was as rough as any Margaret Dumont received. When she was first

Director Mayo supervises the camel sequence

introduced to the brothers, they looked her over skeptically and shook their heads. "Well," she said weakly, "I'll go get dressed." Go get undressed," advised Groucho. Later, when they were playing a restaurant scene, Groucho asked her what champagne she would like. "Mumm's '28," she answered, following the script. Groucho shot back, off the cuff, "I don't care how old your mother is! What champagne do you want?" Finally, when the director at one point asked her to delay her entrance because "we saw you before," Groucho yelled, "and we saw her behind!" Miss Verea survived, but the scenes between her and Groucho are strained and only occasionally funny, lacking entirely that superbly fluid give-and-take that characterized the old Groucho-Dumont exchanges.

Harpo was all but immune to weak scripts. Free to invent his own comic world in the protected precincts of silence, his performance varied little with the quality of the screenplay. Even in the worst Marx films, Harpo is brilliant. In fact, as the writing grows progressively weaker in their last pictures, Harpo shines even more brightly by comparison. His humor is dependent only on the volume of talking around him, not the quality of the gab. In *A Night in Casablanca,* the great mime is as good as or better than ever, as the incomparable film critic James Agee noted in his review for the *Nation.* "I think this is his best performance," he wrote about Harpo. "Of the three, he shows his age the most. He is sadder than before, more acid, more subtle: he looks uncannily like Charlie Chaplin out of character." Agee also delivered the

A scar for Sig Rumann

most balanced appreciation of the film itself. Noting that it wasn't one of their best movies, he goes on: "The worst they might ever make would be better worth seeing than most other things I can think of. Many of the things in this one which by substance and look should be level with their best somehow fall flat . . . after all these years the Brothers are tired. But to anyone who likes them much, I don't think that will get in the way."

Harpo stamps the picture as his own in the opening scene. The most recent manager of the Casablanca Hotel goes the way of his predecessors, poisoned at lunch. Police Chief Brizzard announces, "Round up all likely suspects," echoing Claude Rains' classic, "Round up the usual suspects," from the original *Casablanca.* Harpo qualifies eminently. A policeman discovers him lounging rouguishly against a modest cottage. "Say, what do you think you're doing," the cop barks,

Six shines for the price of one

"holding up the building?" Harpo nods pleasantly. The cop hauls him away, and instantly, the building collapses. Harpo is valet to Heinrich Stubel, a Nazi officer posing as Count Pfefferman, who, is systematically bumping off the managers to gain control of the hotel and locate a cache of valuable art hidden on the premises.

Durability appears to be Harpo's strong suit as valet. He demonstrated this ability to sustain abuse in the employ of Lassparri in *A Night at the Opera*. Here Stubel, a sadist from the tips of his boots to the scar under his toupee, thrashes him for sport. Nothing Harpo does can please his boss. The clown arranges Stubel's shoes on the closet wall in a knife-thrower's pattern around his body, then polishes six pairs at a time by executing a kind of rumba, arms, legs, elbows and bottom buffing the leather. Stubel's reward for this ingenuity—a beating. Harpo helps the Nazi on with his coat, jamming a cane down his back. Another beating. But Harpo, as always, avenges his mistreatment. He extends his vacuuming chores to include the ingestion of Stubel's toupee. The Nazi is confined to the hotel room as a result, because without his

hairpiece, he would be recognized. To amuse himself and kill some time, he instructs his assistant, Kurt, to kill Harpo. Kurt, an expert dueler, squares off against Harpo, who has suited himself up in a catcher's uniform and boxing glove. With eight deft strokes, Kurt divests Harpo of his equipment. Harpo lunges. His sword misses, but his foot crushes Kurt's toes. Kurt closes in for the kill, but his impish adversary, agile as a Fairbanks, casually parries every blow, munching on an apple with one hand and occasionally stifling a yawn with the other. Kurt flails away futilely for a few hours, then drops with exhaustion.

Usually the first comic scene in a Marx movie belongs to Groucho. In *A Night in Casablanca* he doesn't appear for some time. Finally, as Roger Cornblow, motel operator, he arrives to replace the murdered hotel chief. Chico, president of the Yellow Camel Company, greets him at the station. "They'll never let you in," he remarks, looking over Groucho. "Do they let you in?" Groucho asks. "Sure," replies Chico. Returns Groucho: "I'll put a stop to that. I'm the new manager." Groucho has other plans for the hotel. In the lobby, the staff has been assembled to learn what he expects of them. "Never mind the staff," Groucho declares. "Assemble the guests. I'll tell them what I expect of *them*." Groucho expects courtesy toward the employees. "They must learn," he explains, "that a kind word will get them further with a bellboy or a chambermaid than a couple of drinks. Of course a kind word *and* a couple of drinks will get them still further. And if it gets them any further than that, it'll get them kicked

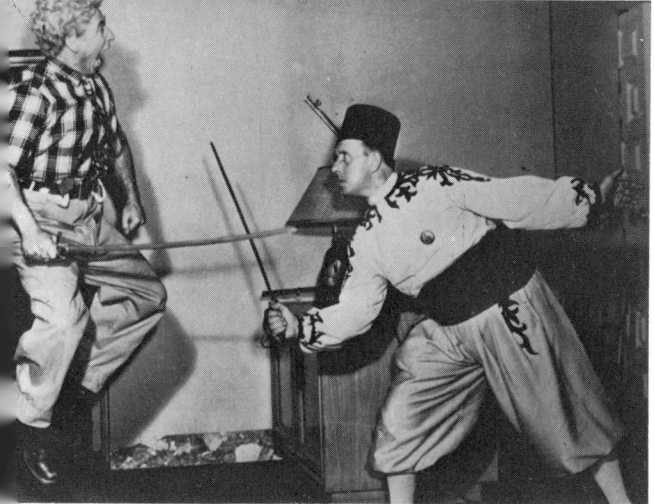

out of the hotel. The next thing we're going to do," he goes on, "is change the numbers on all the rooms." "Think of the confusion," he is told. "Yes," he concedes, "but think of the fun." Groucho demands to know what service he will receive. The hotel will pick up his laundry once a month. "You wait that long," he warns, "and you won't be *able* to pick it up."

Groucho and Lisette Verea square off for the first time when the Rumanian actress, in the role of Beatrice Rheiner, enters the manager's office in search of Stubel's hairpiece. "I'm Beatrice Rheiner. I stop at the hotel," she says. "I'm Ronald Cornblow," he replies. "I stop at nothing." Soon he is shoveling woo at her. "You know, I think you're the most beautiful woman in the whole world." "Do you really?" asks Beatrice. "No," he confesses, "but I don't mind lying if it'll get me somewhere." It gets him an invitation from Beatrice to join her at the supper club. "Why," he asks, "are you falling apart?" "I'll be singing only for you," she tells him. In a parody of the classic Bacall line from *To Have and Have Not,* he replies, "You don't have to sing for me, just whistle." Then, looking over her twenty-four-jewel movement as she saunters from the room, he tells the audience: "That reminds me, I must get my watch fixed."

At the supper club, she is his guest, a dubious honor. Groucho asks her what she wants to drink. "Champagne," she replies. "Waiter" commands Groucho, "bring this lady a cheese sandwich and charge it to *her*." They move onto the dance floor, cheek to cheek, not out of romance but necessity. Chico and Harpo have

Kurt crosses swords with a master

"I'm Beatrice Rheiner, I stop at the hotel."

"I'm Ronald Kornblow, I stop at nothing."

decided to earn some money by securing tables for everyone waiting in line. Their method is simple. They set up new tables in the corners, in the aisles, on the dance floor, until the club becomes one crowded stateroom. "This place has a wonderful floor show," Groucho comments, clinging to Beatrice like a man balancing on a small raft. "Too bad it doesn't have a floor."

Oh, for the days when Groucho was only pitched down the stairs. In *A Night in Casablanca* he is battered by a taxicab and nearly jolted to death in a plummeting elevator. In fact, the whole plot revolves around the efforts of Stubel to kill him with dispatch and attempts by Chico to kill him with kindness. Harpo learns that Beatrice will lure Groucho to her room so that Stubel, as jealous lover, can bust in and shoot him. Ordinarily a mute would write the message. But Harpo can't write, so he tells Chico this way: he steps on Chico's corn, then blows in his face. "Cornblow!" exclaims Chico. Harpo starts eating from an imaginary bowl. "Eat-a chop suey, eat-a-rice, eat-a soup," interprets Chico. "soup, rice, souprice, souprice, suprise. You gotta surprise for Cornblow?" Whistle. Whistle. Harpo bumps into Chico. "Somebody's

gonna bump him off. Who's gonna bump him off?" Harpo flashes a cigar. "A cigar, a cgar, a scar." Harpo counts on his fingers. Chico gets it: "The count with the scar." It's going to happen in some room, but whose? Harpo whistles and outlines a curvy form. "Snake, big snake." Harpo shows his legs. "Garter snake ... oh, ho, that's-a no snake ... a lady's room." Which lady? Harpo imitates a B-29, shortens it to "B," then adds a twist of his wrist. "B-twist, b-twist, Beatrice!!" and Chico is off to warn Groucho.

"I wish *they'd* tell me," Groucho tells Chico on hearing the news. "I don't mind being killed, but I resent hearing it from a character whose head comes to a point." Chico tells him he needs a good bodyguard. "What I need is a good body," Groucho replies. "The one I've got isn't worth guarding." "But, boss," Chico pleads, "if I'm-a you bodyguard, I watch over you like a mother watches her babies." "Is it a pretty mother?" "What's the difference?" asks Chico. "Well," Groucho answers, "if the mother's pretty, I'll watch the mother and you can watch the baby."

But Chico would rather watch Groucho, which he does with a tenacity unheard of in the man who man-

"I only rented them for an hour."

aged to lose Groucho's picture in *Duck Soup,* Joe Helton in *Monkey Business* and the land deed in *Go West.* First he and Harpo devour Groucho's dinner under the pretense of protecting him from poisoning. "This food doesn't look any more poisoned than any other hotel food," Groucho vainly protests. Later, when Groucho corners Beatrice in her apartment, Chico hounds him and Beatrice's hound hounds him. Groucho arrives for his rendezvous, carrying his own romance with him—a table, champagne, and flowers. "Ah, roses," exclaims Beatrice. "I shall keep them forever." "That's what you think," Groucho shoots back. "I only rented them for an hour." "Oh, Mr. Cornblow." "Call me Montgomery," he implores. "Is *that* your name?" "No," says Groucho, "I'm just breaking it in for a friend." Groucho would sit on Beatrice's lap, but her lapdog, Frou-Frou, has beaten him to it. "If he had good manners," Groucho says, "he'd get off your lap and give me a seat. He can stand up better than I can. He's got twice as many legs." Just as the pair are snuggling down, Chico knocks at the door. "Hey, boss, you got a woman in there?" "She lives here." "Yeah," says Chico, "but you don't. She'll have to get-a you out.

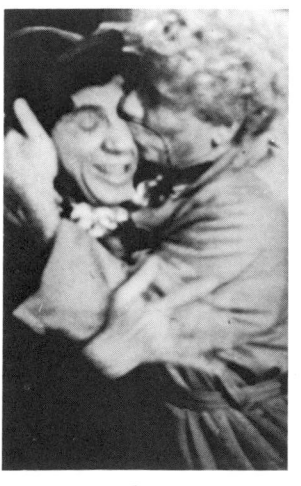

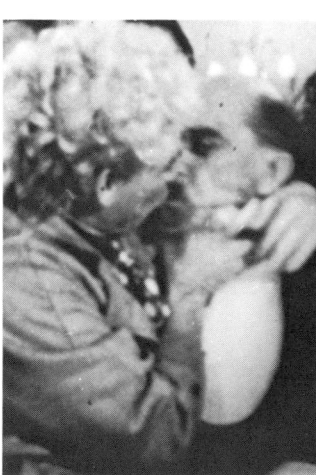

Harpo breaks the bank, kisses everyone— and that means everyone

The brothers languish briefly in jail after breaking the bank

Remember, I'm your bodyguard." "I'm too old to have a bodyguard," Groucho pleads. "Then you're too old to be in there," says Chico. Groucho admits the logic of this and piles table, flowers and champagne into his arms, then grabs a phonograph and records. "I wanted to get loaded tonight," he comments, "but not this way."

The two descend to Groucho's room just before Stubel roars in, finding only a note directing him downstairs, where Groucho is about to put the clinch on Beatrice. Chico interrupts again. "I'm crazy about her," cries Groucho. "I've completely lost my head." But Chico is intractable. "Well, put your hat on your neck and get out." He packs up again, toting away his caravan of flowers and furniture, leaving Stubel to storm once again into an empty room. When Groucho finally makes it back to Beatrice's room, stooped as he is with the paraphernalia of passion, he finds the door locked. "It's me," he calls, "the Hunchback of Notre Dame." "Hey, boss," cries a voice from the other side of the door. "You gotta woman out

there?" "No." "Then go away," says Chico. "I got one in here."

Harpo has not been idle. In several spins of the roulette wheel downstairs, he has parlayed a single chip into a fortune, all by betting on number five. Groucho arrives just in time to caution him. "You sure you want to go through with this?" he tells Harpo, who has put his mountain of chips on number five for the third straight time. "Remember what happened in 1929." (A letter from Groucho to Harpo reveals what really happened in 1929. "Remember once, way back in '29," Groucho wrote his brother, "when I suggested a few stocks that would, in time, place you in the same class with Andrew Mellon and Diamond Jim Brady? It was but a few months after this that you were wiped out.") This time, Harpo doesn't heed his benefactor's counsel. As Groucho murmurs, "What a sucker," Harpo hits the jackpot, having retained his magic touch since he broke the "telephone" in *Horse Feathers*. He dives through the chips, then emerges to kiss everyone at the table, finishing with a passionate embrace of an angry bearded little man.

Stubel had at first feigned leaving for Tunis, to have an alibi when he shot Groucho. "Some beautiful women in Tunis," Groucho had remarked at the time." "I'm not interested in beautiful women," Stubel replied. "Then you ought to look up some of the girls *I've* taken out," Groucho advised, instructing his desk clerk, "That man's going to Tunis. Get him a seat by an open window." Now it turns out that Stubel really is leaving for Tunis, having found the treasure in the hotel. As he packs to go, the brothers haunt him. Groucho and Chico spirit his suits back to the closet as fast as Stubel packs them. Then the suits disappear. Then they start walking back to the closet. Stubel takes a stiff drink. Harpo hides in the top of a chest. When Stubel opens it to put some things in, Harpo shifts his weight, and the top cracks down on the Nazi's hand. The clothes keep shifting about the room, seemingly driven by a mind of their own. Stubel unloads shirts onto a table, but Har-

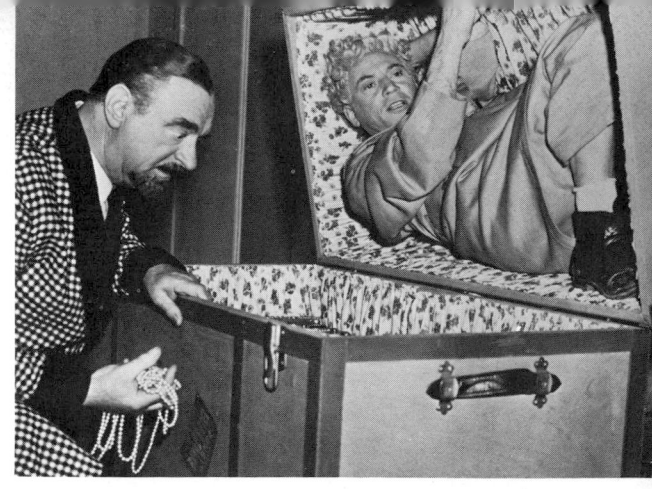

The brothers help Rumann unpack

…oarding the plane: Groucho, at fifty, …ll did some of his own stunt work

Wecome aboard. This is your captain, Harpo Marx

po, hiding beneath, opens the fly leaves so the shirts drop through the table, then tosses them back onto the pile. Stubel unloads some hundreds of shirts before he surrenders to fatigue. Finally, with the heavy thoroughly bats, the brothers sneak into his wardrobe trunks and accompany him out to the airport, where the plane is waiting.

On board, the brothers knock out the crew and take over, Harpo at the controls. It is his finest moment. He becomes a child in wonderland, testing that stick there, flicking this button here, delicately twisting a knob, then sitting back to watch the effects. The brothers revive the pilot as the plane spins crazily about the airport. Harpo knocks him out again and returns to the controls, eyes dazzling, mouth wreathed in a fiendish grin of delight, limbs playing about the dashboard like a lunatic spider weaving a weird web. Some critics have professed to see in this sequence a significance beyond its obvious madcap fun. "The disproportion between the smallness of [Harpo's] effort and the magnitude of the disaster," wrote the distinguished critic Erwin Panofsky, "is a magnificent and terrifying symbol of man's behavior in the atomic age." The brothers might reply that the only bomb involved was registered at the box office. The film does end, however, with a disaster as Harpo plows the plane into the Casbah. But Stubel is unmasked—or better, untoupeed—as the Nazi and the brothers take off, all three of them, after Beatrice, leers the size of the African continent stamped on their faces. Perhaps the real disaster occurred when they caught her.

Once again, the film received mixed notices. "The gags sound as wheezy as an old Model T panting uphill on two cylinders," wrote the New York *Times* critic, recommending the film "with reservations even to the Marxes' best friends." Once again, the brothers retired. And once again, they were accorded a warm funeral oration. Bosley Crowther per-

210

formed the honors. "What did it matter really," he wrote, "if the Marxes' last three or four films had been, comparatively speaking, a little (or a lot) below par? Granted that their 'Room Service' was a trifle out of their line and that 'Go West' and 'At the Circus' were concocted pretty much out of old stuff. The Marx Brothers' old stuff was always good enough for us. And besides, in each of their pictures, no matter how 'stale' the patterns seemed, there were always a few priceless moments that made up for any other lack." The Marx Brothers themselves were showing their age—becoming old stuff. But news of their screen demise again proved premature. They bolted out of mothballs once more and, as Bosley Crowther predicted, provided at least a few more priceless moments.

Harpo giving Rumann another scar

Ilona Massey

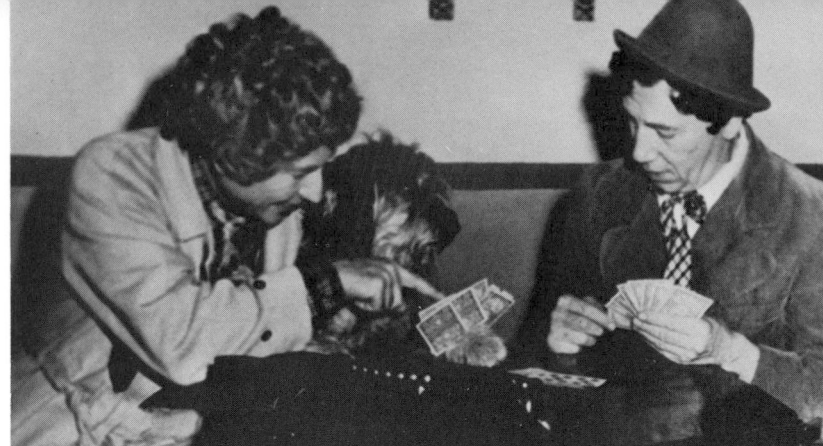

Harpo, Chico, and friend

Groucho and Marilyn Monroe

Leon Belasco

Melville Cooper

Harpo:	HARPO
Faustino the Great:	CHICO
Sam Grunion:	GROUCHO
Maggie Phillips:	VERA-ELLEN
Madame Egilichi:	ILONA MASSEY
Bunny Dolan:	MARION HUTTON
Alphonse Zoto:	RAYMOND BURR
Throckmorton:	MELVILLE COOPER
Mike Johnson:	PAUL VALENTINE
Mr. Lyons:	LEON BELASCO
Mackinaw:	ERIC BLORE
Hannibal Zoto:	BRUCE GORDON
Grunion's Client:	MARILYN MONROE

* * *

Production: Lester Cowan
Presented by: Mary Pickford
Director: David Miller
Screenplay: Frank Tashlin and Mac Benoff
Story: Harpo Marx
Photography: William C. Mellor
Production Designer: Gabriel Scognamillo
Editing: Basil Wrangell and Al Joseph
Music: Ann Ronell
Music Director: Paul Smith
Released by United Artists, March 3, 1950. 85 minutes

Eric Blore

Vera-Ellen

Marion Hutton

Raymond Burr

14 Love Happy (1949)

Love Happy is, on balance, the brothers' weakest picture. But those who love Harpo will rejoice in it. For the first time, he enjoys top billing, credit for the story and, most important, all the screen time he needs to display the full range of his genius. Unlike Chaplin and Keaton, Harpo's lights did not dim with age. He is as spontaneous, responsive and wildly imaginative in *Love Happy* at the age of fifty-eight as he was in *The Cocoanuts* some twenty years earlier. Unfortunately, this time he presides over a shambles. Groucho, just about to launch a successful television career as the emcee of "You Bet Your Life," puts in only cameo appearances at the beginning and end of the film. Chico is still warm and lovable, but without Groucho to play against, his role is diminished by half, leaving him only a translation sequence with Harpo, a piano solo and the ungrateful task of nudging a plot that really needs the full Marxian frontal assault.

So that leaves the field to Harpo. Of the three brothers, Harpo is said by those who knew him to have been the most sane, balanced and content. Although he was the darling of the Algonquin round table in the 1930's, he did not live the fast life of the celebrity. "One thing I am not now and never have been," he wrote in his autobiography, "is a celebrity. Strangers never stop me on the street and ask for my autograph. People don't recognize me out of costume. [He was bald under that great reddish-blond wig.] The public has never heard my voice. In this respect I'm a good deal different from my brother Groucho, who is a genuine, fourteen-karat celebrity."

But if Harpo was a good deal less lunatic off the screen than on it, he did possess a wild streak that belonged to both Harpos. Oscar Levant, one of his Hollywood pals, tells several stories that tie the screen clown and the civilian together. "The first time I met Marie Harriman, Averell Harriman's wife," Levant remembers, "was when I opened a closet door at the Swope home and found Harpo Marx pretending to strangle her. He paused long enough to introduce us." Some time later, Levant was interested in a certain young lady in Hollywood. "I arranged to call a few evenings later at her home," he recalls, "duly appearing with Harpo, whom I presented as my uncle. We were both on the street five minutes later, after Harpo had insulted the butler, chucked the maid under the chin and chased the girl's mother halfway around the house." The stories sound like sequences from a Marx Brothers' film. But the relation between the screen clown and Arthur, née Adolph, Marx does not end with wildness.

"There was nothing naive about

Harpo," wrote the late Ben Hecht. "Harpo's worldly activities had embraced pimps, thieves, whores, dowagers, royalty and statesmen. He had come out of the early vaudeville circuits which were the slums of entertainment. His cruise upward from these lowest of stage alleys to a place among the theater's elite had been full of bawdy adventure. Yet there had come out of it a man mysteriously innocent." And so he appears on the screen, sheltered from the stupidity and menace around him by a radiant purity of spirt—not naive, as Hecht points out, but still totally unsullied. In *Love Happy* he endures torture amenably and waves playfully at his chief tormentor as her thugs work him over. Harpo, like the other brothers, became an increasingly sentimental figure as his film career progressed. But, though softened in *Love Happy,* the essence of Harpo remains constant. He is, to the last, the *enfant terrible* who speaks eloquently the fluid, boundlessly fertile poetry of mime.

Groucho opens the film as Sam Grunion, private eye. His blank business card attests to his motto: "I never tell." "I'm the same Sam Grunion who solved the famous uranium scandal," he tells us. "Scotland Yard was baffled. They sent for me, and the case was solved immediately. I confessed." Saddled with lines like these, Groucho showed both wisdom and charity in limiting his appearance. He hangs around just long enough to set up the plot, then mercifully removes himself, taking with him the worst jokes ever written for him. The Romanoff diamonds are missing and he, who has been after them for eleven years, has trailed them to a group of young actors, "underfinanced and undernourished," who are trying to put on a musical.

Harpo, who works under his own name for the first time since *The Cocoanuts,* gathers food for the actors, snatching a tidbit here and there as customers emerge from a delicatessen. By a stroke of the good for them into his bulging coat. Harpo delicatessen's sidewalk elevator opens and ushers him into a basement filled with absolutely defenseless gourmandise. Harpo needs no flashlight. His face beams in beatific rapture. As a boy, Harpo must have dreamed of such a paradise as he walked about his neighborhood, his face pressed against the windows of local food stores. Even as a wealthy man in Hollywood, he would indulge his childhood cravings by purchasing pound bags of licorice jelly beans. "For a long time after I came into the chips," he once wrote, "I could only buy things in abundance. I bought stuff by the case and the gross, by job lots and truckloads. Soap, thumb-

Groucho as Grunion (private eye in background) with sidekick Eric Blore

arpo in paradise

tacks, dehydrated onion soup—everything."

He is busily clearing the cans into his omnibus trench coat when Throckmorton, store owner and stooge of the nefarious Madame Egilichi, rushes into the basement. He has come to inspect a new shipment of sardines. One tin, bearing a cross, contains the Romanoff diamonds. Throckmorton eagerly pitches the sardine cans behind him like some dog kicking out grass after relieving itself, while Harpo, strategically located, catches the cans in what seems to be eight or ten hands and stuffs them into his bulging coat. Harpo picked up this glorious garment when the boys were on the road in San Francisco during the vaudeville days. It cost him $3 at a hock shop. "When I put it on after the evening show," he recounted, "the coat fell apart at the seams. So that it wouldn't be a total loss, I wore the coat in the act the next day. It was a natural. I couldn't have come up with a better comedy coat if I'd had one custom made. . . . I lined the trench coat with huge panels and pockets—room enough to stash a truck's worth of props in." He might have added "room enough for a delicatessen," for he marches off with one, including the vital sardine can.

Madame Egilichi, who chills the screen like some neatly chiseled ice cake in the person of Ilona Massey, has "wasted eight marriages" trying to corner the diamonds. She sends out an alert for the "sardine" thief and winds up with a lecherous tramp in a baffling trench coat. She orders her men to search Harpo (one of them is Raymond Burr, who was to make his reputation as Perry Mason on tele-

The trench coat coughs up its last great cache

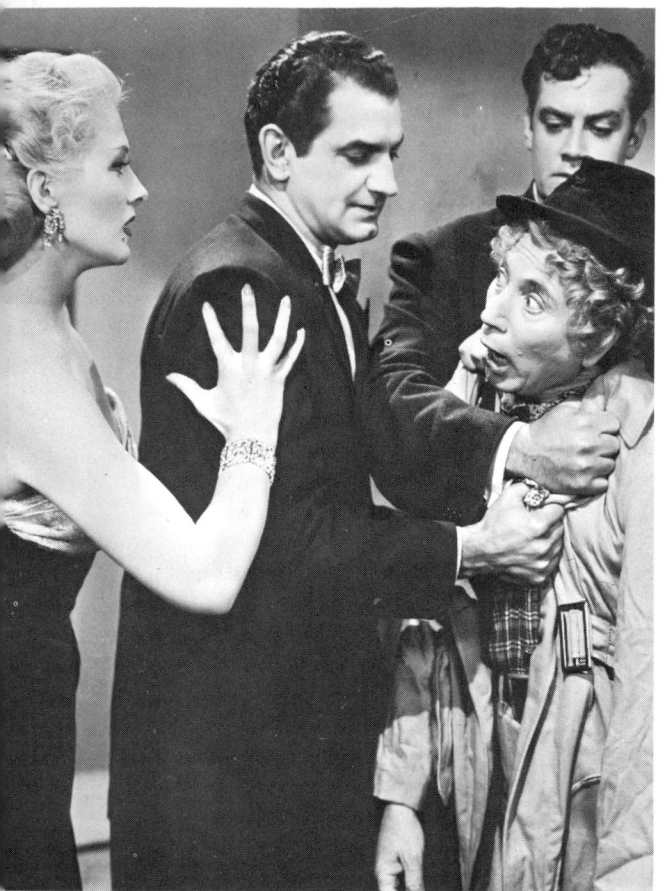

vision). The thugs extract from Harpo's magic coat a "welcome" mat, a pair of legs, a barber's pole, a music box in full swing, rubber tires, a mailbox reading "Moss Kaufman," a block of ice (preserved since *Go West*), a sled and a puppy—but no sardine can bearing a cross.

Next, she tries giving Harpo her famous "whammy," a supersexual gaze that throws men into a helpless trance. "I like you," she purrs. Harpo leans forward, mouth agape. "I like you very much." Harpo leans farther forward, until he is tilted like a lecherous tower of Pisa. But Harpo won't talk. Madame Egilichi's boys work him over. He waves merrily, as though "it" in some sadistic kids' game. He still won't talk, so Madame Egilichi subjects him to a series of cruel and unusual punishments. First, she administers the Hungarian rope

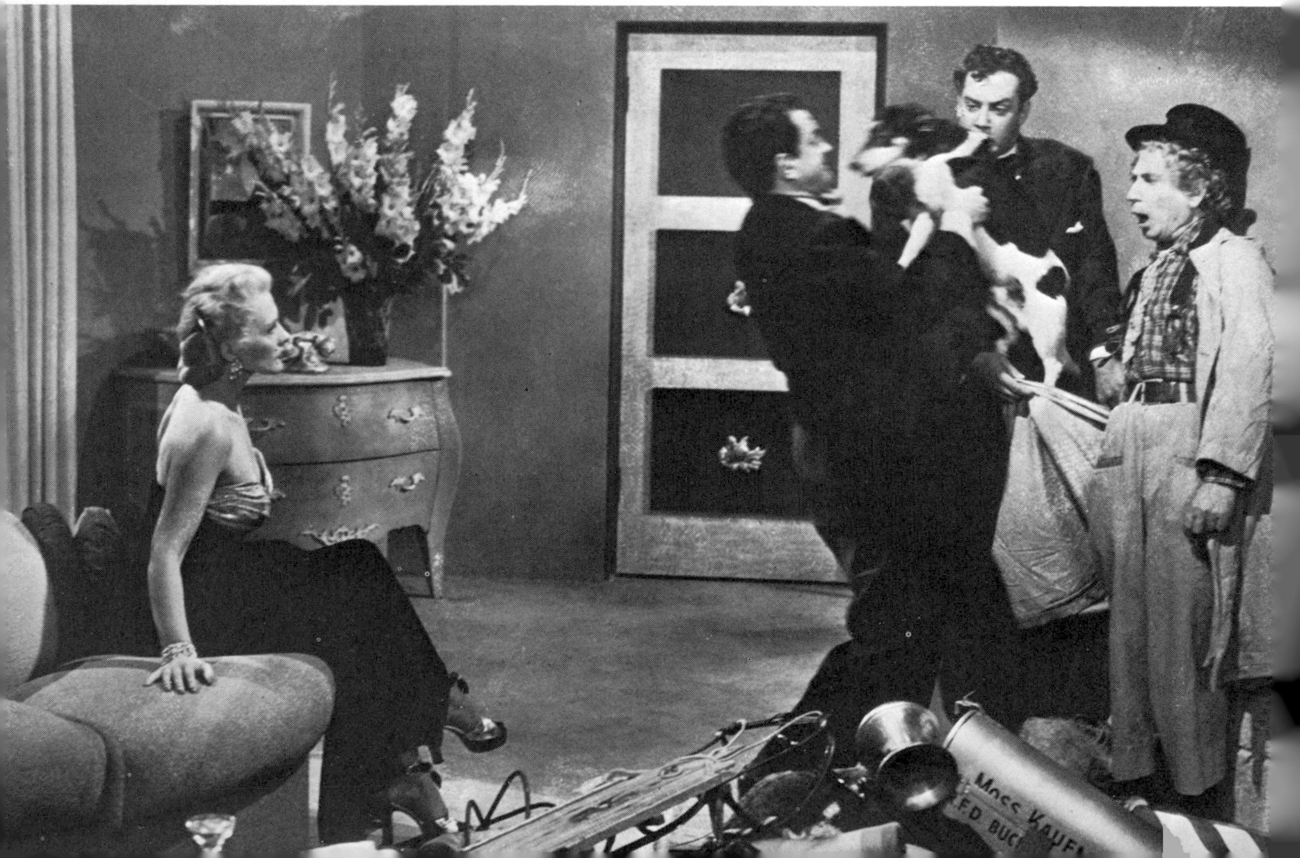

torture, in which Harpo is forced to puff to the death on a king-sized whaling line. Next, she pins her victim to a circular rack, spinning him like some human wheel of fortune until he is as wretched as an astronaut in training. Then she straps him to a chair for three days with food and water just beyond reach. Harpo still won't talk. In desperation Madame Egilichi resorts to the William Tell test. An apple is placed atop Harpo's head and shot through. Harpo foils the torture. He eats the apple—all the while holding a pistol to his head as blackmail.

Obviously, Madame Egilichi is going to get nothing out of Harpo except leers. So she buys a piece of the failing musical comedy and heads for the theater to ransack backstage for sardine cans. Her financing saves the show from the failure which Chico, as unofficial manager of the company, has been trying to stave off. He didn't set out to be unofficial manager. It just turned out that way. "You're hiring peoples that's a-never been heard of," he tells Mike Johnson, the lead dancer and director of the musical. "Well I'm the most unknown and unheard-of actor that's never been on Broadway." "What's your name?" asks the glum Johnson, who sees visions of creditors dancing continually before his eyes. "Faustino the Great," announces Chico. "You never heard of me, huh?" Johnson hasn't. "What did I tell you?" says Chico. Johnson wants to know what Chico is 'unknown' for. "Well the thing I'm most unknown for is mind reading." Chico is unhired but stays around to keep Mr. Lyons, the owner of the props and costumes, from claiming his property.

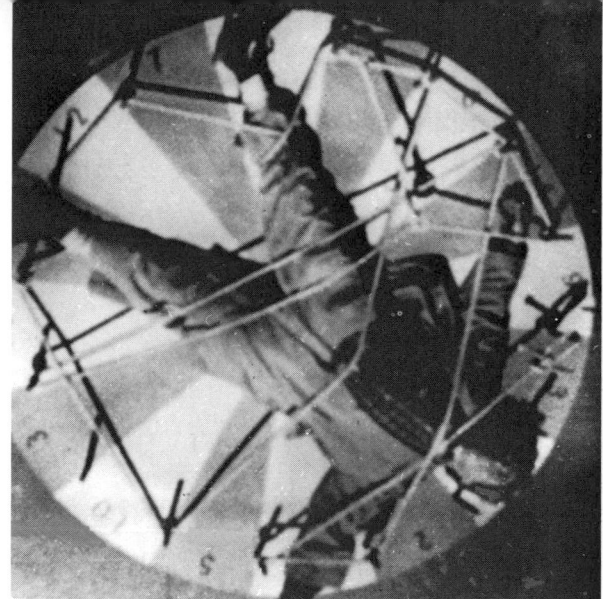

The torture of the wheel and

the ordeal of food and water end with

Harpo winning the William Tell test

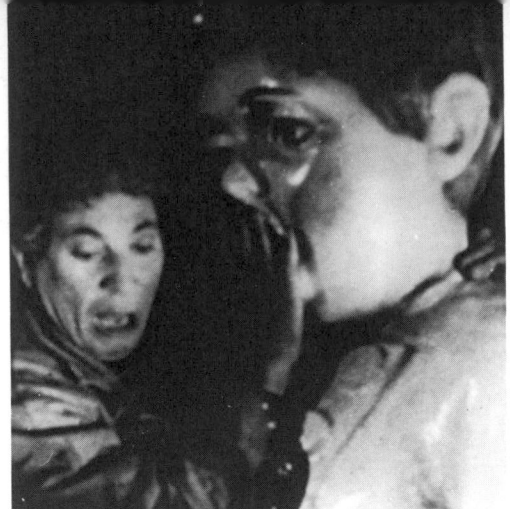

Mr. Lyons has a weakness. He likes to "noodle" on the violin. "Okay," says Chico, sitting at the piano. "You noodle on that. I'll macaroni on this." Mr. Lyons does not know what *pianissimo* is, or *allegro pizzicato*. "You know Jimmy Pizzicato?" asks Chico. "None of the Pizzicatos? What do you know?" "I know pistachio," offers Lyons. "Okay," says Chico, always ready to oblige, "we'll play it." As soon as Madame Egilichi steps into the picture, Chico is ready to oblige *her,* and then some. "You want sardines," he tells her. "I cover you with sardines." Later, he returns. "I no get you sardines," he confesses. Then, laying a thousand tins on the table, he proudly declares: "Anchovies." "I have no use for them," the blond iceberg snaps. "Maybe you like kippered herring," suggests Chico. "Smelts, smoked whitefish. I get you any kind of fish you like. I love you."

But Harpo has the one thing that interests Madame Egilichi: the diamonds, which he discovers while feeding the marked tin of fish to his pet cat. Madame Egilichi is not the only interested party. The Romanoffs, for some strange reason, are interested in the diamonds, too. They send a hired gun named Miles up to Groucho's office to bully him into tracking down the diamonds. "The diamonds," declares the crazed Miles, setting up a large hourglass, "or in one hour you die." "Mackinaw," Groucho says, calling his sidekick, played by the professional Englishman, Eric Blore, "allow me to introduce you to the man who is going to kill me. At the sound of the next bullet, the end of my life will be brought to you by the Bullova Sand Company." "Is your watch running fast," he asks Miles, "or would you like me to drop a little sand into it?" The whole sequence doesn't make much sense, since there is no point to hiring Groucho and murder-

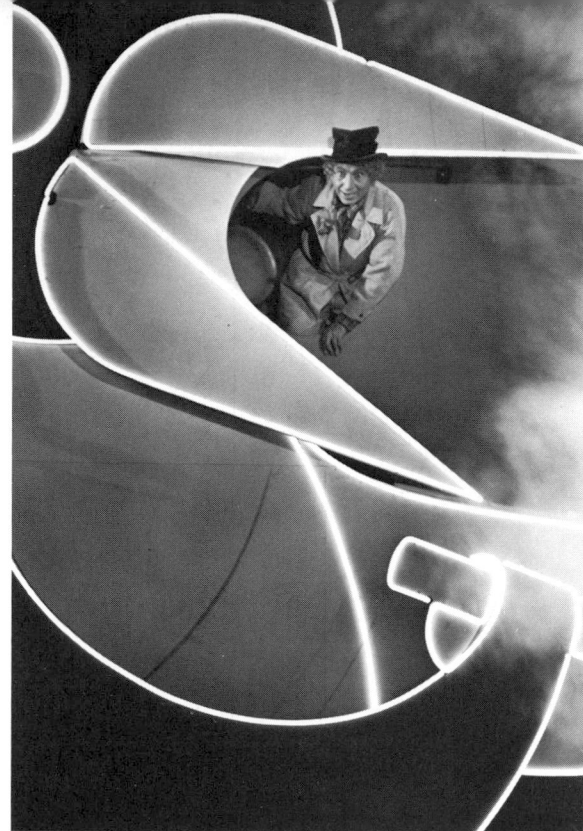

Harpo's last moment of glory: the rooftop chase

ing him at the same time. But a young lady arrives, also for no apparent reason, and saves the scene. Her name: Marilyn Monroe. "Is there anything I can do for you?" asks Groucho. He stops for a moment, reflects upon what he has just said, and tells the audience: "What a ridiculous statement." "Two men are following me," says the young Miss Monroe, who in this early picture appears frizzy-haired, bovine, but as tempting as a strawberry sundae. "I can't understand why," remarks Groucho. He is just about to whisk Miss Monroe off when Miles stops him at the door. "That's been the history of all my romances," he tells the audience, summing up neatly his career as a screen lover.

The film concludes with a memorable rooftop chase overlooking Times Square. Harpo leads Egilichi's henchmen like docile horses over an obstacle course, dangling the diamonds

Harpo escapes from Madame Egilichi's

Care for a smoke?

Groucho in paradise with Marilyn Monroe

under their noses. The setting serves Harpo well. He can no longer rely on rigorous scrambling or Harold Lloyd brinksmanship for laughs. He is simply too old. Instead, he enlists billboards and neon signs as his companions in comedy, emerging with a precious handful of unforgettable images: Harpo, his hand over a great, yawning mouth, impersonating the sleepy boy in Goodyear's "Time to Retire" billboard; Harpo, like some electrified Tom Mix, galloping away from his pursuers on the back of a neon Mobilgas Pegasus which carries him flash by flash by flash into the sky; finally, Harpo seeking refuge in the open beak of the Kool penguin as it belches smoke rings over Broadway. When the crooks catch him, Harpo combats them like some human tear gas arsenal, streams of smoke pouring from his ears and mouth. He finally leads his pursuers up a flagpole, leaps off, and then binds them as neatly as a cowboy hogties a heifer—by swinging on a rope around the pole.

Groucho and Madame Egilichi are also roaming the roof. "Remember me?" Groucho asks when he literally runs into her. She slaps his face. "I mean *before* that," he says. Groucho, decked out in a Sherlock Holmes hat, reminds one of a beagle with a moustache rather than the wolf he really is. Madame Egilichi, pistol in hand, commands the sleuth to search Har-

po. Groucho takes one look at the trench coat and refuses. "Oh, no, I'm not getting into *that*." Then he turns to search Madame Egilichi but stops. "If this were a French picture, I could do it," he tells the audience. In the end, however, it is Harpo who retains the diamonds, marching off into the night with them glittering in his hand, still innocent of their value. It is the last we see of him on screen, as jocular, uncorrupted and impish as the day he marched into the Cocoanuts Hotel and ate the telephone.

The critics were so happy to have the brothers back that they all but overlooked the ignoble vehicle that brought them there. The New York *Times'* critic noted that the brothers "appear to be much better than their material," which must rank as the critical understatement of the Marxes' career. But Joe Phidona, writing for the New York *Herald Tribune,* expressed the feeling of most reviewers and film buffs when he wrote: "The Marx Brothers, in slightly amended form, are back in the cinema world and the event is an occasion for celebration . . . a visit to the Criterion may be regarded as a pilgrimage."

The screen career of the Marx Brothers ends here. They made no more films as a team. Regrettably, no younger men have come along to rule over their comic kingdom. The late Ernie Kovacs and comic writer Mel Brooks have come closest to carrying on the liberated, lunatic tradition of the Marxes. But the world that made the brothers is gone, sealed off from the present except as a frame of reference by which comedy measures itself. Ten years after *Love Happy,* the brothers each tried to explain the death of Marxism. Groucho attributed it to the demise of satire and, until recently, this judgment has stood. Now, however, with the work of Terry Southern, Joseph Heller and the graduates of the improvised nightclub comedy of the 1950's—Alan Arkin, Elaine May and Mike Nichols among them—satire seems to be in a period of resurgence. Harpo posited that "the kind of comedy we made isn't around anymore because nobody took the care we took. We worked with the writers six months, then the writers worked alone for six months. It just isn't done that way anymore." And so it isn't. But Chico cut closest to the heart of the matter. "Twenty years ago, all performers had ideas and developed them on the vaudeville circuit. Before TV, you could do an act for twenty years, developing it as you went along." All that is over. There will be no second coming of the Marxes. But their thirteen films are legacy enough. Each fall, in revival houses from New York to San Francisco, a new generation of young moviegoers joins with the veterans of a thousand Marx showings to discover and rediscover the shyster with the lope, the moustache and the machine-gun wit, the enterprising Italian under the dunce cap and the raggedy blond child-man with the harp, the fallen archangel of silence.

And they lived happily ever after

The Marxes immortalize their palms in cement in front of Grauman's Chinese Theater in Hollywood. Sid Grauman looks on

15 Conclusion

Technically *Love Happy* was not the last Marx Brothers movie. But it was the last in which they appeared as a team. In 1957, Groucho, Harpo and Chico were featured in separate installments of an ill-fated and obscure compendium called *The Story of Mankind*. Groucho swindled the Indians out of Manhattan Island. Chico played a monk who counseled Columbus. Harpo played the harp and Sir Isaac Newton. Otherwise, the brothers pursued their careers independently. Harpo and Chico put in occasional appearances on television variety shows, and both united briefly with Groucho on television's "G. E. Theater" to pull off "The Incredible Jewel Robbery." Brightened by multiple disguises, nonsensical plot twists and ridiculous police lineups, it was hailed as an oasis of comedy in the bleak cathode desert. Groucho spent the 1950's starring as quipmaster of "You Bet Your Life." He also found time to write several breezy memoirs and to coauthor with Norman Krasna an unexceptional stage comedy, *Time For Elizabeth*. Groucho played the title role of the aging hero confronting the perils of retirement when the show played outside Los Angeles. Hollywood director Billy Wilder hoped for a while to make a movie of the brothers' life in which the team would appear briefly, but the project never materialized.

Chico died October 14, 1961, at the age of seventy. "While Groucho, Harpo and Chico were all available," wrote the New York *Times* in an editorial the following day, "there was always an outside chance that they might vandalize the land of cuckoo once more. It can never be. The funniest team of twentieth century mountebanks is broken beyond repair. Alas, poor Chico. Alas, ourselves." Harpo died at seventy, three years later. Groucho, in a letter to Betty Comden, wrote: "Having worked with Harpo for forty years, which is much longer than most marriages last, his death left quite a void in my life. He was worth all the wonderful adjectives that were used to describe him. He was a nice man in the fullest sense of the word. He loved life and lived it joyously and deeply, and that's about as good an epitaph as anyone can have."

Groucho currently lives in Beverly Hills, California, retired except for a few brief television appearances. Zeppo and Gummo, both former theatrical agents, have retired also and live in Palm Springs, California, where they spend much of their time playing golf.

* * * * * * * * * * * * * * * * * * *